5-27-71

LUTHERANS AND ROMAN CATHOLICISM
The Changing Conflict: 1917–1963

LUTHERANS AND ROMAN CATHOLICISM

The changing conflict: 1917-1963

The Catholic
Theological Union
LIBRARY
Chicago, Ill.

MYRON A. MARTY

UNIVERSITY OF NOTRE DAME PRESS
NOTRE DAME   LONDON

For Shirley

PREFACE

THERE IS A difference, I believe, between the purpose a
person has in writing a book and the hope that he cherishes
when it is presented to the public. My purpose, determined
many months ago, is described in the Introduction, for it is
an integral part of the book. My hope, held only vaguely in
mind when the work was begun, has grown as it neared completion, so that today I feel it rather keenly. I think that I am
not abandoning my role as critic and scholar when I express
the hope that this book might play some part in bringing
Lutherans and Roman Catholics into a more evangelical
relationship.

It seems to me that the conflicts and tensions of the past as
they are described in this book, if they are understood more
fully, can lead toward at least a degree of convergence in the
future. Roman Catholics, I believe, can profit from an "as
others see us" look and analysis. I do not know if this has
so far been a concern of theirs, but if it is true that an understanding of the present can grow only out of an appreciation
of the past, this book should prove helpful. Lutherans, I hope,
will use this retrospective look for constructive purposes; it
is not intended to provide material for either ridicule or
glorification of their spokesmen of earlier days. As I point
out carefully in the text, the conduct and attitudes of these
spokesmen were to a great extent reflections of the climate in
which they lived, and they should be so understood.

We seem today to be living in a new climate, but I am
under no illusion that a new era has securely arrived. Large
elements within both churches, shaken by the uncertainty

that comes with change, are no doubt reacting with increased resistance to it. Certain aspects of the tradition and practice within each group are at once too generally accepted within that group to be discarded suddenly, and too strongly disliked, even detested, to be absorbed by the other. Discouraging though this might be, it need not prevent those who see the need for change from working toward it. They must only realize that they cannot expect to build a huge span connecting the two churches in a formal organic relationship. Little bridges here and there, built wherever understanding and agreement can be reached, will in the long run bear greater fruit, enabling Lutherans and Catholics to study together some of the highly pertinent theological questions that have been obscured by the controversies described in this work.

I am indebted to many friends for the assistance they have given me while this book was in progress. Two of them, Father Martin F. Hasting, S.J., of St. Louis University, and Professor Arthur Carl Piepkorn, of Concordia Seminary, St. Louis, merit special mention for their valuable and deeply appreciated counsel. Both are no doubt aware of the book's shortcomings, and it would be improper to hold them accountable for any aspect of its contents.

A note on terminology is in order. For ease of style and in keeping with colloquial practice, I have used the terms "Roman Catholic" and "Catholic" interchangeably, although I always refer to the church as the Roman Catholic Church. In doing so I am not insensitive to the feelings of those who share the attitude of Dr. Piepkorn as he repeatedly expressed it to me: "The term 'catholic' cannot be accorded to the Roman Catholic Church in any exclusive sense, for to concede that designation to them as a denominational description involves a denial of one of the marks of Lutheranism; if the Lutheran communion is not catholic, then it is not Christian and it has no reason for existing." I believe that the way I have handled the problem does not constitute such a denial.

St. Louis, Missouri   MYRON A. MARTY
May, 1968

CONTENTS

xi

INTRODUCTION

IF THE ROMAN Catholic Church today finds itself in the mainstream of American religious life, it is a tribute to its efforts to put itself there, not evidence that it was invited. While other church bodies drifted in or were drawn in, and still others consciously resisted the pull, dikes and levees were being constructed to exclude Roman Catholicism.

Antagonism to Catholicism has been a persistent theme in American history. Social and political accounts of our nation's past are incomplete if they do not include a reference to the steady undercurrent of anti-Catholic sentiment or descriptions of the recurring outbursts of anti-Catholic agitation. In the early days of American settlement Catholics suffered disabilities in every colony, ranging from the denial of the right to vote and hold office to outright exclusion, although how rigidly these disabilities were enforced is not entirely clear. Even Maryland, originally established at least in part as a refuge for Catholics, later became the scene of severe persecution, probably because Catholics were most numerous there.

After the last formal disabilities had been removed, the Roman Catholic Church remained the object of continuing hostility. In the first half of the nineteenth century sporadic anti-Catholic agitation and the cry of "No-Popery" were important elements in the shaping of the Nativist movement and eventually also in the formation of the Know-Nothing party, a party of some influence in the 1850's. Nativism in the latter half of the nineteenth century found expression in the American Protective Association, founded in 1887. Although it is no doubt true that hostility to immigrants was partly responsible for these movements, that great numbers of the immigrants were Catholics certainly increased the resentment. Anti-Catholic sentiment has continued into the twentieth century. It was given most prominent expression first through the cruder tactics of the Ku Klux Klan, and more recently in more sophisticated forms through the arguments of the organization known as Protestants and Other Americans United for Separation of Church and State and through the sharp attacks of the lawyer and journalist Paul Blanshard.

The reasons for this widespread and continuing hostility toward Catholicism are complex, and have changed from time to time during the three centuries that the general sentiment has prevailed. The reasons offered within one opposition group are a major subject of this study. We can, nevertheless, at this point assert that the whole phenomenon of anti-Catholicism is attributable in a general way to the conviction that the Roman Catholic Church constitutes a menace to American institutions, that there exists some kind of a papal plot—to be executed through an authoritarian, foreign-controlled, politically influential hierarchy, abetted by a semi-subversive school system—to take over America or at least to gain a position of advantage in American life. Certain Roman Catholic doctrines and practices aggravate the concern, but this is the heart of the argument.

The intensity of anti-Catholic sentiment has varied through the years, depending largely upon the activities of the Roman Catholic Church and the publicity given to them. The best that Catholics could hope for, however, seems to have been a sort of neutrality or benevolent indifference on the part of non-Catholics. Yet within the past decade a significant change has occurred, as the climate of hostility has given way to one of cautious cordiality. Fears of the the Roman menace, if they do exist, at least do not find popular expression or widespread reception. The old rhetoric, for the present at least, seems to have lost its steam.

How can this change be explained? In part it is attributable to changes within the Roman Catholic Church. If what one opposes changes, then the form and substance of the opposition must also change, and these adjustments are occurring now. In part it is attributable to the realization by church leaders of many denominations that increasing secularity in American life no longer allows for hostile divisions within Christianity. Furthermore, the spirit of ecumenism, with its emphasis on inclusiveness and its minimizing of particularity, also has contributed to more amicable relations. Religion-in-general, it seems, can be interpreted broadly enough to include Roman Catholicism.

If the change in attitude were occurring only within those denominations that traditionally have been inclusive or among those who have been participants in broad religious movements in the past, it might be regarded as merely an extreme in the rhythmic swing of the pendulum, a sign that the spirit of the times has, for the moment, taken control of their better judgment. But when such a change takes place within a denomination that has historically been particularistic and exclusive, it takes on added significance. A denomination that fits this description is the Lutheran Church-Missouri Synod. Through a study of the historical development of the Missouri Synod's conflict with Catholicism we can gain a better understanding of the whole phenomenon of anti-Catholicism and of the extent and significance of the change in attitude toward the Roman Catholic Church. This book is such a study.

The name Lutheran Church-Missouri Synod is somewhat

misleading, since the membership of the church extends far beyond the state of Missouri. In fact, there are member-congregations in all fifty states, in Canada, and in about a dozen Latin American countries; mission outposts are located around the world. The synod is most strongly represented in the Middle West, with more than half of its membership concentrated in eight Midwestern states, but California, New York, and Texas also have large contingents who call themselves "Missouri Lutherans." The Missouri Synod today ranks in size about midway between the other two large Lutheran bodies, the Lutheran Church in America, which is somewhat larger, and the American Lutheran Church. Realignments and mergers within Lutheranism make it difficult to trace the historical relations between these and other Lutheran bodies or to characterize the issues that keep them divided. The Missouri Synod increased in membership from about one million in 1917 to more than two and one-half million in 1963.

The Lutheran Church-Missouri Synod was founded in 1847 as the German Evangelical Lutheran Synod of Missouri, Ohio, and Other States. The designation "German" was dropped in 1917, in part because of anti-German sentiment in World War I, but also because the church was in fact losing some of its immigrant and ethnic character as it became Americanized. In 1947 the present name was adopted.

Throughout its history the Missouri Synod has been characterized by its insistence on a vigorous, assertive confessionalism, and has required its members to accept without reservation the Old and New Testaments as the written Word of God and the only rule and norm of faith and practice, and the Confessions of the Lutheran Church as the true and unadulterated statement and exposition of the Word of God. At various times in its history it has resisted forcefully such deviations as "dead orthodoxy," pietism, rationalism, and modernism, and thus has taken sharp issue with Protestant denominations in which these deviations gained acceptance. In opposing "unionism" it has been particularistic and exclusive, and has generally maintained that fellowship with other bodies can come only when there is complete agreement in both doctrine and practice. It has taken a strong position on many matters which seem to threaten the church and the purity of its teaching, such as lodges, evolution, secularism, and materialism.

In all of these matters the Missouri Synod has been willing to stand alone if necessary. It has sought neither to organize nor to follow crusades against that which it opposed. This applies also to its position on Catholicism. Although it was no doubt influenced both by its German origins and heritage and by the climate of hostility that prevailed in the United States, the anti-Catholicism of Missouri Synod Lutherans was based largely on religious convictions. Because of the synod's independent and even isolated character, parallels with strains of anti-Catholicism elsewhere in Protestantism are coincidental rather than derived. Thus the Lutheran opposition to Catholicism is a fitting subject for a case history.

As a case history, this book has narrowly defined limits. It treats only the period 1917 to 1963. In 1917 Lutherans were celebrating the four-hundredth anniversary of the Reformation with an extra flourish of anti-Catholicism. As we noted, this year also marks the approximate time at which the Missouri Synod began in earnest to shed its German character and to put itself into the mainstream of American religious life. The year 1963 was selected as the terminal date because by then the traditional Lutheran attitudes had been sufficiently challenged to compel Lutherans to undertake a reappraisal of their entire position in relation to Catholicism. Completing the symbolic significance of the inclusive dates, the year 1963 was also the four-hundredth anniversary of the closing of the Council of Trent.

Because this is a case history of the opposition to Catholicism among Missouri Synod Lutherans, anti-Catholic activities outside the synod are referred to only as they relate to the thought and practice within it. Furthermore, all the materials used, with only a few exceptions, were written by Missouri Synod Lutherans or produced by synodical or related agencies. In most instances they were intended primarily for the consumption of Missouri Synod readers. The only exceptions were those which were produced outside the synod but received wide circulation within it, or those which reported some significant extrasynodical activity by members of the synod. The sources used were, with minor exceptions, only those which appeared in print. What was said in pulpits, in classrooms, and in private conversations would no doubt make interesting and significant contributions, but would be difficult to assemble and assess properly. Finally, no attempt is made to present an accurate account of Catholic activities or to correct Lutheran misinterpretations of Roman Catholic teaching. Catholic readers may be dismayed at what Lutherans were told about Catholicism; nevertheless, where Lutheran impressions differed from the actualities, the impressions were obviously the determining factors in shaping the Lutheran attitudes and approaches. It is proper, incidentally, to speak in the plural in this respect, for there was no single or uniform approach even among Missouri Synod Lutherans. General theological agreement has not prevented Lutherans from looking at Catholicism in different ways. Indeed, through the years not only have individual Lutherans viewed Catholicism differently but individual writers have altered their approach as time and events passed.

This study is organized as follows: the first three chapters consider three different levels of approach to Catholicism;

chapters four through seven deal with Lutheran concern over the political power of the Roman Catholic Church as a threat to liberty, particularly to religious freedom; in chapters eight through eleven, four specific theological issues are discussed; the final two chapters are concerned with the reasons for changes in the Lutheran position and the nature and direction that the new position might take.

1

RHETORICAL CRITICISM IN
THE PRESS

In 1917 THE Lutheran conflict with Roman Catholicism was continuing into its fifth century. The differences between the two faiths were real and substantial, the issues were clear, the lines were drawn, and the positions had hardened. The terms for accommodation set by both sides precluded the likelihood of rapprochement, much less of reunion. Lutherans, nevertheless, could not simply ignore Catholicism. They felt constrained to meet in some way the challenge that Catholicism presented. Constructive debate in this situation would have been desirable, but it would have required that the differences be reevaluated, the issues restated, the lines redrawn, and the positions made more flexible, if not softened.

For much of the half century that followed 1917 that sort of debate was apparently not possible. Perhaps constructive criticism provided an alternative to debate or dialogue, but much of the criticism of Catholicism offered by Lutherans was not constructive; some of it was even of the carping, faultfinding, quibbling variety that characterizes popular journalistic criticism. For many of the participants in the warfare with Catholicism this journalistic criticism became so much the style that it appears to have prevented serious discussion of the differences and issues.

A characteristic instance of this type of criticism was displayed when in 1940 a Catholic Congressman protested against the issuance of a Mark Twain commemorative stamp because of Twain's conduct early in life. One Lutheran writer suggested that the real objection was that Twain had ridiculed the saints. Editorializing in the *Lutheran Witness,* he added that, along with Christian Science, Catholicism provides more material for jest, comedy, and humor than almost anything else in the world.[1]

This writer actually took Catholicism most seriously, for he and many others regarded it as a menace to the nation and their church. So dangerous a threat was Catholicism deemed to be that a form of holy warfare was waged against it. It may have been a war of words, but it was warfare nonetheless. Many editorials in Lutheran periodicals were laced with pejoratives, and some were intemperate in language. For example: "Romanism, built upon lies, feeds upon lies, welcomes lies, and employs lies as the principal means of propaganda. There never has been a greater liar than Rome."[2]

The most frequent and most biting spokesman along these lines was Martin S. Sommer, for many years a professor at Concordia Seminary, St. Louis, and coeditor of the *Lutheran Witness,* the official synodical magazine. His attacks on Catholicism grew out of his sincere conviction that the teachings of the Roman Catholic Church and of the pope were in opposition to the teachings of Jesus and that Lutherans must follow God's command to teach what Jesus had taught. He regarded the Roman Catholic Church as the strongest of all the forces in divided Christendom and believed that scriptural testimony could be used successfully in warning against it.[3] Sommer seized every opportunity to criticize Catholicism, contending that it was his constitutional right to do so, and was harsh with those who believed that religious tolerance

[1] Martin S. Sommer, "Mark Twain and Romanism," *Lutheran Witness,* LIX (September 17, 1940), 321.
[2] J. T. Mueller, "The Catholic Church Waits," *Theological Monthly,* III (January, 1923), 18–19.
[3] "Why Write Against Romanism?" *Witness,* LVI (August 24, 1937), 279–280.

implies the absence of religious criticism.[4] In opposing a bill under Congressional consideration designed to prohibit the sending in the mail of any periodical carrying polemical articles, he made a special point of reserving his right to criticize the Roman Catholic Church.[5]

Verbal warfare, unless it is only for exercise, carries with it the intention of incitement to action. Presumably the readers of *Witness* editorials were expected to respond in some way to the revelations and arguments of the editors. One of the possible courses of action open to anti-Catholic Protestants was to join an anti-Catholic organization, or at least to emulate its tactics. The most fanatical such organization in the 1920's, when the *Witness* editorials were most harsh, was the Ku Klux Klan. The editors could not of course approve the Klan's methods, so they had to find some way of dissociating themselves from it. They did so by denouncing both the Klan and the Roman Catholic Church in charging that the church was directly responsible for the existence of the Klan and that the Klan had been driven to desperate measures by Catholic efforts to take over the government. As Sommer put it, "Those whining and protesting Romanists have the greater sin, for they have driven these men to their excesses."[6] On the other hand, he contended that the Klan was helping the church by fighting it, thus giving Catholics a chance to speak of intolerance and bigotry and pernicious secret political activity and to be martyrs.[7]

[4] "The Intolerance of the Tolerant," *Witness*, XLIX (February 4, 1930), 39.

[5] "Liberty at Stake," *Witness*, LXIV (January 30, 1945), 35.

[6] "Catholics and the K.K.K.," *Witness*, XLII (January 30, 1923), 37.

[7] "Helping Romanism by Fighting It," *Witness*, XL (November 22, 1921), 379–380. A more detailed investigation of the Klan, without anti-Catholic overtones, was provided by W. H. T. Dau, *Weighed and Found Wanting: An Inquiry into the Aim and Meth-*

Theodore Graebner, also a professor at the St. Louis seminary and for many years Sommer's coeditor of the *Witness,* pointed out that criticism of both the Klan and the church should not be regarded as a defense of either. Granted that many of the charges of the Klan are true, he argued, it is also true that as long as the church conforms to the laws of Congress and of the various states, it is entitled to the protection of the federal and state powers. This might not preclude violence, but Christians should not participate in it:

We well know that the wealth of the Roman Church before long will be a serious menace to our country. What measures may be needed to remove this menace we do not know. That dispossession by force and in defiance of law may be the final outcome as it was in the French Revolution, when the Church gobbled up half the wealth of France, is not improbable. But as law-abiding citizens we cannot lend our hand to any unlawful act even against an organization so antagonistic to our Church as the Church of Rome.[8]

If action was expected of the readers, and if Klan-type action was not approved, what course might they follow in opposing Catholicism? Sommer asserted that since "the Antichrist is to be 'consumed with the Spirit of His mouth,' . . . the Spirit of Truth," the Christian's task is to "proclaim the Word of God."[9] It is true that in discussing Catholicism the pages of the synodical periodicals were filled with scriptural references. As we shall see later, this was particularly true when the theological differences were under scrutiny, even though we might at first be annoyed and then amused at the

ods of the Ku Klux Klan (Fort Wayne: American Luther League, 1923).

[8] *Witness,* XLIII (October 21, 1924), 379.

[9] "Rome Disturbing the World," *Witness,* XLIV (May 5, 1925), 144.

frequent references to 2 Thess. 2:3–12, the famous Antichrist passage.[10] But the rhetorical critics of Catholicism on occasion ranged far afield, and, from the perspective of the mid-1960's, the connection with proclaiming the Word of God appeared rather tenuous. Looking at the accumulated literature, one is able to discern a pattern of characteristics that may not have been apparent singly at any given time, but which has no doubt had a marked effect in shaping the attitudes toward Catholicism of those who were consistent readers during the first three or four decades of the period under consideration.

Although it was expressed in a more or less subtle manner, perhaps the most distinct and pervasive characteristic was the confidence that the teachings of the Lutheran Church-Missouri Synod were in accord with Scripture and that therefore conflicting teachings of other denominations were in error. For example, in identifying as the distinguishing mark of true Lutheranism its glorious scripturalness, John Theodore Mueller explained that this does not mean that there are no believing Christians in "Romanistic and Calvinistic denominations which still retain the essentials of the Christian faith." Even in these denominations some will be saved. "But," he said, "all these cases are exceptional and

[10] "Let no one deceive you in any way; for that day will not come, unless the rebellion comes first, and the man of lawlessness is revealed, the son of perdition, who opposes and exalts himself against every so-called god or object of worship, so that he takes his seat in the temple of God, proclaiming himself to be God. . . . And . . . the lawless one will be revealed, and the Lord Jesus will slay him with the breath of his mouth and destroy him by his appearing and his coming. The coming of the lawless one by the activity of Satan will be with all power and with pretended signs and wonders, and with all wicked deception for those who are to perish, because they refused to love the truth and so be saved. . . ." (RSV)

must be regarded as miracles of divine grace," occurring not because of, but in spite of, the unscriptural character of these denominations. The only reason differing denominations exist is because of the unscripturalness of the erring factions.[11]

The ramifications of this conviction are numerous; two stand out in regard to the conflict with Catholicism. First, it prompted Lutherans to assume an affected, patronizing attitude toward Catholics, as typified in Sommer's comment that "a true Lutheran does not hate the Catholics: he loves them; and because he loves them, he would gladly share his freedom, his truth, and his joy with them. That is the reason why Lutherans warn the Catholics against the errors of Rome."[12] More important, it led to an unwillingness to see anything good in the Roman Catholic Church and even to an almost hostile desire to prevent contact and exchange with it. For example, in 1922 Sommer criticized a Baptist preacher for commending the Roman Catholic Church on such matters as the copying of New Testament manuscripts by monks, on the sense of reverence and worship the church developed in its people, on its efforts to uphold marriage vows, on its stressing of obedience to authority, and on the service given by an unselfish clergy. Instead, according to Sommer, he should have referred to 2 Thess. 2:7–12, to the tyranny of Rome, and to its false doctrine.[13] On another occasion he denounced a meeting of Catholic and Protestant laymen, sponsored by the Knights of Columbus, for the purpose of allaying religious

---

[11] "Lutheranism in Its Fundamental Opposition to Romanism, Calvinism, and Modernism," *Proceedings of the 23rd Convention of the Central Illinois District,* 1942, pp. 12–13, 21.

[12] "Lutherans Are Debtors to the Catholics," *Witness,* LXV (March 12, 1946), 84.

[13] "Foolish Protestants Helping Rome," *Witness,* XLI (May 23, 1922), 168.

prejudices. The Knights could, he observed, use their own churches for this purpose, but "they prefer to use their own church to *sow* religious prejudice against Luther, Lutherans, and all Protestants, while they would like to lure some foolish Protestants to public halls to tell them that Rome is a mere harmless kitten, and is humbly satisfied with bare tolerance."[14]

Similarly, a well-intended statement by *Our Sunday Visitor* evoked an unenthusiastic response. The *Visitor* had commented that it respected Lutherans above all other Protestants because of their adherence to most of the fundamental teachings of Christ. Sommer queried, as would any good Lutheran, "To which fundamental teaching of Christ does the Lutheran Church not adhere?" Then he added that the differences between Lutherans and Roman Catholics cannot be bridged over by personal pleasantries and mutual personal good will.[15]

Another general characteristic of the rhetorical journalistic response to Catholicism was the tendency to reply directly to Catholic words and deeds. Occasionally this reply took the form of some overt action, as in 1926, when a Chicago Lutheran pastoral conference, in response to the pomp and publicity of the Roman Catholic Eucharistic Congress then in progress, resolved to set aside a day for revealing "the true purposes" of the Eucharistic Congress and to give their own sermons as much local publicity as possible.[16]

More often the reply was in print. Usually the regular periodicals provided the media, but occasionally extra efforts were expended. In 1944 Walter A. Maier, characteristically leaning heavily on the exclamation point of his typewriter, advanced a ten-point program for fighting Catholic propa-

[14] "Jesuitic Politics," *Witness,* XXXVI (February 20, 1917), 55–56.
[15] "Lutherans Respected," *Witness,* LIII (December 4, 1934), 418.
[16] Graebner, *Witness,* XLV (June 1, 1926), 177–178.

ganda. Maier, a professor at Concordia Seminary in St. Louis and editor of the *Walther League Messenger,* a magazine for young people, proposed the development of a propaganda machine similar to that of the Catholics, one which would win favor through the use of the press, radio, tracts, and any other means of influencing public opinion.[17]

The following year the *Witness* commended groups in Fort Wayne and St. Louis which had taken it upon themselves to reply in the papers to the Knights of Columbus newspaper advertisements, and the writer urged more groups to follow the same course.[18] Also in 1945 the American Lutheran Publicity Bureau, an organization loosely affiliated with the Missouri Synod, announced through its official organ, the *American Lutheran,* that the Catholic campaign to win America had brought matters to such a crisis that the Board of Directors was prompted to urge special efforts to meet it. The bureau had already been assisting local groups in meeting Catholic attacks and in some cases in taking the offensive, but now a special Lutheran Reply Fund was being established for this single purpose.[19] Apparently this effort never developed into anything significant, for there are no later reports on its achievements, although the publication of the harshly anti-Catholic pamphlet *The Split Between Roman Catholicism and Christ* can perhaps be related to "The Lutheran Reply."[20]

---

[17] "Fight Catholic Propaganda!" *Walther League Messenger,* LIII (October, 1944), 54–55, 80–81.

[18] Graebner, "Meeting the Knights in the Newspapers," *Witness,* LXIV (March 27, 1945), 100.

[19] "The Lutheran Reply," *American Lutheran,* XXVIII (May, 1945), 4.

[20] [Oswald C. J. Hoffmann], *The Split Between Roman Catholicism and Christ* (New York: The Lutheran Press, n.d. [1945]); *American Lutheran* XXVIII (October, 1945), 4. The booklet is now out of print after the distribution of more than 1,000,000 copies.

The third characteristic apparent in this approach to Catholicism was the heavy reliance on encyclicals, other papal statements, pronouncements of bishops and cardinals, and Catholic encyclopedias and textbooks, as the authority for Roman Catholic doctrine and practice. The authoritarian, hierarchy-oriented tradition in the Roman Catholic Church made this a natural tendency, but if there were any Catholic theologians before the late 1950's they remained largely unknown or unread by Lutheran commentators.

This reliance on official statements of the church showed itself regularly through the years, and the practice of "quoting the popes" to refute a current Catholic position was commonly used. Later we shall call attention to the absolute unwillingness to accept at face value any current Catholic opinion that contradicted in any way the church's formal position. Closely related to this was the popular practice, typified by William Dallmann's article "Why Lutheran—Not Catholic," of exposing Roman Catholic theology by positing an official Catholic pronouncement next to a statement from the Word of God or the works of Luther.[21] It should be noted that this characteristic was not exclusive to the rhetorical journalistic critics. The serious polemicists (not to imply that the critics were not serious) whom we shall consider later also relied almost exclusively on these sources. Only very recently have Roman Catholic theologians received attention from Lutheran writers.

This practice led Lutherans to believe that contradictory opinions within Catholicism were simply deceptive cover and to demand absolute capitulation by Catholics as terms for agreement or fellowship. Theodore Graebner displayed this

[21] Sommer, "The Reformation—The Work of God," *Witness,* XXXVI (October 16, 1917), 318–319; Dallmann, "Why Lutheran—Not Catholic," *American Lutheran,* XXVIII (June, 1945), 6–8.

attitude in the editorial greetings and good wishes he extended to a newly created cardinal in 1921. He commented that if the wishes of the *Witness* were realized, they would prove an even greater blessing to the cardinal than the one received from the pope's hands. The wishes of the *Witness* were, in summary, that the cardinal might reject the Roman Catholic position on the hierarchy, the Mass, Mary and the saints, the priesthood, Scripture, tradition, papal authority, and the doctrine of justification.[22] Similarly, in discussing a speech by Archbishop Schrembs of Cleveland, Walter A. Maier allowed that possibly Rome *is* changing, but he added: "In view of past history, most conclusive evidence of that change would be the specific disavowal of official acts and utterances that are clearly bigoted and intolerant."[23] Along the same lines the *Witness,* editorializing on Catholic-Protestant tensions, commented: "Let Pius XII rescind some of the pronouncements of his predecessors . . . or publish an encyclical in support of the apologies of prominent Catholics in this country, and the hard feelings between the Protestant and the Roman Catholics will begin to disappear."[24]

A persistent emphasis on the history of the Roman Catholic Church and on the distinct continuity between past and present in Catholic practice is the fourth general characteristic in the rhetorical anti-Catholicism of the journalistic critics. In 1917 Theodore Graebner published *The Dark Ages,*[25] a muckraking exposé of conditions in pre-Reformation Europe. Convincingly written, as were all of Graebner's writings, it described in detail examples of perverted religiosity and moral

[22] "To Cardinal Dougherty, Greetings," *Witness,* XL (April 26, 1921), 136.
[23] "Is Rome Changing?" *Walther League Messenger,* XLVIII (March, 1940), 384–385, 414–416.
[24] *Witness,* LXXI (June 24, 1952), 9.
[25] (St. Louis: Concordia, 1917).

decay of medieval life. Graebner contended that this was not the Age of Faith, but rather an age of wickedness, attributable largely to the teaching and practice of the Roman Catholic Church. Veneration of relics, pilgrimages, superstitions, the domination by the financially and sexually corrupt clergy, the monasteries as seats of wickedness, the tyranny of the papacy, the Inquisition, depraved Rome, and many other features of the Middle Ages were portrayed vividly. Factual accuracy is not the important question; rather, the question is, Was it slanted? The answer is that it was distinctly slanted to fix all the responsibility for such wicked conditions as existed on the Roman Catholic Church. Frequent references to this book for many years indicate that it had significant influence in shaping the attitudes of Lutherans toward the Roman Catholic Church.

Another book, not of the same quality, but in the same category and apparently with similar influence, was William Dallmann's *How Peter Became Pope* (published originally as a series of articles in the *Concordia Theological Monthly*).[26] Incoherently put together, poorly documented, and not dealing with the subject in the title, the book is in fact a collection of gossip, some substantiated, about the popes through the centuries. Again, factual accuracy is not the principal concern; rather, we note that this was the sort of diet on which Lutherans were nourished as they faced the problems posed by Catholicism.

In their books both Graebner and Dallmann emphasized the persecution and oppression practiced by Catholicism in the past. Frequent references to conditions in Latin America and to the fate of Protestants in Catholic countries stressed the belief that the church would extend past practices into the present whenever possible and that it does indeed persecute

[26] (St. Louis: Concordia, 1931).

now wherever it has the power to do so. Sommer even contended that when Catholics complain about treatment they are receiving from different governments, they are really complaining because the power to persecute other religions has been taken from them.[27] J. T. Mueller cited a reference to a catechism written by a Jesuit in Paris in 1929 which allegedly encouraged inquisition and persecution. Mueller, for many years a professor at Concordia Seminary in St. Louis, remarked that the chapters of history that tell of the fury of the papacy against all who dared to profess the pure gospel ought to be studied. In a footnote he added that "there are not many periodicals today that dare to tell the world what Rome really is and demands."[28]

The role of the Jesuits in the dark history of the Roman Catholic Church was also stressed. Several times Walter A. Maier went to great pains to show how C. F. W. Walther, an honored founder of the Missouri Synod, had forced a showdown with the Jesuits in St. Louis on whether the Jesuits adhere to the principle that the end justifies the means. The alleged failure of the Jesuits to appear for the showdown meeting was taken to prove that they do indeed subscribe to this principle. He added that just a look at Jesuit writers shows this principle to be accepted.[29] The implication of this emphasis, of course, was that since persecution is now not

[27] "The Wailing of the Romanists," *Witness,* L (September 1, 1931), 297.

[28] "Jesuitism and the Persecution of Protestants," *Concordia Theological Monthly,* X (October, 1939), 787–788.

[29] "A Challenge Which the Jesuits Did Not Accept," *Walther League Messenger,* XXXI (November, 1922), 121; "The End Justifies the Means," *Walther League Messenger,* XL (March, 1932), 420–421, 456. The only extended treatment of the Jesuits, written from a highly hostile viewpoint, was F. J. Lankenau, "The Jesuits," in *Great Leaders and Great Events,* edited by Louis Buchheimer (St. Louis: Concordia, 1922), pp. 224–244.

legal, the Jesuits will find other means of achieving their ends. The modern way the Jesuits have of robbing the people of the sure Word of God was described by another writer in this way:

> These Jesuits are going up and down the land and fooling people with their sleight-of-hand performances, making fools of their audiences, and casting thousands into damnation. By their adroit scene-shifting they slip the Word of God out of sight, and push the fiction and fraud of an infallibility in its place. These are the arts and sciences of the devil, who stalks about in the garb of these Jesuits, and dupes thousands into eternal damnation.[30]

The fear of a return to a policy of outright persecution nevertheless was claimed. When Pope Pius XI exhorted the Dominican Order in 1934 to "rally to the standards of St. Dominic and to drive out heresy" by following the standards of their founder, Maier wrote in the *Messenger:*

> This is dangerous advice; for while Dominic generally disdained the resort to arms, it is a matter of history that he was not completely adverse to spreading Roman Catholicism by the sword. . . .
> To appeal for a re-emphasis of this conversion by-the-sword policy and the spread of this repent-or-be-slaughtered program can be viewed only with more than ordinary alarm. It is tell-tale evidence that Rome never changes.[31]

Sommer, on another occasion, urged that the proposed revision of the Lutheran hymnal retain the phrase in one of Luther's hymns "Restrain the Murderous Pope and Turk" on the grounds that it still applied.[32]

---

[30] G. E. Hagemann, "Why Do Catholics Accept the Deity of Christ?" *Theological Quarterly,* XXI (July, 1917), 142.

[31] "Will Blood Flow?" *Walther League Messenger,* XLII (May, 1934), 524.

[32] "Restrain the Murderous Pope and Turk," *Witness,* LIII (February 13, 1934), 58.

The emphasis on the sordid side of Roman Catholic history was used primarily to show what conditions would be like if the Roman Catholic Church were to gain a dominant position in America. Periodic revelation of current Catholic troubles, in order to place the church in a bad light, is still another general characteristic we note in Lutheranism's journalistic conflict with Catholicism. Here again Martin Sommer was the principal reporter and commentator. In 1924, for example, he commented on a report that when the Loyola University of Chicago football team stayed at the Marquette Hotel in St. Louis, they threw a lot of Gideon Bibles from the windows. He wrote:

> It is time for Protestants to come out in the open to call these offenders by their right names and to hold them to account. . . .
>
> We have known bands of Catholic boys interrupting the services of Protestant congregations and mutilating the property of Protestant churches. Where do they learn and imbibe this vandalism?
>
> Romanists complain of the persecution of the Ku Klux Klan, but give them but half the chance, and they themselves will out-Klux the Klan.[33]

Concerning a report about a defecting priest who had attended a "college of propaganda" in Rome for four years, during which time six of his companions became "totally affected in mind and became inmates of lunatic asylums," Sommer exhorted Lutherans to thank God for Martin Luther and the message of deliverance that came through him.[34] Commenting on a report that well over one-half the inmates at Sing Sing were Catholics, he observed that while it may be true that the prison is located in a region where Catholics are

[33] "The Catholic Church and The Bible," *Witness,* XLIII (January 15, 1924), 26.
[34] "Ex-priests," *Witness,* LIII (October 23, 1934), 370.

in the majority, it is also true that a comparison of conditions in regions anywhere in the world which are predominantly Catholic with Protestant regions will show that unsanitary conditions and sickness, ignorance and beggary, are greater in Catholic communities.[35] Sometimes Sommer's solutions to Catholic problems would certainly have amused Catholics. Noting that the pope was hoping to cut down on lawlessness by Italians in American cities through more active religious ministrations, he asserted that this was not the right means. He urged instead that the pope should introduce them to Luther's Small Catechism![36]

Sommer also took delight in giving statistical reports which he believed reflected against the Roman Catholic Church. He was most happy when he could report that another Catholic priest had defected, especially if the priest had been a Jesuit.[37] But he also took pleasure in reporting the number of persons estimated to be leaving the Roman Catholic Church each year. Not only did his box score show that Catholic gains were diminishing, while Protestant gains were increasing, with the balance in favor of Protestantism, but he also claimed that Lutheran preaching and Lutheran publications were still forcing Catholic authorities to tell their people more of the truth, so as to give at least the impression that they are also teaching the faith in the only Savior.[38] He reported further

[35] "The Religion of Prisoners," *Witness,* LII (January 31, 1933), 37.
[36] "The Pope Ashamed of Italian Emigrants," *Witness,* XLVIII (January 8, 1929), 7. Sommer's editorials were never profound and rarely provocative; most were shallow or innocuous. In reading them today one suspects that they must have been widely unread, a suspicion generally confirmed in conversations with those who were *Witness* subscribers during his tenure as coeditor. It is tempting but unwise to regard him as entirely representative of Lutheran thought.
[37] "Another Jesuit Quitting," *Witness,* XLVII (January 10, 1928), 8.
[38] "Catholics Still Turning Protestant," *Witness,* XLVII (January 24, 1928), 22.

that adult converts to the Roman Catholic Church frequently give the church considerable trouble, for when they find out what Catholicism really is, they become unhappy.[39]

Another way of attempting to discredit the Roman Catholic Church was to refer to the various alleged methods of raising money. Most typical were the assertions that Catholics cling tenaciously to the doctrine of purgatory because it "fills their coffers."[40] In commenting on the efforts of the pope to serve as peacemaker, Sommer observed that "if men were only willing to pay him enough, he would decide every family quarrel."[41] A brief item in the *Messenger* noted that "the pass sign to privilege in the Roman Catholic Church is the dollar sign." In this instance the writer was referring to a report that monks and nuns were buying their way out of cloisters and convents.[42]

Another, somewhat puzzling characteristic of the Lutheran anti-Catholic warfare was the suggestion that somehow, in some unspecified way, there was a secret alliance between the Roman Catholic Church and some other power interests. This idea was expressed infrequently, and then only in tentative terms, but it did play a part in the thinking of those who were shaping the attitudes of the reading constituency in the synod.

In 1922, for example, W. H. T. Dau wrote with concern over the amicable relations between the Masons and the Knights of Columbus.[43] That same month Maier referred to the Jewish interests, the Vatican, and Masonry as the great

[39] "Converts to the Roman Church," *Witness,* LXVII (September 7, 1948), 284.

[40] Sommer, "Masses for the Dead," *Witness,* LVIII (April 4, 1939), 119–120.

[41] "The Pope to the Rescue," *Witness,* XLIII (February 26, 1924), 74–75.

[42] *Walther League Messenger,* XXXIV (May, 1926), 551.

[43] "Masons and Knights of Columbus," *Theological Monthly,* II (February, 1922), 61.

powers trying to rule the world.[44] The following year Graebner suggested that the happy cooperation between the Knights of Columbus, Masons, and Jews leads to a coalition between them for control of political affairs.[45] Later, Graebner was more specific, as he first condemned the good fraternal relations between the Masons and the Knights of Columbus and then speculated on how these good relations could exist, knowing the official antagonism of the Roman Catholic Church to the Masonic Order. He continued:

> We are not guessing when we say that both the Masonic Order and the Roman Catholic hierarchy are part of that Invisible Government which rules national and international politics, and for which the constitutional governments are but screens. Is it possible that in the friendly relations between Masons and Knights of Columbus we are permitted to get a glimpse of the true relation between the heads of both systems?

He did not draw a definite conclusion, but stated simply, "Let us wait and see."[46]

Waiting and seeing had not resolved the question in Graebner's mind by 1940, only by this time he was seeing a different alliance. First he noted that the "back of the dragon of the Papacy has been broken," so that in spite of all its efforts, including propaganda, falsification of history, slander of the Reformers, control of government and education, a vigorous mission and proselytizing program, and Catholic Action, it could not regain the power it once had. He then wondered about the present tie-up between the Roman Catholic Church and the "international Jew." Disclaiming

[44] "Trying to Rule the World," *Walther League Messenger,* XXX (February, 1922), 266.
[45] "Going Shares?" *Witness,* XLII (July 31, 1923), 246–247.
[46] "Shriners and the Knights of Columbus," *Witness,* XLIII (September 23, 1924), 345–346.

anti-Semitism, he was nevertheless puzzled at the friendliness he saw. He concluded:

> We have a right to ask just what is behind this approachment between the Roman Church and the modern Jew. Jewish magazines come to this desk regularly, and recently there was not an issue that did not acknowledge gratefully this new friendship of the Roman Catholic Church. What does it all mean?[47]

The final characteristic shown by those waging journalistic warfare against Catholicism was a strong, perhaps instinctive, tendency to defend Martin Luther against slanderous attacks by Catholic writers. Although the attacks, generally charging Luther with immorality or with responsibility for the rise of Hitler, were recognized as low-level and unfounded, the writers were compelled to reply. The response, usually on the same level as the attack, commonly took one of three forms: citing examples of papal immorality,[48] referring to the judgment of objective historians,[49] or quoting Catholic writers who had spoken well of Luther. "Lies About Luther Refuted by Candid Catholics," a series of articles by William Dallmann, a well-known parish pastor and writer, is perhaps the best example of "replying in kind."[50]

The observer in the mid-1960's, influenced by the develop-

---

[47] "Not Forgetting the Hammer Blows," *Witness,* LIX (January 23, 1940), 19–20.

[48] Sommer, "A Horrible Charge Against Luther," *Witness,* XXXVI (April 17, 1917), 117.

[49] Graebner, "Luther in World Opinion," *Witness,* LXIV (June 5, 1945), 179–180.

[50] "Lies About Luther Refuted by Candid Catholics," *Walther League Messenger,* LIII (June, 1945), 380–381, 408; LIII (July, 1945), 424–425, 453; LIII (August, 1945), 472–473; LIV (September, 1945), 18–19, 34–36. This series was to be continued, but when Maier left the editorship, no further articles were published.

ments of Vatican II, must be careful not to judge too harshly those engaged in the verbal antagonisms of an earlier day. The writers cited in this chapter did not in any sense regard themselves as captious critics, editorial snipers, or petty warriors. They took their work seriously, carried on in God's name, and no doubt believed that they were making a constructive contribution to Lutheran resistance to Catholic aggression and false doctrine. Although they added to the prevailing climate of hostility and suspicion, they were as much the products of that climate as they were its creators. In fairness to these men it should also be noted that since their basic position was one of reaction to Catholic words and actions, their criticism would have been pointless had they found no real targets in Catholic practice or no counterparts among Catholic writers. There were journalistic warriors on both sides.

The Lutheran critics were, for the most part, writing for a closed audience, and could afford at times to be incautious or injudicious. Furthermore, they probably supposed that their readers wanted this type of writing. A letter to the editor in 1957, after the approach of the *Witness* had begun to moderate, inquired about the change. "Has our Lutheranism reached the point of perfection where we do not need an occasional barb to jolt us out of our complacency?" the reader asked.[51]

The real significance of the rhetorical criticism in the press does not lie in its contribution to Lutheran-Catholic relations at the time that it was written. Rather, it is significant because it shaped the mentality of the hundreds of thousands of readers who were exposed to it. We shall have occasion to consider the effect of this in a later chapter.

[51] *Witness,* LXXVI (January 15, 1957), 47.

2

EXERCISES IN POLEMICS

As WE MOVE from a discussion of rhetorical criticism in the press to a look at serious polemics, we shall see that it is difficult to establish arbitrarily three distinct levels of opposition to Catholicism. Because we analyze the writings, and not the writers themselves, some men who were engaged in the criticism described in the first chapter will appear here as serious polemicists. Similarly, because the men whose writings are discussed in these two chapters lived in the same environment and had generally the same theological training, their writings expressed many of the same ideas and exhibited many of the same characteristics. The differences that existed were differences of degree; one should not look for the complete presence or absence of a given idea, attitude, or practice, nor should one assume that the three levels of opposition described here were neatly chronological.

Along with the critics, the polemicists shared the underlying assumption that Rome never changes. Since Rome is always the same, it is not necessary to study either what Roman Catholic theologians are saying currently or the opinions that are being expressed unofficially, even by those in the hierarchy. A look at what has been stated officially at any given point in history is all that is required. This official pronouncement then serves as the subject of the polemics.

The principal distinguishing mark of the polemicists was their concentration on the theological issues. In journalistic attacks one writes editorials about Peter's mother-in-law so that she will not be forgotten, as the Catholics would like;[1] in polemics one is concerned with such basic matters as sin, justification, and the means of grace.

A favored practice of the polemicists, as it was also of the journalistic critics, was to lay Lutheran and Catholic doctrine side by side in parallel columns, citing the source from which each was derived. In *The Split Between Roman Catholicism and Christ* the columns were headed "The Word of Rome" and "The Word of God." Theodore Hoyer, a professor at Concordia Seminary, St. Louis, identified them as "God's Truth" and "Rome's Falsehood" in his widely distributed pamphlet *Why I Am Not a Roman Catholic.*[2] With only parenthetical introductions, Hoyer relied solely on Scripture texts for delineation of the Lutheran position; for the Catholic side only official pronouncements were cited, more than half of them from the canons and decrees of the Council of Trent. The principal difference between Hoyer's work and Dallmann's "Why Lutheran—Not Catholic," referred to above, is that Hoyer was more concerned with the central issues, as it is evident when the topics treated by the two men are listed in adjacent columns:

Dallmann	Hoyer
Justification	The Norm and Rule of Life
Indulgences	Reading the Scripture
The Sacrifice in the Mass	Original Sin
	Christ's Redemption
Transubstantiation	Justification
Denying the Cup	The Assurance of Salvation
Adoration of the Wafer	Good Works
	Purgatory

[1] Martin Sommer, "Peter's Wife's Mother," *Lutheran Witness,* LXVIII (July 26, 1949), 240.
[2] (St. Louis: Concordia, 1953; fourth printing, 1960).

Human Mediators
Mariolatry
Preachers Burned
Bibles Burned
Theocracy
Purgatory
Vain Repetitions
Wrong Cults
Auricular Confession
Celibacy
Monkery
Forbidding to Marry
Forbidding Meats
Union of Church
   and State
Persecution

The Means of Grace
The Mass
Indulgences
Confession (Penance)
Veneration of Angels and Saints
Rulership in the Church
The Use of Secular Power in and by
   the Church
Using Temporal Power to Enforce the
   Teaching of the Church
Marriage

A slightly different practice was followed in the series of short polemical articles by Carl S. Meyer, also of Concordia Seminary, in the *Lutheran Witness* from mid-1957 until the end of 1958. This series, "Let's Investigate," represented the acceptance of a challenge by the Knights of Columbus to investigate the claims of the Roman Catholic Church as the only true church.[3] The very brief articles examined and answered the claims as they were stated in the Knights of Columbus advertisements.

Another series of *Witness* articles to which we shall refer later, titled "Why Pastors Warn Members About the Roman Catholic Church," was written by James G. Manz in 1962. Manz, a Chicago parish pastor, conceded that it was no longer popular to discuss issues like this, but he declared that it was nevertheless necessary, for the differences between the Roman Catholic Church and the Lutheran Church were essen-

---

[3] *Witness,* LXXVI (July 30, 1957), 380.

tially the same as at the time of the Reformation. A friendly approach by Rome, he added, does not change in the least those basic doctrines that split the church in Luther's day.[4]

Manz followed his intention to speak the truth in love and to adhere to a strictly scriptural point of view, but he happened to be writing when the winds of change were strong. Upon the completion of the six-month series he apparently had some misgivings, if not about the content, at least over the timing. He asked: "Could it be that our *Witness* articles on the Roman Catholic Church have introduced a discordant note into the hopeful church unity situation of 1962? One finds considerable emphasis on friendly 'dialog' and on understanding different points of view of the 'separated brethren' of Christendom." He also noted that some Lutheran theologians believe that it is misleading and uncharitable to regard the canons and decrees of the Council of Trent as representative of Roman Catholic teaching and that there can be no doubt concerning the excellent Christian witness being given by such Catholic theologians as Karl Adam, Hans Küng, and Gustave Weigel (to whom, incidentally, he had not referred in his series). In seeking nevertheless to justify his articles, Manz called attention to the limitations of space, to the attempt to write in a popular style, and to the "riddle" of Roman Catholicism. He claimed that the articles were aimed at the laity and clergy who live and work at the grass-roots level and that Cardinal Spellman and *Our Sunday Visitor* are surely more characteristic on this level than, say, *Commonweal*. Finally, he emphasized that Lutherans must be kept informed, for they cannot condone false doctrine.[5]

Of the great abundance of polemical literature in books,

---

[4] "America—Stronghold of Protestantism?" *Witness*, LXXXI (January 23, 1962), 30–31, 44.
[5] "A Discordant Note?" *Witness*, LXXXI (July 24, 1962), 364–365.

magazines, and tracts, we should here take special note of an essay which exemplifies the efforts of a highly partisan observer to deal in a detached fashion with the central theological issues. In the strictest sense of the word, Frederick E. Mayer's "The Holy Catholic Apostolic Roman Church" in *The Religious Bodies of America*[6] should not be called polemical; yet even though he aimed at interpreting the doctrines and practices of the Roman Catholic Church objectively and without bias, he was unable to do so without acknowledging and citing the basic differences between Catholics and Lutherans. The idea that the Roman Catholic Church is basically in error is evident throughout. Nevertheless, it is less judgmental in tone than its predecessor volume, *Popular Symbolics,*[7] published twenty years earlier.

The striking feature of Mayer's work is that although he relied heavily on papal pronouncements and the decrees of Trent, he also acknowledged that "there is probably no other Church which has the capacity for harboring so many widely divergent theological points of view."[8] By distinguishing between Rome's policy and Rome's principle he showed how the church is able to work out a *modus vivendi* for almost every situation.[9] "It is extremely difficult," he wrote, "to determine, with any degree of certainty, the exact position of Rome on many significant points of doctrine."[10] He continued:

> The Roman Church is the most dogmatic and at the same time the least doctrinal Church. There is a fixed

[6] *The Religious Bodies of America* (St. Louis: Concordia, 1954). This work was revised three times, most recently in 1961, by Arthur Carl Piepkorn. The 1954 edition is used in this study because it was entirely the work of Mayer.

[7] Theodore Engelder *et al., Popular Symbolics* (St. Louis: Concordia, 1934), pp. 147–206.

[8] *Religious Bodies of America,* p. 30

[9] *Ibid.,* pp. 106–107.

[10] *Ibid.,* p. 33.

dogmatic limit, but within this limit there is room for divergent and often contradictory opinions. It is difficult to understand how Rome sometimes can be extremely dogmatic in certain theological matters, and sometimes very tolerant. This enigma resolves itself when one understands both the formal and the material principle of Roman theology.[11]

The next twenty pages were devoted to elucidating these two principles. The idea of a monolithic and unchanging church was minimized.

The efforts of the polemicists to concentrate on the principal theological issues naturally had an effect on the tone and content of their writing. They were stern and unyielding without being abusive. They were critical of Catholic history, but did not usually find it necessary to recount tales of dread or to parade the horribles. Consequently we are able to identify a second distinguishing characteristic shared by those engaged in polemics: a more charitable attitude toward the Roman Catholic Church and particularly toward Catholic parishioners, who were usually regarded as good neighbors and honorable fellow citizens. They attempted to make clear that the differences with Roman Catholic officialdom did not in all cases apply with equal force to individual Catholics.

In 1948 Theodore Graebner, whose position on Catholicism had moderated somewhat, wrote that "we are able to distinguish between fellowship with Roman Catholics and other religions, and our attitude toward their personal relation to God." He continued: "We well know and have always taught that there are true believers in our Protestant church bodies and in the Roman Catholic communion. We are far from thinking that only Lutherans will be our associates in heaven."[12] W. Gustave Polack, another St. Louis professor

[11] *Ibid.*, p. 36.
[12] "A Plea for Tolerance," *Witness,* LXVII (January 13, 1948), 14.

and an editor of the *Witness,* commented similarly in replying
to criticism in *Our Sunday Visitor.* He said that Lutherans did
not oppose the Roman Catholic Church because it was large
and aggressive, but rather because of some of its teachings
and also because of the political machinations of some of its
leaders. As for their Catholic fellow citizens, Polack added,
by and large they are devout, conscientious, and law-abiding
people, and Lutherans try to be fair and honorable toward
them. Of the church itself he wrote:

> The Lutheran Church has always recognized the Roman
> Catholic Church as part of the visible Church on earth.
> We recognize its ministry. We hold its Baptisms to be
> valid. We believe that the Holy Ghost also works in this
> part of Christendom through the means of grace. We be-
> lieve that He converts sinners from the error of their ways
> also through the work of this Church. We do not prosely-
> tize among Roman Catholics.[13]

This, of course, differs substantially from the assertion of
J. T. Mueller, cited earlier, that salvation outside the Lutheran Church is exceptional and must be regarded as a
miracle of divine grace.

Just as those carrying on petty warfare had to determine
their relations with the radical anti-Catholic groups, particularly the Ku Klux Klan, so the polemicists had to decide the
extent to which they would agree and cooperate with those
groups and individuals outside the Lutheran Church who
were also engaged in anti-Catholic polemics. It had been a
relatively easy matter to reject and disavow the Klan. The
almost simultaneous rise to prominence of Paul Blanshard
and the formation of Protestants and Other Americans United
for Separation of Church and State (POAU) presented a
problem that was not resolved so easily.

[13] "Dangerous Tensions," *Witness,* XLVIII (November 15, 1949),
371–372.

The formal organization of the POAU was noted by William Arndt in January, 1948. His concern, surprisingly, was not with its aims and methods; rather, he wondered whether such a society, organized for the sole purpose of maintaining separation of church and state, might not itself be a violation of that principle. He concluded that one could not justly accuse it of acting contrary to its own purpose. Because it was not seeking special privileges, the church and state principle did not apply.[14]

Two months later the immediate objectives and the general purposes of the POAU were reprinted in the *Concordia Theological Monthly*. Mayer appeared to be in general agreement but did nothing to promote the organization.[15] In the summer of 1948 the Lutheran Educational Conference, a meeting of education executives from across the country, devoted part of its program to a panel discussion on the POAU's recent "Protestant Manifesto." W. G. Polack pointed out that "we have reached a period in our national history in which the activity of the Roman Catholic hierarchy for special favors to their institutions is becoming increasingly bold and sometimes even brazen" and that if its efforts to receive public funds are successful, "our liberties will be lost." But, he added, it must be clearly understood that this is not a movement against the Roman Catholic Church as such.[16] After other panelists had summarized Protestant and Catholic reaction to the manifesto and considered a presentation on "Luther and the Confessions on the Separation of Church and

[14] "An Organization for Maintaining Separation of Church and State," *Concordia Theological Monthly*, XIX (January, 1948), 64–65.

[15] "A Protestant Manifesto," *Concordia Theological Monthly*, XIX (March, 1948), 216–218.

[16] *Report of the 1948 Educational Conference* (River Forest, Illinois: Board for Parish Education, The Lutheran Church-Missouri Synod, 1948), p. 73.

State," Albert G. Huegli discussed the stand that Lutherans should take on it. He concluded that it would not be wise to join hands with the POAU but that the possibility of being of service to the aims of the manifesto still existed. Such service, however, should be done only after Lutherans had carefully reexamined their position on the issues and brought their practices into line.[17]

Apparently the POAU never received any kind of official sanction in the synod, nor is it recorded that any prominent officials sought membership. On the other hand, neither was there any official disapproval or denunciation, although the *Cresset,* published by Valparaiso University, an institution affiliated with the synod, expressed disfavor with its attitudes and methods on the grounds that there is a vast difference between freedom *of* religion and freedom *from* religion. The kind of religious liberty favored by the POAU, according to the *Cresset,* comes perilously close to freedom *from* religion. Observing that the POAU really offered a choice between Blanshard and Spellman, the *Cresset* refused to choose and contended that there is a middle way which is in keeping both with the ideals of American democracy and with the historic insistence of the church that its message is applicable to every

---

[17] *Ibid.,* pp. 79–81. Stirred by Roman Catholic actions, Lorman M. Petersen, a Peoria, Illinois, pastor, prepared *A Critical Analysis of "A Manifesto" by "Protestants and Other Americans United for Separation of Church and State" and Its Relation to the Lutheran Church-Missouri Synod* (Peoria: Committee on Parish Education and Youth Work, Central Illinois District, The Lutheran Church-Missouri Synod, 1949). He relied heavily on the 1948 Lutheran Educational Conference report and on *Christian Century* articles. His "analysis" was largely devoted to exposure of Catholic abuses and to enthusiastic acceptance of the position stated in the manifesto. He concluded that "for want of something better to uphold the Principle of Separation of Church and State in America, we shall quietly support the spirit and major principles of the POAU" (p. 41).

moment and every activity of life.[18] Some years later the *Cresset* referred to the POAU as a "screwball outfit."[19]

A similar reception was accorded the books by Paul Blanshard. Mayer reviewed *American Freedom and Catholic Power* sympathetically, almost cordially, in 1949, but did not endorse or recommend it. His principal objection was to Blanshard's liberal theology.[20] Carl S. Meyer treated the second edition in much the same way in 1958.[21] Again it was the *Cresset* that spoke the word of dissent. Observing that controversy over questions of church and state is a good thing, it asserted that it becomes a bad thing if it merely stirs the radical anti-Catholic forces to renewed hatred and fanaticism not only in their opposition to Catholicism but to Christianity itself. This, it said, is a real danger when the attack is made by Paul Blanshard.[22] In reviewing another book by Blanshard in 1951, James Savage wrote in the *Cresset:* "Everything is so easy for Mr. Blanshard that it is difficult not to accept his theses. An acceptance, however, would amount to submission to a form of anti-Roman-Catholicism which would be as much a form of tyranny over the mind as submission to Roman Catholicism."[23] Evidently, then, neither the POAU nor Paul Blanshard were ever able to attract a significant following in the Lutheran Church-Missouri Synod.

The polemics have been referred to here as "serious," which in a sense they were. But in really serious polemics the polemicist hopes to be persuasive enough to influence his opponent, and, in turn, he exposes himself to his oppo-

---

[18] "Religious Liberty Week," *Cresset*, XIV (October, 1951) 1–2.
[19] "Rome Elects a New Bishop," *Cresset*, XXII (December, 1958), 4.
[20] *Concordia Theological Monthly*, XX (November, 1949), 877–879.
[21] *Witness*, LXXVII (May 20, 1958), 237.
[22] "Lefts and Rights," *Cresset*, XI (April, 1948), 2–3.
[23] *Cresset*, XIV (October, 1951), 59–60.

nent's persuasiveness. The sharp edge in the Lutheran-Catholic polemics was blunted by the conviction that Rome never changes and the tacit assumption that the Lutheran position is also firmly set. The give-and-take of serious controversy was therefore missing. This no doubt explains why so much of what Lutherans said so fervently and so eloquently strikes the reader as really little more than theological and intellectual exercise, polemics intended only to prove and prove again the rightness of Lutheran teaching.

3

MOVING TOWARD
EVANGELICAL CONCERN

ALTHOUGH OPPOSITION TO Catholicism was unanimous, not all Lutherans agreed upon the methods that should be used in opposing it. In the early years, disagreement with the two approaches described so far was seldom expressed, but by 1960 the journalistic critics seem to have had their day, the party-line polemics were mellowing, and the anti-Catholic expressions of some Lutherans had begun to reflect a tone of evangelical concern. It is this new approach, growing out of dissent with the old, that is the subject of this chapter.

Identifying the common denominators in the journalistic criticism and in the polemics has been fairly easy. It is not so easily done with the more recent approach, for the very certainties that the critics and the polemicists had dealt with were now no longer so certain. The underlying assumption that Rome never changes was being tested by Rome itself, and as the world became acquainted with Pope John XXIII, it became a bit curious to dwell on the idea that he was "the very Antichrist," bent on dominating America, destroying democracy, and leading souls to hell. Furthermore, the increasing power and influence of non-Christian forces in the world prompted the recognition that Christianity, if it had to be divided, should strive at least to ease the hostility growing out of the division.

The writers in this third group were evangelical in their approach, that is, they spoke in the spirit of the gospel. Readiness to seek and to grant forgiveness and to work toward a more perfect expression of oneness in Christ is apparent throughout their writings. In addition, they do not appear to have merely been on exercises; they were genuinely concerned about the specific problem of Lutheran-Catholic relations. This does not mean that they adopted a soft line on Catholicism or that they were prepared to compromise their beliefs; their uniqueness lay entirely in the way they approached the problem.

The early voices in this approach were indeed faint and tentative. In 1934 the *American Lutheran* expressed the notion that Lutheran people secretly resent the attacks by the clergy on Rome. In seventeen years, commented the writer, he had met only one or two people who really welcomed anti-Catholic propaganda. The effect of anti-Catholic preaching on Lutheran people, he observed, is that, without realizing it, they identify themselves with Protestantism (something Lutherans were reluctant to do), and then they try to get rid of all the things they think Lutherans have in common with Catholics, such as spires, crucifixes on the altar, candles, and the chanting of psalms. "We would suggest," continued the editorial, "that there be less violence in the matter of polemics. Our people ought to be taught that many things are based upon ancient usage, and useful to the devotional life of the Christian, and ought not to be discarded."[1]

Otto A. Geisemann, a Lutheran parish pastor in suburban Chicago, was another observer who feared the self-destroying effects of anti-Catholicism. He noted that ever since the *Christian Century* had presented a series of articles on whether the Roman Catholic Church could win America, editorial writers had vigorously pounded their typewriters and denominational orators had held forth with special eloquence. He continued: "We will do well to understand that raving,

[1] "A Suggestion Offered," *American Lutheran,* XVII (September, 1934), 15.

ranting, and denunciation in and by itself will never serve to frustrate any designs which Roman Catholicism may have on America." Implying that this approach hindered the church in its real mission, Geisemann urged that Lutherans proceed to give America a Bible-founded, Christ-centered, freedom-bearing religion. In conclusion he asserted: "Let us give it freely, unceasingly, in season and out of season, and then under God Rome shall not win America."[2] On another occasion Geisemann urged his readers to stop worrying too much about Rome's political maneuvers and about its ability to make headlines in secular journals. Instead, he said, "let us apply ourselves to the constructive task of helpfully, warm-heartedly and earnestly bringing the story of Christ and salvation to famished souls."[3]

A traditional attitude of Lutherans had been the unwillingness to accept at face value any statements of opinion by Roman Catholics if they were not in complete agreement with official pronouncements. Roland H. Bainton, the Luther biographer, although not a Missouri Synod Lutheran himself, took the opportunity to discuss this characteristic in an article in the *Walther League Messenger*. After warning against making Reformation Sunday an annual blast against popery, he took issue with the approach of Paul Blanshard and James Hastings Nichols, who were sharply critical of Catholic practices and suspicious of Catholic aims. He cited the views of John Courtney Murray and other American Catholics which show that there is difference of opinion within the Roman Catholic Church over the official position of limiting freedom for non-Catholics. Perhaps he was speaking more to, than for, Missouri Synod Lutherans when he concluded:

The most grievous aspect of the contemporary liberal fear

[2] *American Lutheran*, XXVIII (April, 1945), 5.
[3] *American Lutheran*, XXIX (May, 1946), 5.

of Catholicism is precisely the distrust which is unwilling
to take assurance at face value. To Protestants we may
say that although by trust we may be duped it were better
to be duped than to live in perpetual suspicion. To Catholics we say that nothing would so clear the air as a
repudiation of the religious liberty clause in the Spanish
concordat by the Vatican.[4]

Not attributable directly to this counsel of Bainton, of course,
but nevertheless apparent, was a tendency among the evangelically concerned toward accepting Catholic statements at
face value.

This does not mean that Catholic viewpoints were becoming any more acceptable to Lutherans or that Roman Catholic
theology was any more plausible than previously. It means
simply that even on the most controversial subjects the evangelically concerned showed respect for the Catholic position
as one honestly arrived at and sincerely held. The book
reviews in the *Concordia Theological Monthly,* the journal
edited by the faculty of Concordia Seminary, reflected this
approach most clearly. In the days when J. T. Mueller was
doing much of the book reviewing, the reviews showed a
distinct, almost willful, lack of understanding of the Catholic
position, and were often used to ridicule and denounce the
writer, his book, and Catholicism in general without real
regard for the book's contents. The reviews of Arthur Carl
Piepkorn, on the other hand, were written objectively and
fairly, and reflected a genuine respect for Catholic writers
and a thorough knowledge of the tenets and practices of
Catholicism.[5]

Another distinguishing feature shown by the evangelically

---

[4] "What About Catholic-Protestant Relations in the U.S.A.?"
Walther League Messenger, LXIII (October, 1954), 14–17.
[5] See for example three reviews by Piepkorn in *Concordia Theological Monthly,* XXXIII (May, 1962), 300–301.

concerned was the emphasis they placed on the beliefs held in common by Lutherans and Catholics. As early as 1928, in the heyday of the journalistic critics, Paul G. Prokopy, a youth work executive, warned that solicitude for truth must not be allowed to degenerate into contempt or disregard for everything Catholic, nor should personal feelings prevail against Catholics as such. "Indeed," he wrote, "the spirit of charity and Christian love should hold sway and cause us to rejoice in such matters as are common to our creeds."[6]

The effort to do this was made incidentally through the years, but as the evangelical approach became more pronounced, attempts were made to identify specifically those areas in which agreement existed. Thus, in 1961 Berthold von Schenk, a New York pastor, wrote a thirty-two page essay expressing a Protestant, but reflecting a Lutheran, view on "factors that unite us." Taking the position that the Reformation was unfortunate, unnecessary, and had negative results for both sides, von Schenk contended that the issues that divided Lutherans and Catholics in the sixteenth century were essentially the same issues that might possibly unite them now, and that their separation on such matters as the Mass, Marian devotions, papal authority, and grace and good works is not as wide as one supposes.[7] Von Schenk no doubt expressed a minority view, if not an isolated one; certainly most Lutheran theologians would not agree that the division results largely from semantics and historical circumstances. But the mere fact that a Lutheran clergyman, even though he was something of a maverick, approached the problem in this way sug-

[6] "To Hate Or Not to Hate," *Walther League Messenger,* XXXVI (February, 1928), 367.
[7] "Factors That Unite Us: Protestant," in *Christians in Conversation,* ed. Peter W. Bartholome (Westminster, Maryland: Newman Press, 1962), pp. 47–79.

gests that the traditional attitude toward Catholicism was in for reappraisal.

In studying the "riddle" of Roman Catholicism, Jaroslav Pelikan, a Lutheran theologian and university professor, also took special note of "the unity we have." Quoting Albert Outler, he pointed out that Protestants and Catholics have the unity of their common history as Christians and their participation, no matter how varied and fragmented, in those saving events of Jesus Christ by which the Christian community was constituted. He contended that these areas of agreement are important because they are also the areas of disagreement and evidence of disunity. According to Pelikan, studying the unity they have is a guarantee against the idea that all the differences between Protestants and Catholics are matters of semantics or of sentiment or of "mere doctrine." "But," he continued, "it is also an antidote against the type of Protestant chauvinism which refuses to think of Rome as anything except our ancient foe and the harlot of Babylon."[8]

Willingness to accept statements of Catholics at face value, expressing criticism in respectful terms, rejoicing in common beliefs, these are all signs of the hopefulness shared by the evangelically concerned. The despair of the critics and the pessimism of the polemicists here gave way to a cautious optimism. This optimism did not rest on the belief that Rome was about to be converted. Pelikan emphasized that Catholicism is here to stay and added that Protestants had better give up the hope of ever converting all Catholics to a Protestant point of view. He urged Protestantism to develop an approach transcending the vacillation between aggressiveness and defensiveness, the usual Protestant posture.[9] In the new approach both

[8] *The Riddle of Roman Catholicism* (New York: Abingdon Press, 1959), pp. 177–178.
[9] *Ibid.*, p. 175.

Protestants and Catholics must recognize the integrity and sincerity of the other, and within this framework they must face the differences between them, hopeful that improved relationships might develop, even though the separation persists.

A variety of forces worked together to help the evangelically concerned develop their position. A most important one was Vatican Council II, first announced in 1959, with sessions held in Rome in 1962, 1963, 1964, and 1965. The effect of Vatican II on Lutherans will be studied in more detail in a later chapter. Here we merely take note of its influence on the thinking of the evangelically concerned. Viewing the council with caution, some early observers detected a powerful current running in the direction of more positive relations with Protestants. The central theme of "reform" shook the foundations of old Lutheran convictions. The never-changing church was consciously setting out to change! It was recognized, even by the most hopeful, that the dogma would not be changed, but that any change, if only in forms and ceremonies or in organization and concerns, would be significant.[10]

One reaction to the new atmosphere in Rome was the suggestion that Lutherans must also find ways of perfecting sound theology and of presenting its witness in a living-for-pleasure civilization. This was offered, not in the former sense of beating Rome at its own game, or of turning back the Roman menace, but in the evangelical sense that the church has a mission to fulfill and ought to seek improved ways of fulfilling it.[11]

In urging prayers for the Vatican Council the *American*

[10] Richard Koenig, *American Lutheran,* XLVI (January, 1963), 16.
[11] Curtis E. Huber, "The Challenge of Rome's Council," *Lutheran Witness,* LXXXI (November 27, 1962), 583.

Lutheran reflected the recent emphasis on the common elements of Lutheran and Roman Catholic faiths:

> Our Roman Catholic fellow-Christians are not merely neighbors; they are brothers in Christ, even though they may be separated brothers and on some doctrines heretical brothers. To the extent that the Gospel of God's grace in Christ is proclaimed as Gospel in the Roman Catholic denomination and the sacraments are administered there as sacraments, so that men and women are reborn into the life that is hid with Christ in God in that communion, the Roman Catholic community is part of the one, holy, catholic, and apostolic Church.[12]

Another force in helping Lutherans develop an evangelical approach to Lutheran-Catholic tensions was the presence of Pope John XXIII. The *Cresset* noted that in him "the Lord of the Church has given the Christian community a wise, irenic, and prophetic voice which, in many areas of Christian concern, speaks not only for the Roman church, but for all Christendom."[13] Even the *Witness* "dared," by its own admission, to speak well of Pope John on his death. Noting that many of their readers would instinctively think of the Lutheran Confessions and their judgment regarding the antichristian character of the papal system, the *Witness* asserted that this judgment still has validity. But then it asked, "Must the *Witness* therefore restrict itself to negative comments on everything Roman Catholic?" Apparently it concluded that it must not, for the editorial proceeded to pay tribute to the Pope for focusing the eyes and hearts of the people on peace, for fostering improvement in the universal religious climate from one of suspicion and hostility to one of openness and frankness. "Though he closed no doctrinal gaps," noted

[12] "The Coming Roman Catholic Council," *American Lutheran,* XLV (October, 1962), 3–4.
[13] "Pacem in Terris," *Cresset,* XXVI (June, 1963), 3.

the *Witness,* "he set up some machinery for building bridges of understanding so that divisive issues could be discussed without prejudice and blinding emotion."[14]

Admittedly it is impossible to distinguish between causes and effects in the new religious climate. No doubt the four remaining trends in the evangelical approach both derived from and contributed to the new situation. Classifying them as causes or effects is much less important than taking note of their existence.

The first of these trends was toward an increasing emphasis on gaining an understanding of Catholicism through a study of its history. Pelikan, noting that the Roman Catholic Church is viewed by outsiders with a mixture of suspicion, fascination, and ignorance, introduced *The Riddle of Roman Catholicism* with an historical review of the origins and evolution of Catholicism. The church would be less of a riddle, he believed, if people understood it in its historical context.[15] For similar reasons Martin E. Marty traced "A Dialogue of Histories," Protestant and Catholic, in *American Catholicism: A Protestant-Jewish View.*[16] Both of these accounts reflect an air of detachment and fair-mindedness. The aim of both writers was to use history as a key to understanding, not as grounds for indictment. The general acceptance of this trend is evident not so much in what was written, but in what was not. The earlier judgments were not renounced, nor was the "Dark Ages" interpretation of Catholic history specifically revised. Yet, if one considers the former emphasis on the more sordid aspects of the Catholic past, there is some significance in the disappearance of these themes from the synodical literature.

The second noteworthy trend among the evangelically con-

---

[14] *Witness,* LXXXII (June 25, 1963), 291.
[15] *The Riddle of Roman Catholicism,* pp. 19–71.
[16] Ed. Philip Scharper (New York: Sheed & Ward, 1959), pp. 29–56.

cerned Lutheran theologians was toward paying more serious attention to their Catholic counterparts. Some of them showed a real understanding of developments taking place in the Roman Catholic Church. The prime example of familiarity with that church's theology and practice and with the writings of Catholic theologians is Pelikan's *The Riddle of Roman Catholicism.* A quick perusal of the backnotes supports the idea that Pelikan had read widely in Catholic literature and that his interpretations had been formulated only after consideration of the several sides to each question.[17]

Awareness of movements within Catholicism did not always mean acceptance or approval. For example, in his little book *Christ or Mary?*[18] Roland Seboldt, a Lutheran clergyman and editor, relied heavily on Catholic sources in making an honest effort to study in a fair-minded way the evolution of Roman Catholic dogma. The book is respectfully written, but disagreement and disapproval are always apparent. Yet a Catholic theologian might read it as an appeal from a concerned brother rather than as simply another anti-Catholic blast.

On the other hand, a number of Lutheran writers were encouraged by some of the things they saw happening in Roman Catholic theology. One such was Ernest B. Koenker, author of *The Liturgical Renaissance in the Roman Catholic Church,* a book that received favorable attention in the *Concordia Theological Monthly.*[19] An article by Koenker in *Una Sancta* observed that the Roman Catholic Church regards

[17] Pp. 241–258. The objectivity of this book is apparently open to question. I regard it as fair and balanced; the St. Louis University library card catalog identifies it as an "anti-Catholic polemic." Reaction among Catholic reviewers was mixed.

[18] (St. Louis: Concordia, 1963).

[19] *The Liturgical Renaissance in the Roman Catholic Church* (Chicago: University of Chicago Press, 1954). Reviewed by Walter E. Buszin in *Concordia Theological Monthly,* XXVI (September, 1955), 716–717.

itself as a church always reforming from within. Showing real familiarity with Catholic sources, Koenker, a Valparaiso University professor, cited six "evangelical trends" in Catholicism: (1) increased Bible study, (2) restoration of wholeness to preaching, (3) catechetical renewal, (4) liturgical developments, (5) the Una Sancta movement (in Germany), and (6) greater appreciation of Luther.[20]

A growing willingness to engage in discussion and exchange with Roman Catholic theologians, a natural effect of familiarity with their writings, is the third trend we note among the evangelically concerned Lutherans. It is difficult to ascertain how extensively Lutherans participated in such discussions on the local level before the end of 1963, the terminal date for this study. No doubt the atmosphere changed more quickly in some communities than in others, to permit some clergymen to meet with their Catholic counterparts for serious, but unpublicized, discussions. On the official level no meaningful exchange was reported. The men who represented the Missouri Synod as observers at Vatican Council II remained just that—observers, for the opportunity to participate was not extended to any Protestants. Perhaps the only significant line of communication opened between Lutherans and Catholics came in the form of a series of meetings between the theology departments of Valparaiso University and the University of Notre Dame. The unpublicized meetings began in 1957 and continued through 1963. Aside from this single effort it seems safe to say that for Lutherans the age of dialog had not yet been ushered in.[21]

---

[20] "Current Evangelical Trends in the Roman Catholic Church," *Una Sancta,* XIX (The Presentation of Our Lord, 1962), 5–12.
[21] These meetings were described in a mimeographed paper prepared by Robert W. Bertram, "Chronology of the Notre Dame-Valparaiso Dialogue, 1957–1964" (April 8, 1964). Bertram was head of the theology department at Valparaiso until he joined the

On an individual basis, however, some Lutherans were involved in debate and discussion. In late 1960 Berthold von Schenk and Jaroslav Pelikan were participants in a colloquy of Catholics and Protestants held at St. John's Abbey, Collegeville, Minnesota. The colloquy, sponsored by the Most Rev. Peter W. Bartholome, Bishop of St. Cloud, was organized around two themes: "Issues Which Divide Us" and "Factors Which Unite Us." Pelikan presented a paper expressing a Protestant view on the first theme, and von Schenk did the same on the latter. These essays, along with two presenting Catholic views, were published under the title *Christians in Conversation.*[22] Neither the colloquy nor the book received wide publicity in synodical publications, although the book was discussed by Richard Koenig in the *American Lutheran.*[23]

The two Missouri Synod Lutherans who seem to have had the most frequent and direct public contact with Catholics were Jaroslav Pelikan and Martin Marty. Both were accorded the unique opportunity of speaking on the Catholic Hour (May 5 and May 12, 1963), and both were invited to write for Catholic publications, including *Catholic World, Commonweal,* and *Ave Maria.* That Catholics should have been given similar opportunities to express their views through Missouri Synod media would have been surprising. Our con-

---

faculty of Concordia Seminary in St. Louis in 1963. It has also been suggested to me by former chaplains, both Lutheran and Roman Catholic, that the military chaplaincy has encouraged theological discussions between Lutherans and Catholics. This is no doubt true, but I could not find reports of meetings, either formal or informal, between representatives of the two denominations. There is also no doubt that military service, by putting Lutherans and Catholics side by side in a common cause, has helped to reduce interdenominational misunderstanding.

[22] (Westminster, Maryland: The Newman Press, 1962).
[23] *American Lutheran,* XLVI (February, 1963), 11, 25.

cern here is not so much with the content of what they said and wrote as with the way in which they approached Catholicism. Marty, a Lutheran theologian and an editor of the *Christian Century,* identified himself in his Catholic Hour address as "standing between hope and suspicion, but making an ideology of neither." Later in the address he summarized his position:

> Sometimes before or after I have participated in Catholic or Protestant discussions someone will ask what I hoped to accomplish. Was I soft on Catholicism, ready to "capitulate" in my Protestant witness? Or was I agressive, and bent on converting the Catholic? It is hard to communicate to this mentality. I must stand silent . . . and patiently, later, explain: we are given a mandate to seek Christ and thus to find each other. We are given an arrow and a road map, and now and then a ride on a vehicle. But we are not promised that in our generation we will arrive at our goal. The full unity of the Church belongs to the Last Things, but its "hope projected backward" into history forces us, calls us to work in the here and now. How much more free we are if we have no time table, no agenda anxiety, no compulsion to be handed merit badges—but only to hear the inviting word of the Lord of one flock![24]

To what extent Marty and Pelikan contributed to the shaping of Lutheran attitudes toward Roman Catholicism is impossible to measure. They may have been more widely read by Catholics, and thus had a greater effect on shaping Catholic attitudes toward Lutheranism. Regardless of the impact of their writings at the time, their long-range contribution to Lutheran-Catholic relations will no doubt be significant, for they showed that it was possible to confront Catholics openly, honestly, and respectfully without compromising their own

---

[24] "The Church and the Council: A Non-Catholic View," Part II (Catholic Hour Address, May 12, 1963).

Lutheran confession. Whether other Lutheran writers will continue in this pattern, whether the Lutheran "man in the pew" will alter his attitudes toward Catholicism accordingly, and whether general Lutheran opposition to Catholicism will become truly evangelical, remain to be seen.

The fourth trend shown by the evangelically concerned was toward recognizing the necessity of bearing the burden of separation. This idea was expressed most clearly by Pelikan. His sermon on this subject, delivered at the Reformation festival in the Princeton University chapel in 1957, was published in the *Seminarian,* the student journal of Concordia Seminary, St. Louis.[25] In expanded form it became a chapter in *The Riddle of Roman Catholicism.* In this address, after expressing a distaste for the clichés and shrill defiance displayed by both Protestants and Catholics, Pelikan observed that although we may hope for a day of reunion, we must, for our lifetime at least, face the certainty of separation. We should therefore learn to live in a divided church, "reverently, discreetly, advisedly, soberly, and in the fear of God" (as the *Book of Common Prayer* says about marriage).

In Pelikan's interpretation this means, first, that as Christians all, Protestants and Catholics have a mutual responsibility to and for each other. Because of the faith they have in common, each side should include the other in its ecumenical concern. Second, both Catholics and Protestants should bear gentle and firm testimony against the other's faults and avoid both the practice of seizing on the scandals and blunders of the other side and the policy of "live-and-let-live." This cannot be done unless each side is informed about what is really going on in the thought and life of the other side. Third, according to Pelikan, both sides must carry on a program of honest self-evaluation, with each generation regarding the Ref-

[25] "Bearing the Burden of Separation," *Seminarian,* XLIX (May, 1958), 22–27.

ormation as an unfinished task and a new responsibility.
Fourth, both sides must make an honest assessment of their
mutual needs and debts; Protestants must find ways of being
more catholic, and Catholics must become more evangelical.
Each side will find its historical identity if Protestants will
recognize that they are what they are because of their Catholic background and if Catholics will acknowledge the extent
to which their church has been shaped by the Reformation.
Finally, both Protestants and Catholics must develop a concern for the total church of Christ and an awareness of the
consequences of their actions for that church. Protestants
must guard against making Protestantism merely the negation
of Catholicism, and Catholics must be careful not to act as
though the Christian cause and the Catholic cause are identical. This sketchy summary does not, of course, do justice to
Pelikan's cogently expressed ideas, but it does at least indicate
the direction of the thought of the evangelically concerned.
Their writings show that these principles were in fact carried
into practice.

It is still too early to judge how widely the evangelical
approach has gained acceptance in the Missouri Synod and
to what extent it actually has replaced the traditional party-
line polemics. We cannot yet tell if it represents the beginning
of a new era in Lutheran-Catholic relations or whether it is
merely a passing phase, prompted by Pope John XXIII and
the Vatican Council. If the view that Rome never changes is
revived, it is not difficult to imagine a reversion to the practices described in the first two chapters. The comparative
silence of the hard-line polemicists after 1961 should not be
interpreted to mean that they have been converted to a different approach. Attitudes ingrained through decades are not
blown away by slight changes in the wind, which in the view
of some is the real extent of the spirit of Vatican II.

On the other hand, in the judgment of others the impact

of the new spirit has been so profound that Catholicism can never again be what it was before Pope John XXIII decided to "throw open some windows." He did not create the fresh air he wished to let into the church; that fresh air was already there, ready to come in. The ventilating experience has made it difficult for Rome to close the windows again. If Catholicism cannot become what it once was, then opposition to Catholicism must also take new forms. In the final chapter we shall return to this matter by considering the form that Lutheran reappraisal might take as attempts are made to develop new relations with Catholicism.

The turning point in the position of the Lutheran Church-Missouri Synod appears to have been reached by late 1963, when the *Lutheran Witness* editorialized:

> This seems certain: as Roman Catholic fathers work to "update" their church, Protestants—Lutherans specifically—will have to work toward updating long-cherished opinions and fixed ideas of Roman Catholicism.
>
> Some of the expressions Protestants have long been using about Roman Catholics will necessarily and in all fairness have to be drastically qualified. Wince though we might at first, we won't be able to escape thinking and speaking of Romanism in much more deliberate and "defrosted" tones.
>
> .　.　.　.　.　.　.　.　.　.　.　.　.
>
> Meanwhile a question Pope Paul asked at a special session with the 65 non-Catholic observers last month is one which Missouri Lutherans, too, ought to be mulling over: "After so many years of separation, after such painful polemics, what else can we do but love one another, listen to one another, and pray for one another?"[26]

[26] "Protestants and the 'New Rome,'" *Witness,* LXXXII (November 26, 1963), 548–549.

4

ROMAN PRINCIPLES AND
AMERICAN PRACTICE

F ROM A DESCRIPTION of the three general approaches of
Lutherans to Catholicism we turn now to an examination of
the principal specific issues which brought Lutherans and
Catholics into conflict. First will be considered the general
ground for Lutheran concern over the political power of
Catholicism as a threat to liberty, particularly to religious
freedom. The following three chapters treat in detail three
major issues which brought the Lutheran position into
sharper focus.

Fear of the actual and potential political power of Catholicism was no passing matter among Lutherans. Through the
years it provided material for a steady stream of articles and
editorials. They were not fighting a chimera; the menace was
real, and their response was serious and often well reasoned
and documented. The arguments and attacks of the Lutheran
writers were directed against the Roman Catholic Church's
stated claims of temporal power and her official, historic position on religious liberty, and against the actual aggressive
practices of the church in the United States and abroad. The
criticism of the stated Catholic position embodied four aspects:
identifying and elaborating the official, historic position; discussing its ramifications; explaining why many people were
not aware of it; and proving that it was still currently held.

In simple terms, the official Catholic position was interpreted along these lines: the Roman Catholic Church rejects
the American principle of separation of church and state, and
favors instead a state in which the government does the bid-

ding of the Catholic hierarchy and works for the advantage of the church. The church must permit freedom of worship for itself alone, for this right can be possessed only by truth, never by error. When it is in the majority, it will not permit other groups to propagate false doctrine. If the Roman Catholic Church finds itself in the minority, it will demand for itself all possible concessions. Therefore, it accepts the American principles of separation of church and state merely for temporary reasons of expediency because Catholics are now only a minority in America. The church's iron fist is still encased in a velvet glove, but there is sufficient evidence that it has not changed, that the age-old spirit of intolerance is still burning brightly within its breast.[1]

This argument was developed most fully by Theodore Graebner in *The Pope and Temporal Power,* a book not published until 1929, but apparently prepared by Graebner in anticipation of the 1928 election.[2] Because it consisted largely of documentation from Catholic sources, it carried an authoritative tone and served a purpose similar to his earlier work, *The Dark Ages.* Later writers relied on it for reference, although they did not always credit it with being their source.

A shorter, more recent delineation of the Roman Catholic position was included in Alfred M. Rehwinkel's *The Voice of Conscience.*[3] A brief outline of Rehwinkel's argumentation serves here as a representative Lutheran interpretation of the

---

[1] This argument was expressed in various ways; see for example: *Lutheran Witness,* XLVII (April 3, 1928), 125; LX (March 4, 1941), 68–69; LXVII (July 13, 1948), 220; and *American Lutheran,* XXVII (August, 1944), 4.

[2] *The Pope and Temporal Power* (Milwaukee: Northwestern Publishing House, 1929). A letter from Graebner to Sommer, March 10, 1928, requested Sommer to read the manuscript of a volume tentatively titled *Rome and the Constitution.*

[3] *The Voice of Conscience* (St. Louis: Concordia, 1956), pp. 131–158.

Catholic teaching on the relation between church and state. Rehwinkel, a Concordia Seminary professor, began by declaring that the power of the Roman Catholic Church was a danger to the freedom of conscience second only to Communism. He characterized this power thus:

> Romanism was the first great totalitarian force in the world. It claimed absolute authority over the total man and it exercised that authority to the fullest extent in all Christendom during the Middle Ages and still does where Catholicism is in undisputed control.
> . . . It is neither slander nor intolerance to make such a claim; it is a statement of fact based upon the official teachings of the church and upon her past performance in history. The common people within the Catholic Church and even the lower clergy have, of course, little or nothing to do in determining the attitude of the church with regard to religious freedom or, for that matter, on any other question of doctrine and practice. The real power in the Roman Church resides not in the people but in the hierarchy. This small body of men, appointed for life by the pope, constitutes the real government of the church which determines its policies and issues the laws, rules, and regulations for the people to follow.[4]

Rehwinkel disputed the claim that the intolerance and unsavory conditions found in the church in Spain, Italy, and the countries of Latin America do not represent the real character of the teachings of the Roman Catholic Church, but are a caricature, a result of the national character of the people or of the social, political, and cultural environment of the country in which these conditions prevail. Acknowledging that vast differences do exist within the Roman Catholic Church, he asserted that in a Protestant environment it is "enlightened, progressive, and even to a degree evangelical," while in the old, solidly Catholic countries it is "backward,

[4] *Ibid.*, p. 131.

tyrannical, morally degraded, and in some areas even semi-pagan."[5] Observers should not be deceived into believing, however, that there are different Catholic churches. There are not. According to Rehwinkel it is merely that the church's "real attitude of intolerance and her unsatiable greed for power come to surface only when she is the sovereign mistress in a country and unhindered by a non-Catholic government or a non-Catholic environment." The old principle that truth can never tolerate error has not yet been fully acted upon in America because conditions are not yet favorable for such action.[6] In the next several pages Rehwinkel described in detail how the Roman Catholic Church is working to achieve a dominant position in America.

To prove that undisputed dominance by the Roman Catholic Church would represent a threat to our religious liberty, he turned to quoting official and semiofficial documents. The first reference was to the fourteenth-century bull of Pope Boniface VIII, *Unam sanctam,* which asserted that the church possesses the power of the two swords, spiritual and temporal, the latter to be used for the church and the former by the church. Then he referred to the 1885 encyclical letter of Pope Leo XIII, *Immortale Dei,* which he termed a mere restatement, in more elaborate form and for modern conditions, of the same ideas included in Boniface's *Unam sanctam.* To show that the ideas expressed by the popes have current application in the United States, Rehwinkel cited Cardinal Gibbons' *The Faith of Our Fathers,* in which the Cardinal discussed Protestant fears of Roman Catholic dominance and attempted to allay them by claiming that if Catholics should gain a majority in a community where freedom of conscience is already secured by law, their very religion obliges them to

[5] *Ibid.,* p. 132.
[6] *Ibid.,* p. 133.

respect the rights held by their fellow citizens. Rehwinkel asserted that Gibbons was just doing his best to make the Catholic position as palatable as possible for his American readers.[7]

To support his argumentation, Rehwinkel directed his readers to the source most quoted by Lutheran critics of the Catholic position, *The State and the Church,* a 1922-volume by John A. Ryan and Moorhouse F. X. Millar, S.J.[8] The position taken by Ryan and Millar is indeed the hard party line against separation of church and state and in favor of their complete union under the Roman Catholic Church. However, Rehwinkel and the many others who cited these same passages failed to discern or refused to take into consideration that Ryan and Millar were there developing what what was to them a Catholic ideal in a theoretical situation, with the possibility for practical application virtually ruled out. They were, moreover, writing for a closed audience, and thus tended to present an extreme view. Alternative views were being expressed by other Catholics, but most Lutheran writers were unwilling to give them credence.

To show that the papal statements, and Ryan and Millar's expansion on them, were in fact current policy, Rehwinkel referred to a *Time* (August 3, 1953, p. 41) article reporting a speech by Alfredo Cardinal Ottaviani supporting suppression of non-Catholic religions in predominantly Catholic countries. He then concluded that it *is* possible for Catholicism to win America and that, in view of the church's long record of intolerance and persecution of non-Catholics and its opposition to the principle of religious freedom for all, "it is neither slander nor a sign of intolerance to conclude and

[7] *Ibid.,* pp. 143–144.
[8] Most writers used the 1940 revision of this work: John A. Ryan and Francis J. Boland, *Catholic Principles of Politics* (New York: Macmillan, 1940).

declare that Catholicism . . . is a threat to the freedom of conscience in America today."[9]

As seen by most Lutheran writers, the claims of the Roman
Catholic Church to temporal supremacy and its principles on
the union of church and state under its dominance had serious consequences for the religious and political situation in
America. The underlying assumption in all their conclusions
was that because of his dominant position in the Catholic
hierarchy, control by the Roman Catholic Church would be,
in effect, dictation by the pope. In fact, it was assumed that
even with the Roman Catholic Church in a minority position
Catholics remained under submission to the pope, even in
political affairs.

By translating the theory into practice a principal conclusion was that the pope was directing Catholics in the arena
of American politics. This meant, according to Graebner, (1)
that, as the assumed sovereign over all civil government, the
pope has instructed Catholics to use their political power in
causing the constitution and laws to be brought into conformity with his teachings; (2) that a Catholic, in order to keep
his obligation, must vote as a Catholic and not as an American citizen; and (3) that the Catholic bishops are sworn to
carry out the wishes of the pope, which includes bringing all
Protestants, as rebels and heretics, under his jurisdiction.[10]

A second conclusion was that a "good" Catholic, that is,
one who keeps his obligation to the pope, cannot consistently
be a loyal American citizen. Graebner cited five reasons to
support this conclusion: (1) the pope denounces our form
of government, (2) he claims full sovereignty not only over
Catholics but over all Christians, (3) the first allegiance of
Catholics is to him as the king of kings and as exercising

[9] *The Voice of Conscience,* pp. 153–158.
[10] *The Pope and Temporal Power,* pp. 20–21.

sovereignty superior to our constitution and government, (4)
he instructs them to use their vote, and (5) those who owe
allegiance to the pope are actually under the sovereignty of
a foreign potentate.[11]

Because these convictions were so firmly held by Lutherans, statements by American Catholics affirming their loyalty
to America and to our form of government were taken with
more than one grain of salt. Concluding that "Romanism is
difficult to square with Americanism," Carl S. Meyer wrote:

> The record of the Roman Catholic Church speaks loudly.
> Even in the middle of long and involved arguments, often
> bringing only partial truth, it is evident that the protests in
> favor of democracy and Americanism must be modified.
> Even when statements are brought from American bishops
> of the Roman Catholic Church, these statements must be
> taken in the light of the pronouncements of the Roman
> pontiff, for his is the supreme voice in the Roman Catholic
> Church, also for the American hierarchy.[12]

That there were many Catholics who were patriotic, loyal,
and wholehearted Americans was readily acknowledged by
Lutheran observers. The point was carefully made that it was
the official Catholic teaching and the temporal and political
power of the pope, not the average American Catholic, that
constituted the threat to America. Martin Sommer contended
that many Catholics themselves shared Lutheran fears. Any-
way, he observed, if Rome becomes politically powerful, "the
fine, sociable, upright, loyal Catholics whom we know, and
whose character and patriotism we honor and admire" will
be of very little help.[13] The real concern of the Lutheran

[11] *Ibid.,* pp. 19–20.
[12] "Romanism and Americanism," *Witness,* LXXVII (August 26,
1958), 404.
[13] "Our Catholic Fellow-Citizens," *Witness,* XLVII (March 20,
1928), 111.

writers was that the average American would not agree that the Roman Catholic Church stands for principles which would destroy American liberties if they were put into practice, that it is ready to persecute to the death all who differ from it in doctrine, and that it is subversive of the American constitution.[14]

Why were most Americans unaware of the danger posed by the Roman Catholic Church? This was due, according to Graebner, to the work of Cardinal Gibbons, the ablest spokesman of the Roman Catholic Church in the United States, who was able "to conceal the unscriptural doctrines of priest-power and the sacraments" and "could make the superstitious practises of Rome appear eminently reasonable as an expression of religious faith." Graebner commented on an article by Cardinal Gibbons in a 1909 *North American Review,* written in response to the controversy stemming from Theodore Roosevelt's statement that it would be unwarranted bigotry to refuse to vote for a Catholic candidate for the presidency or any other office. Calling the article a masterpiece of subtle, sophistical reasoning, Graebner wrote:

> It was gentle in manner, heavily surcharged with admiration for American institutions, vibrant with love of country, conciliatory in tone, and breathing a spirit of broad tolerance. Nothing here of the tone which characterized Roman polemics in former ages. The careless reader was convinced that the Cardinal, for one, would prefer the rigid separation of Church and State in the United States to continue forever, as a most desirable arrangement for all parties concerned. And still, there was in this article not one word of retraction. Gibbons asserted that the Church teaches obedience to magistrates "in all things morally permitted and *belonging to the domain of civil society*," and suggested that Catholics would not be bound to obey the

[14] Theodore Graebner, "Cardinal Gibbons Dead," *Witness,* XL (April 12, 1921), 119.

Pope if he "were to issue commands in *purely* civil matters." The words which we have italicized, in Roman interpretation leave the door open for every form of Roman oppression; but only those versed in Roman theology could perceive the deception here practised. The general public was effectively lulled to sleep. The soundly American character of the Roman priesthood in this country has been received ever since without question.[15]

Thus, in effect, Graebner refused to take a statement at face value, and asserted that the American people had been duped into complacency by the smooth talk of a Roman Catholic prelate.

As through the years the Catholic threat failed to materialize, and as Catholics in the United States continued to prove themselves to be loyal American citizens, Lutherans periodically felt compelled to call attention to the official Catholic teaching to prove that it had not changed and that the church was still opposed to separation of church and state and to religious liberty. Any apparent change in Catholic practice was regarded with skepticism, perhaps as something offered as narcotic for Protestant consumption.[16] The usual approach was simply to call attention to the fact that the encyclicals of the past had not been renounced and that the belief that the church has a right and duty to pronounce with supreme authority upon social and economic matters had not been abandoned. Carl S. Meyer referred to numerous encyclicals to show that the claims of the Roman Catholic Church remain essentially the same but that they have been restated in terms of cooperation of the state with the church. "In this way, to borrow Burkhardt's simile, the ship of the Roman

[15] *Ibid.*
[16] William Dallmann, "Catholic Toleration," *Concordia Theological Monthly,* XX (December, 1949), 945–946.

Church has learned to float."[17] As recently as 1960 Carl
Eberhard insisted that the papal claims to temporal power,
expressed in *Unam sanctam* in 1302, still stand and that
American Catholics are not excepted. He cited a May, 1960,
Vatican newspaper which said that it is absurd to try to separate the believer from the citizen. The paper continued: "A
Catholic can never prescind . . . from the teachings and directives of the church. *In every sector of his activity he must
inspire his public and private conduct by the laws, orienta-
tions, and instructions of the hierarchy.*"[18]

Statements in Ryan and Boland's *Catholic Principles of
Politics* provided the basis for James G. Manz's charge that
the Roman Catholic Church constitutes a threat to American
freedom. Acknowledging that Roman Catholic authorities
have stated their opposition to outright conversion of non-
Catholics by physical force, Manz pointed out that these same
authorities still insist that Protestant doctrine and worship are
false. The Ryan and Boland statement that particularly
disturbed Manz was this:

> If these [activities] are carried on within the family or in
> such an inconspicuous manner as to be an occasion neither
> of scandal nor of perversion to the faithful, they may prop-
> erly be tolerated by the state. . . . Quite distinct from the
> performance of false religious worship and preaching to
> the members of the erring sect, is the propagation of false
> doctrine among Catholics. . . . Against such an evil, they
> have a right of protection by the Catholic state. . . . Since
> no rational end is promoted by the dissemination of false
> doctrine, there exists no right to indulge in this practice. . . .
> Error has not the same rights as truth.

[17] "The Role of the Church in the Political Order," *Concordia
Theological Monthly,* XXVII (December, 1956), 913–935.
[18] "Church and State," *Witness,* LXXIX (September 20, 1960),
484–485.

Of this Manz observed: "This is *modern* Roman Catholic teaching. It is small comfort to Protestants when they are told that there are many 'milder interpretations' of the Roman position. *If these policies are ever carried out in the United States, it will mean the end of our freedom.*" He continued:

> Is it any wonder that millions of loyal Americans are deeply disturbed about the growing political power of the Roman Catholic Church in the United States? Are we loyal and faithful as Christians and as citizens of our free land if we simply choke back our deep concern and maintain a discreet silence?[19]

If the official Roman Catholic position was to instill fear in the hearts of Americans who daily witnessed a Catholic practice which was apparently so much at variance with that position, it was necessary for them to see evidence that the Roman Catholic Church actually was intolerant when it was in a position of dominance and that the church was working assiduously to achieve dominance in the United States. Lutheran writers attempted to provide this evidence. They were not reluctant to point to the Roman Catholic Church's record of intolerance, both historical and current, and they resented the charge that in so doing they were guilty of bigotry themselves.[20]

In an earlier chapter it was noted that an important theme in Lutheran anti-Catholicism was the emphasis on the more sordid aspects of Roman Catholic history. References to the "Dark Ages," to the Inquisition, and to persecution and oppression were frequent. Efforts by Roman Catholics to disavow responsibility were rejected. For example, in protesting against a film which showed the Spanish Inquisition in action,

[19] "Threat to Freedom," *Witness,* LXXXI (June 26, 1962), 310–311.
[20] Walter A. Maier, "Bigot! Bigot!" *Walther League Messenger,* XXXVII (October, 1928), 72–75, 109–110.

Catholics in Manchester, England, contended that the Catholic Church had disclaimed all power to punish errors of the mind with the sword, that where the secular powers still punished heresy in this way the church was obliged to plead for mercy on behalf of the heretics, and that pope after pope had protested against the arbitrary conduct of the Spanish kings in using the Inquisition. Graebner dismissed their arguments as "about the boldest perversion of history that we have recently found in Roman Catholic pronouncements."[21]

Similarly, attempts by Catholics to claim any credit for the development of democracy or freedom were rejected summarily. Of the claim made in *Our Sunday Visitor* that "out of the depths of her teachings came the Magna Carta and all the other democratic forms of government recognizing the right of the people to a voice in the government of their affairs" Graebner asserted that Pope Innocent III had (1) by edict annulled the Great Charter, (2) absolved King John for his part in its enactment and released him from his obligation to keep the solemn oath he had made to his subjects, (3) suspended Archbishop Stephen Langton from the exercise of his office, (4) excommunicated the barons, and (5) laid the kingdom of England under an interdict, cutting off the people from all religious privileges except Baptism.[22]

Concerning current practice the Lutheran writers maintained that wherever the government was controlled by the Roman Catholic Church there was a large measure of freedom for that church, but all others had rough sledding. Graebner remarked that "Romanism demands tolerance because Protestants profess to be tolerant, but she would not

[21] *Witness,* XLIII (January 1, 1924), 13.
[22] "New Light on the Origin of Democracy," *Witness,* LV (June 16, 1936), 197–198.

give them the same tolerance if she had power because she does not profess to be tolerant."[23]

There were numerous examples to which they could point. William Arndt cited a statement of G. Bromley Oxnam concerning problems faced by chaplains in Roman Catholic countries. Oxnam warned that continuation of a policy of discrimination against non-Catholics in Catholic countries was the surest way to develop religious conflict in the United States.[24] Conditions in Spain provoked frequent comment. In 1924 J. T. Mueller referred to King Alfonso as a "devoted slave to the Pope" and said that Spain is a picture of what Europe would have been "had not Luther restored the light of Gospel truth."[25] More than two decades later Graebner reported that a United Nations subcommittee had voiced its deep horror at conditions in Franco's Spain. Franco, he said, had come to power with the blessing of the pope and had restored the Roman Catholic Church to power it had not known there in a long time.[26] In 1955 the *American Lutheran* complained that Americans based in Spain could not be married unless they consented, in terms similar to those of the prenuptial contract here in the United States, to having their children raised as Roman Catholics. It called attention to the letter that the synod's president, John W. Behnken, had written to Secretary of State Dulles in which he protested the working out of an agreement to this effect and claimed that an American principle was at stake.[27] Expulsion of Protes-

[23] "Freedom of Religion on Catholic Countries," *Witness*, LX (October 28, 1941), 364.
[24] "Religious Liberty and the Roman Catholic Church," *Concordia Theological Monthly*, XVI (October, 1945), 710.
[25] "Spain's Faith and Achievements," *Theological Monthly*, IV (April, 1924), 120–121.
[26] "Variant Interpretations of Despotism," *Witness*, LXV (June 18, 1946), 205.
[27] "The Long Arm of the Vatican," *American Lutheran*, XXXVIII (February, 1955), 5–6; the Behnken letter was reprinted on p. 14.

tant missionaries from Ethiopia by Mussolini[28] and the threat of withholding the sacraments from those in Malta who refused to obey the directives of the bishops there[29] are just two of a host of similar references to other countries that might be cited.

One area that received particular attention was Latin America. In 1944 the *American Lutheran* referred to a new school law in Argentina as an example of tolerance and democracy after the Roman model. The law required the teaching of the Roman Catholic religion in all primary, secondary, and some other schools. Only those pupils could be exempted whose parents belonged to other religions and asked to have them excused. Religious teachers were to be appointed and textbooks selected by the government, but they had to be approved by the ecclesiastical authorities. This, according to the *American Lutheran,* clearly reveals what America may expect along these lines if and when Catholic Action succeeds in making America Catholic.[30]

The *Cresset* drew some encouragement from developments related to a similar event in 1960. In calling attention to the attempt of the Puerto Rican hierarchy to force Roman Catholics into voting against the party of Luis Munoz Marin, it noted that Cardinals Spellman and Cushing had voiced objection to this attempt to bind consciences on political questions. They inferred from this that the danger that American Catholics would give in to similar ecclesiastical pressures need not seriously disturb non-Catholics. But the fact that it had occurred in Puerto Rico was still a matter of concern.[31]

---

[28] Graebner, "Freedom of Religion in Catholic Countries," *Witness,* LX (October 28, 1941), 364.

[29] William Arndt, "Does Rome Ever Meddle in Politics?" *Concordia Theological Monthly,* II (October, 1931), 785.

[30] "Religious Toleration," *American Lutheran,* XXVII (February, 1944), 4.

[31] "A Deserved Rebuke," *Cresset,* XXIV (December, 1960), 5.

By far the greatest amount of attention was focused on Mexico. In describing conditions in Mexico and the treatment of Protestant missionaries there, the *Cresset* commented that this is how Rome shows its true colors when it is in control: "For a true evaluation of papist policy and the blessings which any country enjoys that is controlled from Rome, we need only examine those countries. . . . Look at Rome and Mexico, where Rome is supreme. One look ought to be enough."[32] Sommer reported that the sorry conditions in Mexico could be blamed on the "fanaticism, superstition, and tyranny of the Roman Catholic Church," which had "goaded on many people to doubt, rebellion, atheism, and even hatred of religion."[33]

Of particular concern was the conflict in 1926 and 1927 between the government of Mexico and the Roman Catholic Church. Graebner and Sommer took frequent note of attempts by "Roman Catholic agents" and the Knights of Columbus to pressure the United States government into intervening or breaking off diplomatic relations with Mexico because of the persecution of Roman Catholic churches there. Sommer reported that according to the Mexican ambassador the reasons for the anti-Catholic activity were that the Catholic priests owned eighty percent of the real estate and movable property, they exercised political control and denied the people the right to run their own government, and they brought poverty to the masses by making them work for low wages and not providing education.[34] "The entire tone of the [Roman Catholic] propaganda," remarked Graebner, "is that which preceded the Spanish-American War, when the brutali-

---

[32] "Rome in Mexico," *Cresset*, VIII (September, 1945), 6–7.
[33] "Who is to Blame for Conditions in Mexico?" *Witness*, LIII (September 25, 1934), 337–338.
[34] "Romanism Troubling Mexico," *Witness*, XLV (May 4, 1926), 148.

ties of General Weyler in Cuba were brought to the attention of the American public."[35]

Graebner was distressed not only by the intolerance and oppression that was occurring in countries under Catholic domination but also by the necessity of reporting it. He acknowledged that the *Witness* would be read by many American Catholics who would never become guilty of such intolerance themselves. He had never met a Catholic in the United States, not even among priests and members of orders, who would ever interfere with the religious practice of others. It was not simply the American principle of religious freedom that restrained them; they had never been trained otherwise than to respect the faith of their fellow citizens. But the Roman Catholic Church in Protestant countries is one thing, and in Latin America and southern Europe it is another. "And what it is in Catholic countries is the living expression of Roman theology concerning the article of separation of Church and State."[36] This comment by Graebner expresses accurately the attitude shared by most Lutheran writers.

The problem, then, from the Lutheran perspective was to prevent Catholic dominance and thus to preserve religious freedom. Lutheran writers were therefore concerned with Catholic aggression both on a worldwide basis and in the United States, for they feared that wherever it occurred it might lead to Catholic dominance.

The international aims and actions of the Roman Catholic Church were reported frequently and in relation to many different countries and regions of the world. Here we shall take note of the three main events that provoked particular

[35] "Will Uncle Sam Meddle in Mexico?" *Witness,* XLV (August 24, 1926), 277.
[36] "That Strange Paradox—Catholicism," *Witness,* LXVIII (May 3, 1949), 141–142.

concern among Lutherans: World War I, the Lateran Agreement of 1929, and World War II. In each of these events Lutheran writers saw efforts by the Roman Catholic Church to increase its power and enhance its prestige.

As his actions were interpreted by Graebner, the pope had hoped to use World War I as a means of reestablishing the papacy as a temporal power and of promoting Catholic ascendancy in Europe. This idea was developed most fully in *The Pope and Temporal Power,* where he cited three forms of evidence. First there were statements by Catholic leaders to this effect. He quoted Archbishop John Glennon of St. Louis as having commented after an interview with the pope in June, 1914, "We may hope that out of it the Cross will conquer once more."[37] Also cited was a comment in a Catholic newspaper in St. Louis: "The late Cardinal Rampolla always said that a general European war would undoubtedly restore Rome to the Pope. If Italy does not get into this war while it is on she will have to get out of Rome when it is over."[38]

Second, he called attention to the massive propaganda favorable to Catholic ends that was circulated around the world during the war, and he reprinted some excerpts from it.[39] Third, he insisted that the Roman Catholic Church's determination that the pope be represented at the peace conference was a sign that he wanted to consolidate his wartime gains. Graebner quoted a statement by Cardinal William O'Connell of Boston which claimed that Americans should welcome the presence of the pope at the peace table, and that the fourteen peace points of President Wilson showed little

[37] *The Pope and Temporal Power,* p. 59.
[38] *Ibid.,* p. 58.
[39] *Ibid.,* pp. 69–87. This volume was literally a clip-and-paste job. The manuscript is in the archives of Concordia Historical Institute.

practical divergence from those offered by the pope.[40]

Although the pope was not represented at the Versailles Conference, and the restoration of temporal power to the papacy did not come until a decade after the war's end, Graebner believed that the Roman Catholic Church had made considerable gains through the war. In writing of the death of Benedict XV he stated that this pope had played a master hand in the war, that he was the only power that had emerged from it with enormously enhanced prestige. "The Pope won the war."[41] A second gain was the formation of the Catholic International, an organization which grew out of the International Catholic Conference at The Hague in 1920. The various branches of this new organization, according to Graebner, were to be the instruments by which the Roman Catholic Church was to bring about world conquest.[42] The third achievement, in Graebner's view, was that although the papacy was not officially represented in the newly formed League of Nations, seventeen of the original thirty-two signatory nations were Catholic-dominated. This was seen as a possible step toward ending the separation of church and state and bringing the civilized world under the dominance of the Vatican.[43] The fourth Catholic gain issuing from the World War was that the Versailles Conference opened the way for further extension of papal dominance in Europe by excluding the Protestant Hohenzollerns from the German throne. There was no such prohibition against a Catholic Hapsburg in Germany or on the throne of a united Austria and Germany. Graebner intimated a sort of domino theory, by which papal power would be extended over all of Europe and

---

[40] *Ibid.,* p. 63.
[41] "Pope Benedict," *Witness,* XLI (January 31, 1922), 34.
[42] *Ibid.,* pp. 34–35.
[43] *The Pope and Temporal Power,* p. 66.

eventually over South America.[44] By 1930 he was convinced that the pope and Mussolini were working hand in hand, with the pope assuming that whatever was good for Italy would be good for him.

The Lateran treaties between the pope and Mussolini in 1929, bringing to an end the fifty-nine-year-old split between Italy and the Vatican, were seen by Missouri Synod Lutheran observers as the second major effort of the Roman Catholic Church to gain world dominance. Graebner devoted the final chapter of *The Pope and Temporal Power* to a discussion of the history and implications of the 1929 accord.[45] In discussing it in the *Witness* he tended on the one hand to play down the significance of the event by calling it a "meager victory" and a "colossal piece of arrogance."[46] But on the other he was concerned because no matter how small the territory given to the pope, it still made him a temporal ruler and gave him a base from which to extend his temporal power. Because he could grant citizenship to lay Catholics anywhere in the world, the way was now open for increasing his influence in every country where he had adherents.[47] Possible additional consequences frequently cited included Vatican membership in the League of Nations and diplomatic recognition by every country in the world, including the United States. Sommer added that it must also be remembered that the pope had established the worst of all temporal rules—a tyranny, in which he exercises executive, legislative, and judicial powers.[48]

---

[44] "Mussolini, Pope, and Empire," *Witness,* XLIX (May 27, 1930), 179.

[45] *The Pope and Temporal Power,* pp. 144–156.

[46] "'Impertinent Doubts' About the Pope's Victory," *Witness,* XLVIII (March 5, 1929), 82–83.

[47] "The Pope Shows His Hand," *Witness,* XLIX (November 25, 1930), 402–403.

[48] "The Temporal Power of the Pope," *Witness,* XLVIII (October 29, 1929), 357.

The third major event which, in the view of these Lutheran observers, the Roman Catholic Church attempted to use to further its own interests was World War II. It is difficult to determine any particular pattern in the Lutheran reaction. There was simply the certainty that it was being used to Rome's advantage; how this was being done was a source of puzzlement.

The failure of the pope to do anything to prevent Mussolini's advances in Ethiopia was the first incident to prompt Lutheran comment. One commentator said that the pope had done nothing because centuries before the Ethiopians had repelled Portuguese efforts to take them over. This was a setback for Rome such as Rome never forgets.[49] Another said that this showed the helplessness of the pope, even though he ought to have been in a position to do something.[50] Graebner commented that nothing was done because it was not to the advantage of Rome to intervene. He continued: "Before long the test may come, and we shall know whether the Pope's temporal power will be cast into the balance for war or for peace. Of one thing we are sure in advance—it will be made to serve the interests of the Roman Church."[51]

Graebner had observed earlier that the pope had his own political plans for the restoration of the Hapsburg dynasty in Austria,[52] so the 1938 Anschluss was interpreted as a setback to Roman Catholic hopes of returning to a position of primacy there.[53] Other papal designs could not be interpreted

---

[49] W. F. Hiller, "The Pope, Mussolini, and Ethiopia," *Witness,* LIV (September 24, 1935), 326–327.

[50] Arndt, "Why Does the Pope Not Stop the War?" *Concordia Theological Monthly,* VI (December, 1935), 950.

[51] "The Pope and World Peace," *Witness,* LIV (October 8, 1935), 348.

[52] *Ibid.*

[53] "The Reunion of Austria with Germany," *Witness,* LVII (March 22, 1938), 92–93.

so readily. One theory advanced by Graebner was that the pope had hoped to use the League of Nations as a lever for gaining recognition as a sovereign state and, beyond this, to achieve such aims as a Hapsburg Austria, a greater Poland ruled by the Hapsburgs, a Danube Union ruled by the Hapsburgs, and a Hapsburg Spain. The rise of Hitler, the revolution in Spain, and the extension of Italian power in the Balkans had thwarted these aims. Would these things have happened if the United States had been in the League of Nations? Graebner intimated that they would not and that Rome would thus have achieved its aims.[54]

The *Cresset* speculated on another possibility. It wondered if the Vatican was changing its policies and attempting to appease the Axis. At first the pope and the Fascists in Italy had got along, but after Mussolini fell under the influence of Hitler, the pope seemed always to oppose the actions of the Axis in Poland, The Netherlands, Belgium, Luxembourg, Norway, and Finland. The *Cresset* admitted being stumped by what the friendliness with the Fascists had come to mean.[55]

After the war a third interpretation of papal strategy was given tacit endorsement by at least one reviewer. In commenting on a book that accused the Vatican of sponsoring the Nazi and Fascist regimes in order to further its own cause, and of encouraging the attack on Russia by Hitler in the hope that Russian doors would be opened to the Roman Catholic Church, this reviewer remarked that the volume "reveals some of the maze of political intrigue" of which the Vatican had purportedly been guilty.[56]

[54] "Rome Dreams of Her Lost Dominions," *Witness,* LIX (March 19, 1940), 92–93.

[55] "The Pope and the Fascists," *Cresset,* III (September, 1940), 3–4.

[56] August W. Brustat, review of D. Tomitch, *Those Responsible for the Second World War* (New York: Agora Publishing Company, n.d.), in *American Lutheran,* XXX (May, 1947), 21.

During the course of the war occasional perplexity was expressed over such things as the establishment of diplomatic relations between Japan and the Vatican. ("Does the Pope sometimes move in a mysterious way to gain whatever objectives he has in mind?")[57] But generally the concern was simply with preventing the Roman Catholic Church from making gains through the war by being represented at the peace table. The *Cresset* commented already in 1942 that if the pope were allowed to have his delegates at the conference, it would be "the greatest step forward in international political influence that the Papacy has achieved since the age of the Reformation."[58] Walter A. Maier, taking some liberty with the realities, thought it was necessary to keep the pope from the peace conference because, as he interpreted it, the purpose of the war was to guarantee all the people of the world religious freedom, something which the pope had consistently opposed.[59]

Regardless of the various theories advanced or the observations made by the Lutheran writers, however, they all centered around one consistent theme: the Roman Catholic Church would use World War II in whatever way it could to advance its own power and prestige. Others ought to be aware of the church's intentions and do all in their power to prevent its success.

The other part of the Lutheran fear of increasing Catholic power centered on the rising influence of the Roman Catholic Church in the United States. It was assumed that, unless thwarted, this influence would eventually lead to dominance. Although this fear was no doubt most intense in the decades

[57] "Nippon and the Vatican," *Cresset*, V (June, 1942), 8–9.
[58] "The Pope's Christmas Message," *Cresset*, V (March, 1942), 8–9.
[59] "We Are Fighting for Religious Freedom," *Walther League Messenger*, LII (February, 1944), 244–245, 277.

prior to the 1950's, Lutherans were still not completely at ease about Catholic intentions in the 1960's. Numerous incidents gave Lutheran writers the opportunity to express their apprehensions and to call attention to Catholic aims. Some reactions were rather amusing, such as the 1959 editorial in the *Lutheran Witness* raising objection to the possible choice of the marigold as a national flower. A Catholic paper had supported the idea in noting that it would be an appropriate national flower in a country which the Roman Catholic Church has placed under the patronage of the Immaculate Conception, but the *Witness* claimed that naming the marigold the national flower would glorify Mariolatry and be another step toward making America Catholic.[60]

Some developments were reported with reluctance. Reminding its readers that for seventeen years it had opposed every attempt to fan the fires of religious animosity, the *Cresset* related that according to Joseph C. Harsch of the *Christian Science Monitor* the activities of Senator Joseph McCarthy were having the effect of increasing the proportion of Catholics in government service. The dismissal rate for Protestants in some departments had become extraordinarily high, and some employers were reportedly hiring Catholics to protect themselves. This, said the Cresset, must be examined.[61]

Other matters also received passing attention, such as Catholic blocking of the showing the movie *Martin Luther* on a Chicago television station, and enforcement of Catholic practices in medical matters, even in hospitals built with funds coming from federal and even Protestant sources. But there were some matters that were of rather continuous concern. Three of the most important were Catholic activity in education, including the efforts to receive government funds to support church schools; attempts to establish diplomatic relations

[60] "Shall It Be?" *Witness,* LXXVIII (February 24, 1959), 82.
[61] "An Unpleasant Question," *Cresset,* XVII (May, 1954), 4–5.

with the Vatican; and the question of Catholic loyalty and responsibility in political office, particularly in regard to the presidency of the United States. Each of these matters is given separate attention in the following three chapters. Three others are treated more briefly here: Catholic Action, Catholic influence in the nation's press, and the workings and doings of the hierarchy of the church in the United States.

The Catholic Action movement, an attempt to involve the laity in the work of a church that had traditionally been dominated by its hierarchy, was watched carefully from its inception and its introduction into the United States, although not all references to efforts to make America Catholic were identified with it. Graebner called attention to it already in 1922. He observed that, scrutinizing its aims and program, which were primarily educational and benevolent, one is prompted to ask, Why so tremendous an organization for such comparatively unimportant tasks as those stated? He wondered whether this might be the beginning of a Catholic party in the United States.[62] Some years later he commented that when Catholics announce their intention to mobilize the world of Catholics to action, it behooves Lutherans to sit up and take notice. After calling attention to some of the activities of the National Council of Catholic Men, at that time the Catholic Action organization in the United States, he again speculated on the possibility of a Catholic party.[63]

The *Cresset,* in its very first issue, also described the activities of Catholic Action and commented on its intention to make Catholicism a determining factor in American life. Perhaps the *Cresset*'s generally more moderate position in regard to Catholicism is reflected in the fact that it acknowl-

---

[62] "Putting the IKA into America," *Witness,* XLI (February 14, 1922), 55–56.
[63] "Catholic Action," *Witness,* L (October 13, 1931), 348–349.

edged Catholic Action's intention to make Catholicism *a,* not *the,* determining factor.[64] Quite a different treatment was Alex Guebert's essay in the *Concordia Theological Monthly* in 1939. Guebert noted that through Catholic Action the church hoped to "introduce its ideals into all phases of American life, civic, economical, political, cultural." Previously, when the burden lay with the priesthood and religious orders, progress was not fast enough, so now it was being shifted to the laity. Guebert saw in Catholic Action "an unmistakable echo of the principles of Jesuitism." He concluded:

> Rome never changes. It desires to bring back a state such as that which obtained in the Middle Ages, when the Pope at times was the absolute ruler also in things temporal. . . . In spite of Biblical terminology Rome's position is essentially pagan and hence cannot be a blessing to anyone.[65]

After 1939 Catholic Action did not receive prominent attention in Lutheran periodicals, although the Catholic intention to make America Catholic was repeatedly referred to.

One of the means by which it was assumed that America might be made Catholic was through Catholic control of the press. Through the years the Lutheran writers regularly complained of all the publicity favorable to the Roman Catholic Church appearing in newspapers and periodicals. W. H. T. Dau commented that "the newspapers are the ass on which Antichrist is riding into his Jerusalem."[66] Sommer's observation characterized the Lutheran attitude:

> The Roman Catholic Church does very little direct advertising, but whoever reads the daily and periodical press attentively and intelligently cannot but notice that there is

[64] "Catholic Action," *Cresset,* I (November, 1937), 4–5.
[65] "Catholic Action," *Concordia Theological Monthly,* X (February, 1939), 128–131.
[66] *Theological Monthly,* IV (May, 1924), 150–151.

a gentle, yet persistent and continued effort made to present to the mind of the reading public as many stories, data, and items of information as possible which will produce an even more favorable opinion of the Roman Catholic Church. Attacks upon Romanism are all but excluded from the public press. Some one is watching that.[67]

The other side of the complaint was that Protestant churches, and particularly Protestant clergymen, were often ignored or put in as bad a light as possible. It was generally agreed that the Roman Catholic Church really did not need a press of its own because it fared so well in the public press. When it did not fare well, economic pressure was used to compel the publisher to change his approach. Whenever possible the Lutheran writers called attention to evidence which would support their two-sided complaint.

Of the many things that rankled Lutheran observers perhaps the most irritating were the activities of the Roman Catholic hierarchy and the publicity given to them. Ironically, by their commentary they themselves were contributing to the publicity of which they complained. One of the sharpest criticisms directed at the hierarchy, particularly the cardinals, was that they were guilty of divided loyalty. "This membership in the papal court," said Polack in writing of the appointment of new cardinals, "is as incongruous as if an American citizen were at the same time an official at the court of a foreign ruler."[68] Other things, too, disturbed: Cardinal George Mundelein of Chicago being given a whole day by President Roosevelt, the special treatment given by the American ambassador to the Cardinal upon his arrival in Rome, adjournment of Congress in respect to the pope on his death

[67] "Roman Catholic Propaganda," *Witness,* XLIII (January 15, 1924), 25–26.
[68] "The Pope Appoints New Cardinals," *Witness,* LXV (January 29, 1946), 42–43.

(and that after hearing glowing speeches and passing fulsome resolutions), the appointment of Joseph Kennedy as the President's special representative at the coronation of the new pope,[69] the kissing of Cardinal Samuel Stritch's ring by Chicago Mayor Edward J. Kelly[70]—these were typical of the events that drew bitter comment from Lutherans.

It is possible, as we have done in this chapter, to record and document the Lutheran reaction to the Roman Catholic threat to religious liberty, but it is impossible to convey the seriousness with which Lutherans regarded this danger. Unless we can project ourselves back into the climate of the 1920's through the 1950's, we may be guilty of thinking that the Lutheran writers were unduly concerned. They were convinced, however, that the Roman Catholic theory of religious liberty and Roman Catholic practice in the United States and around the world were inimical to American principles and Lutheran welfare. They were compelled to write of the things which they had seen and heard.

[69] J. Frederic Wenchel, "Whither America?" *Witness,* LVIII (March 21, 1939), 97.
[70] Thomas Coates, "The Cardinal's Return," *Walther League Messenger,* LIV (April, 1946), 10–11.

5

PAROCHIAL SCHOOLS AND PUBLIC FUNDS

IN MANY RESPECTS the Roman Catholic Church and the Lutheran Church-Missouri Synod find themselves on the same side of the educational fence. Many ideas in their philosophies of education are held in common. Both stress religious training and therefore maintain their own parochial schools. In the two most important judicial decisions guaranteeing the right of free choice in selecting educational institutions, *Meyer v. Nebraska* and *Pierce v. Society of Sisters,* each church aided the other with at least moral support.

Yet certain issues concerning education have brought the two groups into sharp disagreement. We shall not discuss here the predictable Lutheran reaction to such things as nuns in their garb teaching in public schools, or Catholic attempts to censor public-school textbooks, or even such well-publicized cases as the clash between Protestants and Catholics over control of the public schools in North College Hill, Ohio. These and other similar incidents were all regarded as segments of the larger effort to make America Catholic, and of course this effort met with strong resistance from Lutherans.

The concern in this chaper is rather with the broader issue of public financial support for church-related schools and the response of Lutherans to the avowed intention of Catholics to procure such support. We shall necessarily also examine the official Missouri Synod position and the differing opinions of various Lutherans concerning government aid for Lutheran parochial schools. Finally, we shall consider the extent to which the Lutheran position was shaped in reaction to Catholic policy.

Although the hierarchy of the Roman Catholic Church did not take an outspoken position on the matter until recently, some Catholics have argued through the years that their schools are justly entitled to appropriations from state funds. In the late 1940's, when the question of federal aid to education came into prominence, Catholics contended that if a law granting federal aid was enacted, their schools must be included among the recipients. They recognized that without it their schools would be unable to compete with public schools. This demand sharpened the issue and made it the object of national attention. We are here principally concerned with the federal-aid question; references to aid from state governments are included incidentally.

The efforts to obtain government monies for Catholic schools were generally based on an appeal to fairness and justice. As the debate over federal aid intensified, it was necessary for the church to crystallize its arguments and to show the legality of this aid. The Department of Education of the National Catholic Welfare Conference therefore prepared a legal study on "The Constitutionality of the Inclusion of Church-Related Schools in Federal Aid to Education." The specific conclusions of this study were presented in an address by Monsignor Frederick G. Hochwalt in 1962 before the National Lutheran Educational Conference, a meeting of educators from various Lutheran synods. Although the study was made in 1961, it reflects views that had been developing over several decades and serves here as an expression of the official Catholic position:

1. Education in church-related schools is a public function, which by its nature, is deserving of governmental support.

2. There exists no constitutional bar to aid education in church-related schools in a degree proportionate to the value of the public function it performs. Such aid to the

secular [endeavors of the] institution may take the form of matching grants or long-term loans to institutions, or of scholarship, tuition payments, or tax benefits.

3. The parent and child have a constitutional right to choose a church-related institution meeting reasonable state requirements as the institution in which the child's education shall be acquired.

4. Government in the United States is without power to impose upon the people a single educational system in which all must participate.[1]

The third and fourth conclusions represent traditional Lutheran beliefs, but there is no doubt that the first two have been consistently rejected and even deplored by most Lutherans. At least part of the opposition was due to the fear that the Roman Catholic Church would profit greatly from any government aid. That Lutheran schools would also benefit was usually discounted as a point of consideration. Lutherans prided themselves on their willingness to finance their own schools without outside assistance. When Oswald C. J. Hoffmann, well-known Lutheran Hour speaker and director of information for the Missouri Synod, debated the issue of federal aid to church-related schools with Monsignor Hochwalt on national television, his summary conclusion typified the Lutheran position: "Freedom has its price and that price in the case of denominational schools is good hard cash."[2]

Lutheran writers were not reluctant to express their various objections to seeing Catholic schools benefit from federal aid. One view was expressed by August C. Stellhorn, the Missouri Synod's secretary of schools. After outlining his

[1] "Some Educational Problems with Reference to Church and State: As a Catholic Sees It," *Papers and Proceedings of the Forty-Eighth Annual Convention, National Lutheran Educational Conference* (Cleveland, Ohio, 1962), pp. 56–57.

[2] Transcript, "CBS Reports: Should Private and Parochial Schools Receive Federal Aid?" (April 6, 1961), p. 28.

general reasons for opposing a federal-aid proposal and rejecting aid for Lutheran schools, he concluded: "In the end we may lose our own schools but help to support those of the Roman Catholic Church through taxation."[3] Some feared that money they might receive would eventually lead to Catholic dominance in the United States. J. T. Mueller judged Catholicism in the United States to be "almost disgustingly aggressive" and declared that all their educational agencies are used "in the interest of Romanist propaganda." As a powerful minority, they are insisting upon privileges which they would use to their own aggrandizement and "ultimately, in opposition to our very democracy and its prerogatives for our free citizens. It is just for this reason that non-Catholics are so very averse to considering Rome's plea for government support for its schools."[4]

W. G. Polack was concerned for a similar reason. He argued that Catholics regard their schools as "stopgaps" and that the pope has never really sanctioned them except as a temporary, emergency measure.[5] The inference, of course, was that government aid would be a step toward the establishment of a system that the pope could approve, presumably a public-school system controlled by Catholics. The *St. Louis Lutheran,* at the time a bitter foe of any form of government aid to church-related schools, asserted that "Catholicism is not so much in need of government funds as it is determined to foist upon the American way of life the Catholic doc-

[3] "The Federal Aid-to-Education Bill," *Lutheran Witness,* LIX (February 6, 1940), 40–41.
[4] "Catholic Schools and Government Aid," *Concordia Theological Monthly,* XVI (April, 1945), 280–281.
[5] "Roman Catholic Propaganda," *Witness,* LXVI (December 30, 1947), 429–430.

trine of the subserviency of the state to the advancement of Catholic interests."[6]

Catholics were naturally aware that a large part of the Protestant reaction against federal aid was based on their fear that Catholics would benefit from it. When *America,* a Catholic magazine, pointed this out, William Arndt replied that they were using flimsy argumentation. He doubted that this was the chief reason for the Protestant position and remarked: "And if this were the motive, could Rome complain? Its own record of intolerance and bloody persecution of dissenters has been such that no state can be blamed for being very cautious before adopting a course which would be particularly advantageous to Romanism."[7]

Some Lutherans, however, saw danger in making such harsh judgments or in taking such dogmatic positions. When Roland A. Dede, a Wisconsin pastor, wrote a caustic article pertaining to efforts of Catholics in Wisconsin to obtain free bus transportation for children attending parochial or other private schools,[8] Arnold C. Mueller was moved to reply:

> The article . . . is a polemic against Romanism. I share with the brethren these misgivings regarding the Roman Catholic Church which has publicly condemned our democratic form of government and would not hesitate to break down and even erase the distinction between Church and State. . . . But we must not permit the threat of Roman Catholic aggression to carry us to an extreme position that even can be assailed and perhaps overthrown.

Mueller, a Board of Parish Education executive, pointed out

[6] Reprinted in the *Witness,* LXVI (March 11, 1947), 80.

[7] "Catholics and Religious Liberty," *Concordia Theological Monthly,* XVI (November, 1945), 794–795.

[8] "Shall the 'Little Kids' Ride or Walk?" *American Lutheran,* XXIX (January, 1946), 11–13.

that Lutherans in the state of Missouri were working to get the very things opposed by Dede and by the two pastoral conference resolutions Dede had appended to his article. He added that Dede's views were in conflict with those of the synod's Board of Parish Education which had been adopted by the 1944 Synodical Convention. In refuting Dede's arguments Mueller urged that fear of Catholic domination be put aside for the time being and that the matter be looked at without prejudice.[9]

Another Missouri Synod official, Arthur L. Miller, executive secretary of the Board of Parish Education, recognized that the Catholic issue would have to be met. In discussing the whole question of federal aid to education he suggested that John A. Ryan and other Catholic leaders be confronted with their statements about using the schools as the wedge to make America Catholic. In this way it could be determined whose views prevail in the Roman Catholic Church.[10]

Unwillingness to see the Roman Catholic Church receive federal funds for its schools was only a corollary to a larger concern, however, for many Lutherans sincerely believed that a fundamental principle was at stake. Lutheran observers vacillated between the conviction, on the one hand, that the American system of church-state relations could not allow for church-related schools to receive public funds, and the fear, on the other, that such aid would be enacted and the system destroyed.

When George Johnson, director of the National Catholic Welfare Conference, wrote in the *Atlantic Monthly* that there was no reason why a method for providing government funds could not be discovered which would fit our American circumstances, Paul Bretscher demurred and raised some

[9] *American Lutheran*, XXIX (April, 1946), 14–16.
[10] "Federal Aid for Education," *Lutheran Education*, LXXXIII (February, 1948), 343.

pointed questions: Who would administer the funds? Would nonreligious people allow their funds to be used for religious purposes? Would those who support their own religious schools be willing also to support others? He urged that authorities on church-state matters keep their eyes wide open.[11] In his television debate with Monsignor Hochwalt, Oswald Hoffmann asserted that "a demand for direct governmental assistance to the instructional program of a parochial school constitutes a frontal attack upon the traditional policy of separation of church and state."[12]

James Manz intimated that some Protestants regard the Catholic drive for government funds for its schools as a threat to the American system just as distinct as that posed by the freethinkers and secularists who would like to see the church deprived of its rights, position, and favors.[13] He commented that although Catholics are making an all-out effort to get federal aid, in the belief that the very existence of their schools is at stake, others believe that our public-school system and our entire church-state arrangement will eventually collapse if government aid is given to church schools. He thought that this issue might well be the greatest internal problem facing the nation. The money, he said, is far less important than the principle; the future, not the present, is what counts. For him it was a no-compromise issue: "Expediency, seeking the 'middle of the road,' and the quoting of platitudes will not suffice."[14]

The attempt to get funds was also harshly criticized by

[11] "Will Rome Score Another Victory?" *Lutheran School Journal,* LXXV (May, 1940), 394–398.
[12] Transcript, "CBS Reports," pp. 6–7.
[13] "The American Way," *Witness,* LXXX (October 17, 1961), 493–495.
[14] "Federal Aid to Parochial Schools," *Witness,* LXXX (October 31, 1961), 516–517.

Carl S. Meyer. He declared that if Catholics want their own schools, they should be willing to pay for them, just as Lutherans should be willing to pay for Lutheran schools. "We believe in parochial schools," he wrote, "but we do not want to see them the cause for breaking down the established American practices for the separation of church and state."[15]

Not all those who were concerned expressed themselves in such drastic or alarmed terms. But even when they dealt with the problem more objectively, they had to acknowledge its far-reaching significance. Albert G. Huegli, a political scientist and probably the synod's foremost authority on church-state relations, believed that "government financial aid to church schools creates serious difficulties for the operation of the American pattern" and that "we would need to disregard the fundamental understanding of the American pattern in church-state relations if we were to encourage government subsidy." He contended that if the churches that maintain schools mean what they say when they establish them, subsidizing their programs must be subsidization of their religious philosophy. Therefore, if the restriction against outright aid to these schools is dropped, "the whole American pattern will need to be re-evaluated."[16] No doubt Huegli was aware that the American pattern as it was affected by the question of federal aid had been reevaluated periodically by Lutherans

[15] "What About Parochial Schools?" *Witness*, LXXVII (July 1, 1958), 308.

[16] "Church and State in Education: As a Protestant Sees It," *Papers and Proceedings of the Forty-Eighth Annual Convention, National Lutheran Educational Conference* (Cleveland, Ohio, 1962), pp. 52–53. That Dr. Huegli's ideas were modified is apparent in his article in the March, 1966, *Cresset*, "The New Look in Church-State Relations." The new look, as he saw it, "involves a decline in the American system of tension between church and state, and an assertion of cooperative activity quite unlike anything that has preceded it." He referred to the new arrangement as "the American pattern updated" (*ibid.*, pp. 9–14).

for more than two decades, for he himself had participated in such reevaluation. In fact, the most pronounced characteristic found among Lutherans, either when they wrote individually or when they acted as a group, was that although they were willing to take a definite stand, they were unwilling to be dogmatic in that position. They preferred to allow for the possibility of reconsideration and revision if circumstances made this necessary. Perhaps this also explains why Lutherans, unlike Catholics, did not concentrate on the legal and constitutional aspects of the problem. As long as they could discuss it in theoretical terms of policy and principle, they could tacitly maintain the option for a change of heart and mind. A court decision would have closed the options.

The fact that the Missouri Synod had parochial schools of its own also contributed to the refusal to take an absolute stand. Lutherans could never identify with a dogmatic position like that of the Protestants and Other Americans United for Separation of Church and State. Huegli acknowledged this at the 1948 Lutheran Educational Conference during a panel discussion on the manifesto of the POAU, in which he stated:

> I am of the opinion that our subscription to the Manifesto at this time would be embarrassingly inconsistent. We Lutherans have a parish school system, too. We have taken advantage of public support from taxes through the acceptance of free textbooks and free bus transportation. We had a right to do this, of course, following previous Supreme Court decisions. But we could scarcely join an organization which is striving to overthrow those decisions and which upbraids Catholics for taking advantage of them.[17]

Rather than Lutherans identifying with the POAU, he urged

[17] *Report of the 1948 Educational Conference* (River Forest, Illinois: Board for Parish Education, The Lutheran Church-Missouri Synod, 1948), p. 80.

a reevaluation of the Lutheran approach to the concept of separation of church and state. The policy thus having been clarified, Lutheran practices should then be brought into line with it.

The paper presented by Arnold C. Mueller at the same conference suggested the direction that such a reevaluation might take. In an interpretative study of the First Amendment he urged a *simple* rather than an *absolute* separation of church and state. This would make the relationship between church and state fluid in the sense that it would allow for changes in legislation and practice. He saw this as the alternative to a completely secularized society. It is true that he was dealing specifically with two recent Supreme Court decisions and did not at all recommend direct aid to church-related schools, but his paper is significant in that it allowed for adjustments in church-state relations which would be favorable to religion without precipitating the collapse of the system.[18]

Huegli and Mueller were not the first to recommend study and to suggest allowance for the possibility of change. Already in 1939 the *Lutheran School Journal* had editorialized on "Government Subsidy for Private Schools":

> Where do we stand in the controversy? Traditionally with the opponents. But our policy may change. At all events here is a situation which should claim our full attention. To view it intelligently, we must be informed, and the position we take must be the result of careful, calm, deliberate judgment.[19]

Significantly, Theodore Graebner responded favorably to this editorial in a personal letter to the editor. He commented that he considered it as proof of an open-minded attitude that is

---

[18] *Ibid.*, pp. 30–42.
[19] "Government Subsidy for Private Schools," *Lutheran School Journal*, LXXIV (May, 1939), 388–389.

so very necessary when dealing with the problem of state subsidies.[20]

Incidentally, the Missouri Synod might eventually have followed a different course if Graebner, who held influential positions in the synod and who was recognized as something of an authority in church-state matters, had advanced publicly the views he expressed in private. There he stated that there was no question at all in his mind that any church that does educational work for the state has a right to accept subsidies. The burden of proof rests, not on those who would accept subsidies, but on those who would prohibit their acceptance. It certainly would not do, Graebner asserted, simply to quote in an offhand way the principle of separation of church and state.[21]

The Missouri Synod at its triennial national convention in 1941 formally recognized the problems raised by the government-aid issue. It resolved that further study of the movements and countermovements regarding governmental aid to education should be made under the supervision and direction of the Board of Parish Education (then known as the Board of Christian Education) in order to be prepared to meet any eventuality that might arise in this area.[22]

On the basis of a report prepared by a committee appointed to study the question the Board of Parish Education formulated a policy on state support for church-related schools which the 1944 Synodical Convention adopted. This policy was reaffirmed in 1947 and 1950. In 1953 it was again reaffirmed until new developments might make a reappraisal desirable or necessary. It is proper, therefore, to regard the

---

[20] Letter to W. C. Kohn, May 4, 1939.
[21] Letter to Milton G. Kuolt, March 16, 1939.
[22] *Proceedings of the Thirty-Eighth Regular Convention of the Lutheran Church-Missouri Synod*, 1941, p. 133.

terms of this policy as the official and consistently held position of the Missouri Synod.

The position taken in 1944 was distinctly ambivalent. It distinguished between the two aspects of the school program. The social service aspect, which includes such things as library services, lunches, health service, and transportation, was seen to be distinct from the teaching aspect, which involves curriculum, teaching, and philosophy of education. Of the former it provided:

> The social service program should in equity be available to all children of school age irrespective of their school association. . . . The State can grant to children in church schools this program, since rendering this service does not promote the religious tenets of the Church. . . . The Church can accept this program as it is offered and may even be within its rights in demanding it.[23]

In this respect the Lutherans appear to be in agreement with the Catholic position.

The teaching aspect of the school's program was regarded in a different way. Because of the character of the teaching program the church may not subject it to the supervision, control, and direction of the state. When the state contributes tax money, it has the right to control the expenditures, sanctioning both the purpose for which and the manner in which the money is expended. Acceptance of state funds would therefore imply submission of the teaching program to state control. If the state should offer financial aid and at the same time relinquish the rights of supervision, direction, and control, "the church might under conditions accept this subsidy without becoming guilty of wrongdoing." Nevertheless, the state still has the right to reassert control of the expenditures

---

[23] *Proceedings of the Thirty-Ninth Regular Convention of the Lutheran Church-Missouri Synod*, 1944, p. 132.

of tax money or to withdraw subsidy at any time. Either action could produce disastrous consequences, possibly the collapse of the parochial schools that had become dependent on it.[24]

This aspect of the official policy emphasized the real fear with which most Lutherans reacted when they considered the possibility of government aid for their schools. It was in this fear, and not in the fear of Catholicism or in concern over the breakdown of our church-state system, that the *fundamental* objection to government aid appears to have rested. It is therefore ironic that little point was made of the fact that Catholic schools, too, would be exposed to the danger of federal control if they accepted government funds.

Returning to the 1944 statement of official policy, we note that a concluding paragraph stressed a principal difference between the Lutheran and Catholic positions:

> The argument that the State is not being asked to subsidize religious teaching of sectarian schools, but only the teaching of the secular branches is specious and invalid, for all teaching in church schools—also the teaching of the secular branches—becomes a part of the teaching program. . . . Secular branches are taught in the light of the religious tenets of the Church.[25]

This, however, was an *obiter dictum* and did not represent the heart of the argument, namely, that acceptance of government funds exposes the receiving schools to government control.

As we have seen, the 1944 policy was reaffirmed at subsequent conventions and therefore remained the official position. In 1961, because of the national attention focused on the question of federal aid to education, the Board of Parish

[24] *Ibid.,* pp. 132–133.
[25] *Ibid.,* p. 133.

Education issued a guide for the parishes of the Lutheran Church-Missouri Synod and noted that each congregation would have to determine its own course of action—an indication that the official position was not binding. Essentially this was a restatement and updating of the earlier position. It again differentiated between the social service and the teaching aspects of the school program, and was more precise in defining what is included in the teaching program: teachers' salaries, buildings, equipment, and textbooks. The new statement confirmed the belief that "any substantial Federal aid for the instructional program, in spite of protestations to the contrary, would in the very nature of the case involve the Federal Government in at least a measure of control of the schools that receive the funds." It observed that "accepting such aid would have a tendency to interfere with the mission and purpose of the church" and that by resisting the temptation to request or accept government funds "the church will give continued support to the policy of separation of church and state and will retain its freedom of action in education."[26] This statement was approved by the 1962 Synodical Convention.

Most of the articles and editorials in Lutheran periodicals were consistent with and supported the official policy, for, as Arthur L. Miller noted, it represented a tested consensus in the synod. It did not represent a unanimous point of view, however, because some members of the synod still maintained different opinions on this controversial matter.[27] Even though an official position had been reaffirmed regularly for almost

[26] The 1961 statement and the 1962 synodical resolution are included in Arthur L. Miller's excellent, concise essay "Current Issues in Church-State Relations," in *Legal Aspects of Lutheran Parish Education,* ed. Peter A. Zadeik, Jr., Twenty-First Yearbook of the Lutheran Education Association (River Forest, Illinois, 1964), pp. 47–79.

[27] *Ibid.,* p. 61.

twenty years, it was not a closed matter. Just as the synod, by a process of reevaluation and reconsideration, had been led to maintain its position through the years, so others, by a similar process, were led to develop dissenting ideas. One wishes that Graebner would have expanded upon his privately stated thoughts, but there is no record that he did. As a matter of fact, the dissenters who expressed themselves in print were few.

One who did was Neelak S. Tjernagel, a professor at Concordia Teachers College, River Forest, Illinois, who believed that the fears of federal control were exaggerated and unfounded. He said that in favoring state aid he was not moved by the interests of the church nor by a sense of sympathy for those who pay twice, but rather by a national and civic sense of responsibility. He wrote in *Lutheran Education:* "I am convinced that tax support for private Christian education is clearly, urgently, and vitally in the national interest of the United States of America." It was his contention as a historian that the founding fathers did not intend to secularize education. Because religion must be a major part of one's educational experience, and because religious diversities do not permit religion to be taught in the public schools, the only solution is to allow tax monies to be designated as subsidies to private Christian schools. This Tjernagel saw as a means of forestalling moral collapse in the nation.[28] Unfortunately he did not deal with such practical matters as how and to whom these funds would be distributed. Although he favored aid only to private Christian schools, one wonders whether he would have made it available to Jewish groups, Mormons, Christian Scientists, and even to atheists if they were to demand them.

[28] "State Aid and Christian Education," *Lutheran Education,* XCV (June, 1960), 491–494.

Another critical observer, John Strietelmeyer, *was* moved by the interests of the church as he outlined his views in an address to the Conference of Education Executives of the Lutheran Church-Missouri Synod in December, 1962. Strietelmeyer, a Valparaiso University professor and the managing editor of *Cresset,* suggested the direction that the synodical position might take in the future. His remarks were based on his conviction that the parochial school system of the Missouri Synod is basic to the maintenance of a theologically concerned and theologically competent laity and that therefore this source of strength must not be lost. After taking note of certain social and economic signs of the times, he concluded that "all enterprises which rely for their funds upon persuasion rather than compulsion are going to have a harder and harder time of it in the years to come." Caught in the squeeze will be the parochial schools. He continued:

> And so, it seems to me, we can either say, "All right, we will maintain our schools on our own as long as possible and let them go," or we can say, "Our schools are too important to sacrifice. If the only way to keep them going is to assert our rightful claim to public assistance, we will assert that right."
>
> There may be those who would quarrel with my contention that we may claim public assistance as a right. And, I would qualify my statement to the extent of granting that it is not a legal right. But, I do insist that we have a moral right to expect the state to take cognizance of the fact that we are, in our schools, doing an educational job which, if we were not doing it, the state would have to do.

In discussing how government aid to church-related schools could be reconciled with the American system of church-state relations, he recommended a pragmatic, functional approach:

> The state's legitimate concern in education is to ensure that its people are adequately prepared for responsible citizen-

ship. . . . I would maintain that the school which satisfies these legitimate concerns of the state is doing the job for which the state allocates money to its educational budget and is, therefore, entitled to share equally in that budget with all other schools that are doing essentially the same job.

As far as a proposal for a policy was concerned, Strietelmeyer said that for the moment he would recommend nothing more than "an assertion of our moral right to share in whatever assistance the Federal government may choose to offer to the public elementary schools." His principal concern was with keeping all schools "in the same boat."

It is only at that point where there is a considerable likelihood that the public school will be offered assistance that will further widen the gap between its resources and those of the parochial school that I would recommend pressing our claim to consideration.

On the particular question of federal control, a matter of great concern in the traditional Lutheran position, he said:

We are faced with the prospect of increasing government control over our schools whether we accept public funds or not, and the limits of that control will be set not by any state or Federal constitution, but by public opinion as it is reflected in the thinking and rulings of those members of the public who happen to be justices of Federal and state supreme courts.[29]

Although this study on the Lutheran approach to Catholicism concludes with the year 1963, it is more concerned with marking turning points in Lutheran thought than in observing inclusive dates. In fact, 1963 was selected as the terminal date because it seems to have been a year of turning points. There-

[29] The remarks by Strietelmeyer were quoted by Arthur L. Miller in *Legal Aspects of Lutheran Parish Education,* pp. 61–63.

fore, this study would be incomplete if it would not at least take note of the fact that the remarks of Strietelmeyer were reflected in the proposal of the Board of Parish Education (of which Strietelmeyer was a member) to the 1965 Synodical Convention. The resolution on federal aid enacted by that convention showed a significant revision, even a reversal, of the official synodical position.

The question posed at the beginning of this chapter can be clarified: To what extent was the Lutheran position shaped in reaction to Catholic policy? Naturally it is impossible to give a conclusive answer to this question, for we have no way of knowing what the Lutheran position would have been if the Catholic policy had been different. The nature of the relations between the two churches having been what it was, that they might have espoused an identical policy through the years is hardly likely. Nevertheless, some observations in response to the question are possible.

As a starting point, we can conclude that if the synodical fathers were sincere, and if the editors and commentators were honest—and we have no reason to believe that they were not—the perennial fear that government control was tied to government money should have been constant, regardless of Catholic policy, for this was the heart of the Lutheran position. Therefore, although their devotion to the principle of separation of church and state and their fears that Catholic demands threatened this principle cannot be overlooked, the fundamental Lutheran policy should not have been affected by anything Catholics did or said. Any change in attitude would have had to come from a change in other circumstances.

The basic differences that existed on this issue, however, provided a vehicle for expression of anti-Catholic sentiment. The effect of this was threefold: first, it made it natural for Lutherans to take a polarized, more inflexible position than they might have otherwise taken. This seems to have been particularly true in the Hochwalt-Hoffmann television debate. At the time *Cresset* commented that its heart was with Hoffmann, but it questioned the wisdom of taking too rigid a position.[30]

Furthermore, it prompted an exaggerated expression of the fears of Catholic dominance in America and of the impending destruction of our church and state principles if Catholic schools should receive government support for anything beyond social services. We are looking at it from a different perspective, of course, but it is hard to believe that five and ten years ago people thought in terms of "status quo or collapse," rather than adjustment and evolution.

Finally, the basic differences between Lutherans and Catholics seem to have prevented any meaningful discussion and exchange of ideas on their various positions. There is no evidence that before 1960 Lutherans studied seriously what Catholics were saying. They were therefore in danger of contending with a caricature of the other side's real position. Had such discussion taken place a decade ago, a mutually acceptable approach might have been worked out. The recent Lutheran reversal of position comes rather late in the game. Abandoning or reshaping principles in the face of necessity opens one to the charge of following a course of expediency.

[30] "Federal Aid to Private Schools," *Cresset,* XXIV (March, 1961), 3–4.

6

WASHINGTON AND THE VATICAN

THE SPECTER THAT had been haunting Protestants for decades finally became a reality late in 1939. In a dozen years the reality was gone, but the specter persisted. Lutherans shared in the general Protestant apprehension of this specter. Walter A. Maier and Theodore Graebner had begun to alert them to its dangers already in 1921.[1] J. Frederic Wenchel, the *Witness*'s "Washington observer," had added his warnings in the 1930's.[2] So President Franklin D. Roosevelt's appointment of Myron C. Taylor as his personal representative at the Vatican, with the rank of ambassador, did not come as an uncushioned jolt.

Being prepared for it, however, did not relieve the distress it created. During Taylor's tenure as Roosevelt's personal envoy and as President Truman's special representative, and continuing through Truman's attempt to appoint General Mark Clark as ambassador, the issue of diplomatic recognition of the Vatican provided a ready subject for the wits and pens of Lutheran writers. For ten years after Truman's move misfired, the specter was pushed far to the background. When it was not dragged to the fore during the 1960 presidential campaign, one might have supposed that it had disappeared and that in at least one respect a turning point in the Lutheran

[1] *Walther League Messenger*, XXX (December, 1921), 179; "The Vatican and Diplomatic Relationships," *Theological Monthly,* I (August-September, 1921), 225–234.
[2] "Rome Marches On in Washington," *Lutheran Witness*, LVII (April 10, 1938), 142.

attitude toward Catholicism had been reached early.

But specters show a remarkable viability. So we should not be too surprised at the report of the *Witness* in 1963 that many people were uneasy about Rome's secular advances and that much of this uneasiness was about to be revived in the United States because there were feelers here and there to explore how citizens might react to some sort of official diplomatic representation at the Vatican. The *Witness* pointed out that much of the concern was due to the fact that Rome had never repudiated its ancient thesis that secular government derives properly from the consent of the Roman Catholic Church. After reviewing the arguments advanced in support of diplomatic representation at the Vatican, the *Witness* remarked that neither these arguments nor the winsomeness of Pope John nor the capability of Pope Paul prove the need or the value of such a move. The misgivings expressed on this subject in the past, the editorial concluded, are not outdated.[3]

Lutheran observers did not differentiate between the specter and the reality of diplomatic recognition; their writings give little indication that they would have acknowledged such a distinction. In their view the reality was the specter personified. Our principal concern in this chapter will therefore be with the mystery of the specter and the apprehensions that the personification of the specter produced among Lutherans. The term "mystery" is used advisedly; the mysteriousness of diplomatic relations with the Vatican lay in the suspicion that there was something in the whole matter that was inexplicable, that there was more to it than was apparent on the surface. The tack of some writers, particularly Graebner, was to call attention to this mysteriousness and then either to unravel the mystery or to indicate that it simply could not be explained.

[3] "The U.S. and the Vatican," *Witness*, LXXXII (August 6, 1963), 371–372.

The Lutheran writers were aware that some nations did maintain diplomatic relations with the Vatican. In discussing the ties that had been established with some thirty-one countries by 1921, Graebner referred to the efforts of the hierarchy in the United States "to worm itself into a quasi-official relation to the National Government." He called attention to field Masses, to the Pan-American Mass held each Thanksgiving Day, and to Cardinal Gibbons' receptions in Washington. Then came the explanation: "Every encroachment of the Roman hierarchy in this country upon the forbidden ground of politics has had but one ulterior aim—the recognition of the Pope as a temporal ruler." Examples showing the Roman Catholic Church working in that direction were followed by the second explanation: the Catholic masses are being primed for the day when with the weight of their numbers they will demand that diplomatic relations be established between the Vatican and the White House. And finally: "That world-dominion is the hope of the Vatican, who can doubt?"[4] This, of course, was the standard interpretation of the mystery.

Walter A. Maier used a different starting point. He charged that European countries, in establishing diplomatic relations with Rome, were "hitting the Canossa trail." In the United States, too, "papal propaganda" was inducing many to "take the trip to Canossa." The papal propaganda he referred to included such things as the news coverage given to new cardinals, to movies being "sold out to Rome," and to the respect shown to the Roman Catholic clergy by government officials.[5]

The statements of President Roosevelt at the time of the death of Pope Pius XI in 1939, in which the President

[4] "The Vatican and Diplomatic Relationships," *Theological Monthly,* I (August-September, 1921), 225–234.
[5] "Where Do We Go from Here? to Canossa?" *Walther League Messenger,* XXXII (June, 1924), 586–587, 628–630.

referred to the Pope as the "Prince of Peace," were taken by Graebner to mean that the United States was moving toward diplomatic recognition of the Vatican.[6] The friendly relations between the President and Cardinal Mundelein, the adjournment of Congress in respect to the late Pope, and the appointment of Joseph Kennedy as the President's special representative at the coronation of the new pope were interpreted by Wenchel, a Lutheran pastor in Washington, to mean that a papal legation would soon be placed in the capitol.[7] Earlier he had reported the construction of a $500,000 building on Massachusetts Avenue, marked with a large sign reading, "future home of the apostolic delegation." Although he considered this to be presumptuous, it was taken as one indication among others that "Rome marches on in Washington."[8]

After the official announcement of Taylor's appointment the concern intensified. Graebner recalled the 1936 visit to the United States by Pope Pius XII, then Cardinal Eugenio Pacelli, and the mystery surrounding its purpose. He concluded that perhaps there was some connection between that visit, the erection of an ambassadorial mansion, and the appointment of a personal envoy to the Pope.[9] Even deeper mysteries were intimated. Recounting that the President's letter to the Pope, to the president of the Federal Council of Churches, and to a prominent Jew, were all published on the same day that the Pope announced his peace program, Graeb-

---

[6] "Coming Closer—The Capitol and the Vatican," *Witness,* LVIII (March 21, 1939), 94.

[7] "Whither America?" *Witness,* LVIII (March 21, 1939), 97.

[8] "Rome Marches On in Washington," *Witness,* LVII (April 10, 1938), 142.

[9] "When the Pope Was in America," *Witness,* LIX (January 23, 1940), 24. It was not, in fact, an ambassadorial mansion that was being constructed.

ner wondered what exchange of ideas had preceded this "strangely coordinated action."[10] When Archbishop Schrembs of Cleveland addressed a meeting of Christians "(let us say, Gentiles)" and Jews, presumably for the purpose of stating the position of the Catholic hierarchy in response to criticism on the envoy issue, Graebner wrote:

> We shall assume that the reader remembers some earlier comment of ours on the strange affinity which is developing between Catholics and Jews, a spiritual flirtation, which comes perilously close to a denial of fundamental Catholic doctrines. A Jew is certainly, according to Roman teaching, on the way to perdition. . . . We have the right to ask, Why this unnatural alliance between those Jews who reject every Christian doctrine, and the Roman hierarchy? What is behind it? Somewhere in the European scene is the answer.[11]

The mystery surrounding the whole matter of Taylor's appointment was not solved even after his mission was underway. Graebner wondered what kind of understanding there was among European governments at war that would permit Taylor to come and go from Rome.[12] President Truman's retention of Taylor as his special ambassador to the Vatican was seen by Wenchel as evidence of the powerful influence of the Catholic hierarchy in Washington. According to

[10] "The American Envoy to the Pope," *Witness,* LIX (January 9, 1940), 4–5.

[11] "White House and Vatican: Reply to an Archbishop," *Witness,* LIX (February 20, 1940), 58–59. This article was also published as a tract by Concordia Publishing House. It criticized the Archbishop for trying to show, by quoting *Immortale Dei,* that diplomatic recognition constituted no threat to the American principles of separation of church and state. He showed how Archbishop Schrembs had omitted some paragraphs which indicate the exact opposite. Graebner had obviously done his homework in preparing this article.

[12] "The Archbishop Makes a Proposal," *Witness,* LXI (October 27, 1942), 372.

Wenchel the Pope's conduct during World War II had caused him to lose standing, so the hierarchy was doing everything possible to restore his prestige.[13]

A related incident also prompted conjecture. Reportedly, Francis P. Matthews, after having been appointed ambassador to Ireland, told the press that his new job was going to be more than just that; he was going to be the President's representative on the continent of Europe. The *Witness,* recalling that Matthews had been for a long time the head of the Knights of Columbus, wondered what his appointment might mean. The White House had no comment, but rumor in Washington connected it with the Vatican.[14]

President Truman's nomination of Mark Clark as ambassador to the Vatican in late 1951 was also clothed in mystery. The *American Lutheran* commented that the real reasons behind the nomination were known only to Truman, but it speculated on various possibilities: it was a way of getting General Clark out of the political way; it was an attempt to embarrass the Republican party; the President was trying to curry favor with Catholic authorities for political purposes; he was trying to jeopardize the chances of certain potential political foes in 1952.[15] The *Witness* took its own guesses: Was it an attempt to win Catholic votes? Was it related to the effort to wage war against Communism on all fronts? Was the Vatican a sounding board for world events that would give us an official ear to the ground?[16]

It was, in fact, the failure of both Presidents Roosevelt and Truman to state clearly the purposes they hoped to accom-

---

[13] "Washington Letter," *Witness,* LXV (June 4, 1946), 195.
[14] "To the Vatican?" LXX (August 7, 1951), 261.
[15] "The President's Mistake," *American Lutheran,* XXXIV (November, 1951), 5–6.
[16] "Ambassador to the Vatican," *Witness,* LXX (November 13, 1951), 376.

plish by having a representative in the Vatican that encouraged speculation. This omission compelled both supporters and critics to discover intentions and provide explanations.[17] The reaction of the Lutheran writers, once they were confronted with the reality, was to condemn the whole idea of such representation and to meet every purported interpretation with an objection. There is no need to distinguish between the Roosevelt-Taylor, the Truman-Taylor, and Truman-Clark phases, for the arguments were essentially the same.

The principal and most frequently expressed charge was that diplomatic recognition extended by our government to the Vatican "is a direct violation of the principles laid down in the First Amendment of the Constitution." These were the words in the official reaction of John W. Behnken, president of the Lutheran Church-Missouri Synod. He contended that diplomatic recognition constitutes preferential treatment for one religion.[18] Walter A. Maier denounced it for the same reason, but in more emotional terms, on his nationwide Lutheran Hour broadcast.[19] Frederick E. Mayer saw the issue as being much more basic than simply a political argument:

> It is not a political question at all. For Protestants it is chiefly a theological problem. . . . The question is: Does

---

[17] In *The Challenge to Isolation* (New York: Harper, 1952), Vol. I, William S. Langer and S. Everett Gleason draw on a variety of sources to put together the purposes Roosevelt probably had in mind: he hoped to pool his influence and join his efforts with the Pope to prevent the spread of war and to provide a just peace; the wealth of information available to the Vatican from areas and sources more cr less closed to the American government would be of immense practical value; he shared the Pope's anxiety to deter Mussolini from dragging Italy into the war at Hitler's side (p. 348).

[18] *Witness,* LXX (November 13, 1951), 370.

[19] January 1, 1940.

the Pope possess two swords, the spiritual and the secular? Does he control the temporal and eternal weal and woe of all mankind? Official representation at the Vatican is in effect an affirmative answer to these questions. Most American Protestants find an irreconcilable clash between the democratic principles of our Government and the totalitarian principles of the papal empire. The Papacy represents the most thorough form of totalitarianism in the history of the world.[20]

The argument that as ruler of the Vatican, a temporal state, the pope qualified as a temporal ruler met with ridicule among Lutherans. Graebner referred to the Vatican as "the 120 acres on the Tiber." Behnken asserted that the Vatican had received preferential treatment, not because of the "tidbit of territory" under its political control, "but because of the numbers of people over whose lives it claims spiritual control." The claim that recognition of the Vatican would coordinate our opposition to Communism was dismissed by Behnken as appearing "somewhat specious" in view of the success Communism had achieved in certain European countries where the Vatican has achieved the greatest "ecclesiastical domination."[21]

Would not being represented at the Vatican provide the United States with a good listening post? The *American Lutheran* wanted to know what kind of political and social information it would listen for. Must we presume that this great country is dependent on such a little state for information? Or would the information be colored and edited to the advantage of the Vatican?[22] The *Witness* saw some serious

[20] "The Case Against Vatican Representation," *Concordia Theological Monthly,* XXIII (March, 1952), 221–226.
[21] *Witness,* LXX (November 13, 1951), 370.
[22] "Listening Post," *American Lutheran,* XXXIV (December, 1951), 3.

consequences growing out of this possibility. For one thing, this would mean that not only would the pope know what our enemies are doing but he would also know what our friends are doing. Furthermore:

> More serious even than this is the implication it has for our missionaries. If Roman Catholic missionaries are potential informers to their home government . . . could not our future enemies assume that all missionaries are spies for some foreign power? Would not our own missionaries be among the first to fall victims when a war is declared?[23]

What about the argument that thirty-seven other nations are represented there? According to Lewis W. Spitz, a Concordia Seminary professor, this should have no bearing on the action of the United States. The ecclesiastical arrangement in many of those countries may make it advisable for them to have a representative at the Vatican, or at least has dulled their awareness of the impropriety of such an arrangement. Many Americans came to these shores to escape an intolerable connection between church and state. Does not the fact that the United States was represented at the Vatican from 1848 to 1868 provide an historical precedent for representation? Spitz argued that it does not. The representative then was not an ambassador, but simply a chargé d'affaires who was accredited to the Papal States to deal exclusively with civil and commercial matters. Besides, at that time the Papal States comprised 16,000 square miles, with a population of 3,000,000, and there was no other sovereign government in Rome. The unification of Italy changed all this.[24]

Even though the recognition of the Vatican as a temporal

---

[23] "An International Spy Ring?" *Witness*, LXX (November 13, 1951), 377.

[24] "A U.S. Ambassador to the Vatican?" *Witness*, LXXI (January 8, 1952), 7. Technically, the United States representative had been a minister, a rank above a chargé d' affaires.

state might have some harmful effects and put some American institutions to a test, should not the United States give it a try in the hope that the good achieved would more than compensate for the evil? Lutherans could never agree to this. Their judgment that the pope looked out only for himself, as was stressed in a previous chapter, would never allow for that. Although it was not written directly in response to this question, Graebner's comment would apply: "Our President and his Secretary of State should know something about the record of fingers burned by those who have committed themselves to political arrangements with the Pope."[25]

Was there any truth in the assertion of *Our Sunday Visitor* that the sending of Martin Graebner as the Missouri Synod's representative to Lutheran war victims in Europe was more significant than the appointment of Taylor to the Vatican? According to Theodore Graebner, "Even the superficial reader will observe that it is one thing to confer with European Lutherans in their postwar distress for the purpose of rebuilding their schools, churches, and organizations, and an altogether different thing to talk world politics with the Pope."[26]

None of these arguments, therefore, was convincing to Lutherans, for they had an answer for all of them. They remained concerned about the serious consequences that diplomatic relations would have on the United States. In fact, they were concerned about the consequences of the consequences. They could see grave ramifications developing from such an arrangement.

Establishment of diplomatic relations would have the effect of recognizing the pope as a temporal ruler. The secondary

[25] "Mr. Taylor's Role at the Vatican," *Witness*, LXIV (February 27, 1945), 68.
[26] "Two Kinds of Ambassadors," *Witness*, LXVI (September 9, 1947), 292.

effect would therefore be that the dual affiliation of Catholic
American citizens would be officially acknowledged, contrary
to the concept of undivided loyalty of citizens to their own
country.[27] According to Catholic claims, if Catholics must
make a choice between loyalty to any other secular government and loyalty to the pope, they will have to make their
decision in favor of the pope.[28]

Regarded as even more serious than this were the secondary consequences that could result from this violation of the
principles laid down in the First Amendment. First, it would
open the way for actions and developments which could, in
time, take away religious freedom.[29] Official recognition given
by the government to Catholicism was seen as especially bad
because of the Catholic teaching that separation of church
and state is contrary to the will of God and can be tolerated
only so long as the Roman Catholic Church is unable to make
its own the official religion.[30] Second, although it would not
change things immediately, it would be the first step toward
recognizing the primacy of the Roman Catholic Church in
American life. And, finally, it would mean that the Vatican
would be represented in Washington, D.C., and make Catholicism the only religion with official representatives who
would have direct access to the President and other important
areas of government.[31]

On most of the points of conflict with Catholicism Lutheran

[27] Graebner, "An American Ambassador to the Vatican?" *Witness,* LV (December 1, 1936), 405–406.
[28] "To the Vatican?" *Witness,* LXX (August 7, 1951), 261.
[29] James G. Manz, "Ambassador to the Vatican?" *Walther League
Messenger,* LX (February, 1952), 15–17.
[30] Graebner, "An American Envoy to the Pope?" *Witness,* LIX
(January 9, 1940), 4–5.
[31] Manz, "Ambassador to the Vatican?" *Walther League Messenger,* LX (February, 1952), 15–17.

writers could only warn of the error in Catholic doctrine and the evil in Catholic practice, and urge their readers not to be deceived. In the case of diplomatic recognition of the Vatican, however, the situation was different; they could encourage overt action against a specific, tangible danger. Their recommendation was of course not drastic. They simply urged their readers to bring pressure to bear on the nation's lawmakers to see that diplomatic relations would not be established. The *Lutheran Witness,* the *Walther League Messenger,* and the *American Lutheran* all encouraged the writing of letters to the President, the State Department, and congressmen. The *Witness* even printed sample letters that might be used as guides.[32]

The impression has no doubt been created here that Lutheran opposition on this issue was unanimous. Among the official or quasi-official periodicals it was, with the exception of the *Cresset,* which voiced occasional dissent. In 1946 it editorialized on "the other side" of the Taylor mission in pointing out and accepting the validity of some of the arguments supporting representation at the Vatican. It encouraged Protestants to consider whether maintenance of such representation for purely political reasons was a real menace to our nation's welfare, and it added that opposition to an embassy is hardly an effective weapon against the papacy.[33] In 1950 it reviewed some of the arguments in favor of diplomatic relations with Rome and concluded that the sending of an envoy to the Vatican does not confer any special advantages upon the Catholic population of the United States, nor does it imply any approval by our government of Roman Catholic

[32] Graebner, "The State Department Explains," *Witness,* LXV (May 21, 1946), 173.
[33] "The Other Side of the Taylor Mission," *Cresset,* IX (August, 1946), 7–9.

theology. As a strategic post, the *Cresset* favored maintaining some sort of diplomatic representation there.[34]

There is obviously no way of determining how this dissent affected the outspoken editors of the other periodicals. It probably had little effect. We can imagine, though, that another item of dissent must have caused at least mild dismay among the members of the editorial committee of the *Lutheran Witness*. It came in the form of a cordial letter from a prominent Missouri Synod layman. The recipient, Theodore Graebner, was addressed as, "My dear Professor." The layman was John W. Boehne, a Republican congressman from Indiana, who was elected several years later to the Board of Directors of the Missouri Synod.

The letter, under the congressional letterhead and dated January 15, 1940, referred to a recent editorial by Graebner on the matter of an American envoy to the Vatican. Boehne remarked that he had noted the objections raised by Graebner but that he could not arrive at the same conclusions. In explaining, he acknowledged his belief that the pope did indeed qualify as a temporal ruler and that this nation has always found it proper to have an ambassador or minister to every friendly country or nation. He was sure that in his choice of Taylor, President Roosevelt had in mind only a representative as far as the government of Vatican City was concerned. Furthermore, Congressman Boehne wrote, if the United States, through such a personal representative, can effectuate a peace throughout the world, it certainly does not matter whether he works with a Catholic, a Protestant, or a Jew.

[34] "Envoy to Vatican?" *Cresset,* XIII (May, 1950), 3–4. A broad spectrum of opinion was represented among those who published the *Cresset.* Theodore Graebner, whose views were quite in contrast with those expressed in this editorial, had been associated with the *Cresset* since 1937.

The President's motives, Boehne believed, were of the very highest.

A bit of the consternation this letter must have caused is apparent in the small, yellow note still clipped to the letter in the Graebner files in the Concordia Historical Institute. The note from Graebner to the editorial committee reads:

January 22, 1940

I think we ought to publish this with a note. Please pass on: Sommer, Polack, Schick, Graebner.

This requires caution. M.S.S.

Why with a note? W.G.P.

Better not publish. G.V.S.

The letter was not published, and the editorial position was apparently unaffected.

It is difficult to assess fully the significance of the Boehne letter. On the one hand, it shows that the editorial position of the *Witness* was not easily diverted, that the editors were convinced of the validity of their policy. On the other, it emphasizes that allowances must be made for exceptions to the apparent near-unanimity among Missouri Synod Lutherans on this issue.

7

1928 AND 1960: TWO TESTINGS OF AN ABSTRACTION

THE QUESTIONS OF federal aid to education and diplomatic recognition of the Vatican were not matters of moment for the ordinary Lutheran layman. He may not have even known that they were hotly debated issues. If he did know, he very likely did not participate in the debate. He may have nodded his head in assent to the synod's party line or simply shrugged his shoulders indifferently. He was never driven to the point where he had to make a commitment to one position or another.

The candidacy of a Roman Catholic for the presidency of the United States was a different matter, however. The layman might have avoided the debate, but if he was to exercise his citizenship responsibilities, a decision could not be avoided. This issue has arisen twice in the history of the United States. Both times it provoked national debate and both times Lutheran writers and observers participated in it. Because of the necessity of decision by each citizen, it might be assumed that what they had to say was watched more closely by their readers. Whether their readers were looking for guidance or for conformity with their own ideas is of course uncertain.

The 1928 campaign did not elicit the amount of commentary that might have been expected from Lutheran writers. No special tracts were printed, and the number of articles and editorials in the periodicals was slight. One book was apparently prepared, but for some reason was not published until after the election.[1] Although the possibility of electing a Catholic president was discussed as early as 1924, a discreet silence was maintained from May of 1928 until after the election. A letter from Graebner to an inquiring reader indicates that the *Witness* was prepared to comment if it should become necessary, but that even without such specific comment, the editors believed that the *Witness's* attitude toward the political aspirations of the Roman Catholic Church would be remembered. Whether circumstances would arise in the campaign which would compel them to make specific application of their attitude regarding Rome as a political force would, according to Graebner, depend on developments. He added that, speaking only for himself, he could not conceive of any such developments.[2]

The desire to avoid taking what might be regarded as a partisan stand during the campaign does not mean that they were indifferent to the possibility of a Catholic president. They had shown their position on this long before Alfred E. Smith became a candidate. They had frequently discussed it in hypothetical terms. Just a listing of titles of some of the articles and editorials they wrote is enough to show that it was not an open question. In the *Walther League Messenger* Walter A. Maier described what conditions would be "If Rome Ruled,"[3] and Graebner asked, "Is the Roman Peril Real?"[4] J. T. Mueller, in "The Candidate of the Holy See," reported that the Secretary of State of the Vatican had issued a statement on the possible candidacy of Alfred E. Smith,

[1] See note 4, Chapter Two.
[2] Letter to Karl Kretzmann, September 10, 1928.
[3] *Walther League Messenger*, XXXIII (October, 1924), 74–75, 121.
[4] *Walther League Messenger*, XXXV (June, 1927), 622–623, 665–666.

claiming absolute indifference and *denying* that he was the candidate of the Holy See. Mueller commented: "Rome saw the rising of a tide of opposition which it was not ready to meet at this time, and therefore it poured on the tempestuous waves the oil of a conciliating falsehood."[5]

When a Protestant minister was reported to have said that there should be no objection to a Catholic president, Martin Sommer asked, "Is it Jesuitry or Stupidity?" and commented that "no one can blame Protestants if they warn their people earnestly against the religious errors of Rome and beg their fellow-citizens to vote against any candidate for the Presidency who is a faithful son of the Roman hierarchy."[6] In referring to the answers given by Smith to questions raised by Charles C. Marshall in the *Atlantic Monthly,* Sommer asked, "A Catholic President—A Joke or a Menace?"[7] This type of writing, coming as only a segment of the larger attack on the Catholic position on religious liberty described in an earlier chapter, explains why it was not necessary to deal with the 1928 campaign in direct terms.

Immediately after the election, when the charge of political partisanship would be meaningless, Graebner was ready to discuss it further. He noted that the campaign had been dirty and vicious, more so than usual, and that the most bitter controversies had raged upon a field which Americans had always tried to avoid in political campaigns, religion. That Hoover's wife was a Catholic, that Hoover was an evolutionist, and that the prohibition issue was involved, had added to the complexities. He pointed out that at no time during the campaign did a Catholic churchman deny the correctness of the fundamental allegation concerning Catholicism and religious liberty. He praised the conduct of Lutheran pastors and

---

[5] *Theological Monthly*, VII (July, 1927), 213.
[6] *Lutheran Witness,* XLV (November 2, 1926), 360.
[7] *Witness,* XLVI (May 3, 1927), 157–158.

laymen, who, he thought, had conducted themselves during the campaign with superior good judgment. Their expressions were careful and moderate, and never descended to insinuations against the sincerity and good Americanism of the candidates. In reminding his readers that it was not bigotry to discuss religion in the campaign, Graebner noted that Smith himself had raised the issue. He concluded: "We do not look upon the election of Mr. Hoover as a victory for Protestantism. But the defeat of Mr. Smith was a defeat for Romanism."[8]

Graebner gave the election another retrospective look in *The Pope and Temporal Power*. Here he showed point by point that Smith's position on religious liberty and separation of church and state conflicted with the official, historic teaching of the Roman Catholic Church and that Catholic periodicals did not endorse Smith's disclaimers.[9] Graebner's attitude is characterized in this observation:

> The Roman Catholic parishioner, whether oiler on a freight steamer or President of the United States, must acknowledge an authority higher than the federal constitution, higher than any law, the authority of the Pope at Rome. Whether digging a canal in Illinois or writing opinions as Chief-Justice of the United States, he has an Italian boss.[10]

Such an attitude was not out of step with the times. Jaroslav Pelikan referred to the 1928 campaign as the "high tide of suspicion and resentment against Roman Catholics in public life," and added that all the prejudices and anxieties about Vatican domination of America had received a new

[8] "The Political Campaign," *Witness,* XLVII (November 13, 1928), 379–382.
[9] *The Pope and Temporal Power* (Milwaukee: Northwestern Publishing House, 1929), pp. 128–143.
[10] *Ibid.,* p. 132.

lease on life.[11] Lutherans were therefore not the only ones who never really considered the possibility of a Catholic president except in hypothetical terms. Alfred Smith, to many non-Catholic observers, was not a distinct individual, a real, live candidate, but rather a symbol in the hypothesis.

When the possible nomination of a Catholic as a candidate in the 1960 presidential election was first discussed seriously, it appeared that the 1928 pattern might be repeated. In February, 1958, the *Witness* asked if it was too early to scrutinize the religious views of potential Catholic candidates for the next presidential election. The editorial pointed out that the religion of a Catholic candidate is more important than for any other because the official doctrine of the Roman Catholic Church concerning church and state implicitly condemns the United States Constitution and opposes the idea of religious liberty. Although probably not all Catholics accept these pronouncements of their church, the editorial continued, they have never been repudiated and are therefore binding on all loyal Catholics. Therefore, "If the candidates are members of the Roman Church, the issues *will* be raised. Religious liberty would be at stake. The question *must* be raised. Citizens dare not be asleep. It is not too early to scrutinize."[12]

Although the first reader reaction charged the editors with wanting to aggravate religious differences and with dignifying a sinister form of bigotry,[13] letters published later indicate that the editorial had struck a responsive chord and that the 1928 approach might be favorably received. One reader commented that "our people should know the great danger lurking in Roman Catholicism"; another asked if it was bigotry

[11] *The Riddle of Roman Catholicism* (New York: Abingdon Press, 1959), p. 104.
[12] "Too Early?" *Witness*, LXXVII (February 11, 1958), 59.
[13] *Witness*, LXXVII (April 28, 1958), 179.

simply to quote facts. Andrew Melendez, a minor synodical official with a strong background in Latin American affairs, wrote that "the election of a Roman Catholic president would be another step for her avowed intention of conquering America." Among other references he cited the textbook by John A. Ryan and some statements of Leo XIII.[14] The 1928 pattern was definitely apparent.

But by 1958 another point of view had arisen within the Missouri Synod. It was first given expression in the *Cresset* in the same month in which the *Witness* editorial appeared. The *Cresset* editorial asserted that there were "quite a number of good reasons for questioning Senator John F. Kennedy's qualifications for the presidency without resurrecting that old bogeyman of Roman Catholic intrigue." The *Cresset* agreed that religion is not purely a private matter, for it is certain to have an effect on a person's conduct; but assuming that the candidate is a devout Roman Catholic, "we know of nothing in the teaching of his church which would make it any more difficult for him to faithfully execute the office of president than it would be for a devout Lutheran or a devout Presbyterian or a devout Jew to do so." Pointing out that Catholics have served in every public office on every level of government without having given grounds for suspicion of divided allegiance, the *Cresset* declared that if we mean what we say about representative government, it is about time that Catholics were given a voice in public affairs commensurate with their numbers.[15]

When the *Cresset* stated that it knew of nothing in the teaching of the Roman Catholic Church which would impede a Catholic President in the faithful execution of his office, the editors were not professing ignorance. Had that been the case

[14] *Witness,* LXXVII (May 20, 1958), 235.
[15] "Back to 1928?" *Cresset,* XXI (February, 1958), 4.

they could quickly have been edified through a reading of Ryan and Boland's *Catholic Principles of Politics* and the properly selected and marked encyclicals. A reading of *The Pope and Temporal Power* might have done the trick. They were instead expressing a point of view. They were maintaining that the whole matter ought to be looked at in a different way.

The editorials in the *Witness* and the *Cresset* represent two fundamentally different approaches to the problems raised by the candidacy of a Catholic for the presidency. The attitude that each individual person eventually developed depended on the extent to which he accepted one view or the other.

According to the traditional point of view, in determining the advisability of electing a Catholic to the presidency one should consider these questions: (1) What has the Roman Catholic Church stated officially on the matters of religious liberty and separation of church and state? (2) Has the Roman Catholic Church confirmed this historic position by recent or current pronouncements or practice? (3) Has the church specifically renounced what it has said in the past? (4) Will the candidate specifically repudiate the church's official position or dissociate himself from it? (5) If he does, will the church accept such action on his part, or will it believe that it was done with "mental reservations"? In this viewpoint the emphasis is on Roman Catholic *theory* and on finding practices, either historical or current, that substantiate this theory. The whole question is considered as an *abstraction*. The candidate is merely a symbol which must conform to the abstract pattern.

From the other point of view, different questions are raised: (1) What was the context in which the Roman Catholic Church originally made its statements on religious liberty and separation of church and state? (2) Does the diversity in thought and practice within the Roman Catholic Church suggest that, in the practical situation, Catholic teaching need not be hostile to American principles? (3) Has the Roman Catholic Church in the United States demonstrated that it can adapt its practice to American ideals and thus implicitly lay aside the official pronouncements? (4) Has the candidate demonstrated by past and present conduct that he will put the best interests of the United States ahead of any dictation from his church? (5) If he has done this, has he found any support from others within his church? (6) Should we be completely deceived by the candidate, are there any protections against his using his office to the advantage of his church at the expense of treasured American principles? Those whose point of view prompts them to ask these questions are concerned with the dynamic role played by the candidate and with the here-and-now, *concrete* situation. If they can find satisfactory answers to these questions, they have no objection to seeing a Roman Catholic elected to the presidency of the United States.

It must be emphasized that these are the *fundamental* questions in the *pure* viewpoints. Critical observers, of course, raised many other pertinent questions and examined the issue from other perspectives. Furthermore, even though the nature of the questions that a person asks reveals the type of answers he expects, few persons could find satisfactory answers to all the questions of either point of view without at least some misgivings on some points. Some were not doubt torn by the head-and-heart problem: intellectually they espoused one side or the other, but because of experience and training they could not quite bring their heart along.

In contrast to the discreet (or smug) silence and apparent unanimity of thought in 1928, the 1960 campaign provoked fundamental disagreement among Lutheran observers. It would of course be highly improper to speak of an official synodical position on this question, but in 1960 there was not even a party line.

The *Witness,* for its part, had little to say after it first raised the question in early 1958. Not until mid-September, 1960, did it venture further comment. Then in an editorial it asked, "Is There a Religious Issue in the Presidential Campaign?" The editorial acknowledged the right of Senator Kennedy, on the basis of his qualifications, his record in office, and the principles enunciated by the platform of his party, to seek the presidency of the United States. It deplored the dirtiness of the campaign on the religious issue and urged readers not only to avoid such tactics themselves but, in accordance with the First Amendment, to tolerate the free exercise of Catholicism in the United States without imposing any restraints by force or smear. "However," it continued, "in this very amendment . . . many Americans find valid cause for concern when a candidate . . . is affiliated with the Roman Catholic Church." Pointing out that Kennedy himself had acknowledged this concern, it continued:

> The one question Americans have the constitutional right to ask, the one question that must be answered if the religious issue is to be eliminated from the campaign, as it should be, is this: Will Senator Kennedy be permitted to follow his own course . . . or will the Roman Catholic Church, which officially opposes church-state separation, bring the weight of papal pressure to bear on his conscience?

The editorial then cited evidence in Catholic periodicals that many of his fellow churchmen did not accept Kennedy's statement that, whatever one's religion in his private life may be, "for the officeholder nothing takes precedence over his oath to uphold the Constitution and all its parts—including the First Amendment and separation of church and state."

Continuing, the editorial quoted from Roman Catholic statements in 1302, 1885, and 1948 which emphasized the church's traditional antipathy toward religious liberty and the American principles on church and state. In acknowledging that some Catholic laymen, theologians, and prelates appear to have become "Americanized," the editorial asserted that "there are no *'American* Catholics,' for all are simply members of the Roman Catholic Church in America." Even though the *Witness* accepted the sincerity of Kennedy's pledge to uphold the cherished American principle of separation of church and state, it concluded:

> If the Roman Catholic Church speaks out—humbling and painful though it may be—and approves Senator Kennedy's pledge to uphold the Constitution . . . with all of its implications, he will be free to campaign solely on the basis of his qualifications, his record in office, and the principles of his party's platform.
>
> If the Roman Catholic Church, however, by silence now lets it be known that the Roman Catholic Church holds fast to the doctrine of the two swords, voters of America will continue to have valid cause for concern when a Roman Catholic aspires to the nation's highest office. And there will be—at Senator Kennedy's expense—a very real religious issue in the 1960 presidential campaign.[16]

This attitude, expressed in the official organ of the Lutheran Church-Missouri Synod, leans strongly toward the traditional position as outlined earlier. Similar ideas, with particular emphasis on Catholic aggressiveness in the field of education, were expressed in a widely distributed tract written by a Concordia Seminary professor and produced by the synodically owned publishing house.[17]

An article in the *Cresset* by Paul Simon, a Lutheran and a member of the General Assembly of the State of Illinois, conformed generally with the other point of view. The editors

[16] *Witness,* LXXIX (September 20, 1960), 485–486, 499.
[17] Carl S. Meyer, *A Catholic President?* (St. Louis: Concordia, n.d. [1960]).

of the *Cresset* expressly associated themselves with his ideas. Simon first enunciated in some detail his "theological prejudices," particularly deploring not only the division that prevails within Christianity but the acrimony with which this division is perpetuated. Then he discussed a variety of objections to the candidacy of a Catholic and showed that *in practice* these objections can be met.[18]

The general uniformity of thought on the Catholic candidate issue in 1928 had made comment and debate unnecessary, but in 1960 the diversity of thought made it essential. Both the traditional and the modified positions had their spokesmen; all that was needed was a forum through which their ideas might be expressed. Fortunately for those Lutherans who wished to reevaluate their attitudes and to increase their understanding on this issue, such a forum was created by the *American Lutheran*. Published by the American Lutheran Publicity Bureau, the *American Lutheran* was a nonofficial monthly magazine which had achieved a sort of quasi-official recognition among Missouri Synod Lutherans. Its circulation did not compare with that of the *Lutheran Witness,* but it enjoyed a fairly wide readership among the clergy and the church leaders.

From April through August, 1960, the *American Lutheran* opened its columns to invited contributors in a "Symposium on a Roman Catholic President." The contributors, most of them members of the Missouri Synod, represented a broad range of ages and backgrounds, and came from all parts of the country. The contributors were free to express their own views, apparently with no interference from the editors.[19]

---

[18] "Roman Catholicism and the 1960 Elections," *Cresset,* XXIII (April, 1960), 6–9.
[19] The editorial opinion of the *American Lutheran* stated in September, 1959, p. 4, was not in step with the views expressed in most of the symposium articles.

Had the responses in the symposium simply been "more of the same," that is, a consistent reaffirmation of the traditional Lutheran attitude toward Catholicism in matters of religious liberty and separation of church and state, twenty-nine articles covering twenty-four pages would have been unnecessary. But the contributors' viewpoints ranged from a fairly solid affirmation of the traditional position to full acceptance of the modified point of view. The greater number, surprisingly, leaned toward the latter, although almost all who did acknowledged certain misgivings. Some simply tried to present the best arguments for each side. Only a few identified themselves as forthrightly opposed to seeing a Catholic elected, and they couched their opposition in such suggestive phrases as, "Does a man marry only his bride or does he marry into the family too?"[20] and "The things that are more certain in days like these are to be preferred to the things less certain."[21]

There is no need here to cite the customary evidence used to support the traditional position, no matter how cogently it was enunciated in the symposium. Our concern is rather with the arguments marshaled by those who looked at the religious issue from the modified point of view. A survey of the articles turns up some interesting and significant ideas, and indicates that a new approach to Catholicism was indeed developing. Something is lost, of course, in pulling these arguments out of their context, but citing a few of them here is necessary to show the change that was occurring.

In discussing the necessity of understanding the past of the Roman Catholic Church in its proper perspective, Richard Luecke, a Missouri Synod pastor, pointed out that any church

[20] Carl S. Meyer, "Symposium on a Roman Catholic President," *American Lutheran,* XLIII (May, 1960), 11.
[21] Gerhard Lenski, "Symposium," *American Lutheran,* XLIII (April, 1960), 8.

with a history reaching back to the medieval period, with a record of having adjusted in many ways to many sorts of political regimes, is able to provide plenty of fodder to feed the fears that non-Catholics share.

But the way of charity and wisdom is to read a church's tradition of words and deeds without "chronological snobbery." The never-omitted citations from the "Syllabus of Errors" (1864) of Pius IX opposing "the separation of church and state" and supporting traditional monarchy must be understood in terms of the running gunfire between the papacy and French liberalism. This differed from the American system as an "established liberalism" or "totalitarian democracy" differs from the established pluralism of the First Amendment. Even the sober two-realms theory of Leo XIII . . . appeared in statements colored by that controversy. Leo allowed a preference for democratic forms of government provided natural law and authority were upheld; and Pius XII positively endorsed democracy in view of the rise of modern totalitarian states without specifying any form of cooperation or concordat. The point is that many historical Roman Catholic actions, pronouncements, and attitudes frequently cited . . . were not addressed to the American scene, and the conditions to which they were addressed are not the case here.[22]

Luecke and several others referred to a recent booklet, *Roman Catholicism and Religious Liberty* by A. F. Carrollo de Albornoz (distributed by the Department of Information of the World Council of Churches), to show that for every Catholic theorist who still speaks of some sort of "Catholic America" as an ideal, there were many who reject any such goal for America.[23] On this point Thomas Coates, a professor at Concordia Senior College in Fort Wayne, reported:

Chillingly Dr. de Albornoz recalls from past papal docu-

[22] "Symposium," *American Lutheran*, XLIII (June, 1960), 14.
[23] *Ibid.*, pp. 14–15.

ments as impressive an array of pronouncements against religious liberty as any anti-Catholic organization in America could hope to assemble. But he matches this with at least as impressive a summary of alternative doctrinal viewpoints by theologians and members of the hierarchy who have not been disciplined, silenced, or successfully contradicted.[24]

Many of the contributors were equally satisfied that the official, traditional position of the Roman Catholic Church had also been contradicted in practice. John Strietelmeyer called attention to the striking contrasts within Catholicism from country to country and even from diocese to diocese and urged that these differences be recognized. He gave a specific example:

> Francisco Franco is a Roman Catholic. If he were a serious contender for the Presidency of the United States, I would oppose him with every legal means at my disposal as a man who is hostile to the most basic institutions of our country. But Konrad Adenauer is also a Roman Catholic. I would thank God if I could find among this year's candidates . . . a man of his wisdom, courage, and capability. And I would vote for him.[25]

Many contributors stressed the demonstrated loyalty of Catholics within the United States. A former chaplain and the editor of a Lutheran youth magazine, Alfred Klausler, said that among the Catholic politicians he had met, some of whom he had come to know very well, he had yet to hear one of them utter a sentiment or word that would show that loyalty to the Vatican superseded loyalty to the United States. "Their only loyalty to the Vatican is in spiritual matters and they are emphatic in so stating."[26] Paul Simon wrote, "In

---

[24] "Symposium," *American Lutheran*, XLIII (July, 1960), 10.
[25] "Symposium," *American Lutheran*, XLIII (April, 1960), 6.
[26] "Symposium," *American Lutheran*, XLIII (May, 1960), 13.

practice I have never seen Roman Catholics falling down like dominos when the church takes a stand on legislation."[27]

Several of the contributors referred to formal attempts to bring the Roman Catholic Church's official teaching into line with practice. George Lindbeck, a lay theologian in the Lutheran Church in America, pointed out that as a human institution the Roman Catholic Church is incapable of permanently resisting change even when it tries to do so. He went on:

> It is simply blind prejudice on our part, therefore, to ignore or refuse to believe the clear evidence that Roman theologians are engaged in transforming the meaning (even while trying to preserve many of the words) of the traditional statements about the proper relation of church and state. Furthermore, if the Vatican is half as clever as we usually accuse it of being, we will expect it not only to tolerate, but eventually approve, the newer interpretations.

Lindbeck thought this might still be far in the future, but he urged that in the meantime we should "joyfully recognize that a Roman Catholic candidate for the presidency is simply agreeing with many of the highest leaders of his own church" when he endorses American principles.[28]

Along the same lines Reuben Hahn suggested that "one of these years Rome will find a graceful way of backing out of certain traditional attitudes" on matters related to the candidacy controversy, and he thought that possibly this longed-for day might be hastened by a serious consideration of the issues in the current election.[29]

Richard Luecke pointed out that "to ask the Roman Catholic Church to 'come clean' at this time, perhaps through a proclamation by its chief pontiff, is to ask something on the

[27] "Symposium," *American Lutheran,* XLIII (April, 1960), 9.
[28] "Symposium," *American Lutheran,* XLIII (July, 1960), 14–15.
[29] "Symposium," *American Lutheran,* XLIII (June, 1960), 13.

basis of a protestant prejudice concerning Roman Catholic authoritarianism." But he added that we *can* ask Senator Kennedy to declare himself forthrightly.[30] None of the contributors, not even those who opposed his candidacy, denied that in word and deed Kennedy had demonstrated his loyalty to the United States and his belief in American principles. They were willing to accept his performance at face value.

Whether the Roman Catholic Church itself accepted Kennedy's position at face value was not a matter of particular concern to those who had moved away from the traditional point of view. Believing as they did that the church was earnestly attempting to update its official teachings, they apparently saw no reason to be concerned if some in the church criticized his views. More important to them was the conviction that our system of government had such built-in protections and that the pressures on him would be so great that even if a Catholic President were to attempt to serve the interests or follow the dictates of his church, he would find it impossible. Many of the contributors shared the belief of Coates:

> It should be evident that there is enough strength and stability in this great republic, and enough devotion to the historic freedoms which are its heritage, that this nation would under no circumstances supinely acquiesce to foreign control of any sort, political or ecclesiastical. Those who entertain this fear would seem thereby to depreciate the resources of our democratic system. . . .
>
> Moreover, it should be equally evident that Mr. Kennedy, or any other Roman Catholic president, would exercise extraordinary care in avoiding even the appearance of giving any preferment to the Church of Rome or of being susceptible to its influence. So delicate is this issue, and so sensitive is the American public to the warnings

---

[30] "Symposium," *American Lutheran*, XLIII (June, 1960), 15.

against papal dictation in our internal affairs, that a Roman Catholic president might well be expected to "bend over backward" in resisting any such influence.[31]

In recounting here some of the evidence used in meeting the traditionalist arguments the impression may have been created that those who had accepted a modified position were busily engaged in refuting and disproving the traditional point of view, keeping a record of points scored. This was not the case. Although they were ready to discuss both positions, they were disturbed that it was necessary to do so. They were afraid that an unwarranted emphasis on the religious issue might detract from due consideration of the more important questions in the campaign and that it might deepen the separation that already existed between Protestants and Catholics.

To the extent that the modified view discussed here gained acceptance in the Lutheran Church-Missouri Synod, the 1960 election marks another turning point in the history of Lutheran opposition to Catholicism. This change, more than others discussed in earlier chapters, is directly attributable to explicit changes within Catholicism. Unless one considers the Declaration on Religious Freedom of the fourth session of the Vatican Council II to be a deceptive front, the more pronounced turning point has come within Catholicism. The Lutheran change was an informed response to the incipient changes in Catholicism.

It is of course impossible to measure the effect of the arguments of the newer point of view on the attitudes of traditionalists in the Missouri Synod. Many of them probably never heard them. Furthermore, it is too much to expect that more than a few of a generation of pastors who had studied under professors with a strongly anti-Catholic bias at Concordia Seminary, and who had continued to be nourished by them

[31] "Symposium," *American Lutheran,* XLIII (July, 1960), 10.

through synodical literature, should greet the newer viewpoint with anything but skepticism. No doubt many of them shared the view that the first Catholic President would be careful, and maybe even the second. But beware thereafter. As one such pastor expressed it: "Shrewdly, Jesuitically, the tragedy of a United States dominated by the resident of a 108-acre Vatican may be realized."[32] If this was their attitude, they must have been constrained to lay a vote for Kennedy on the conscience of their members. The best that might have been expected of them was a benevolent silence.

As far as the laity was concerned, if they were unaware of either the elaborate arguments supporting the traditional viewpoint or the pragmatic conclusions of the "revisionists," they probably were more in step with the latter. Looking at the issue from a practical point of view, they were likely to accept what they saw and heard at face value.

As a postscript, it is worth noting that the presidency of a Catholic was apparently accepted more readily than his candidacy, for during the three years of President Kennedy's administration Lutheran periodicals made hardly a passing reference to his religion. Perhaps this confirms that a turning point had indeed been reached.

---

[32] August C. Brustat, "Open Forum," *American Lutheran,* XLIII (August, 1960), 15. The only published pastoral conference resolution on this subject reflects the traditional attitude. *Witness,* LXXIX (January 26, 1960), 26.

8

SCRIPTURE AND TRADITION: THE POINT OF SEPARATION

IN DISTINGUISHING BETWEEN temporal and theological issues in the Lutheran conflict with Roman Catholicism we are drawing a distinction that most Lutheran writers have not made. Catholicism has always been regarded as one powerful force. Effective opposition to this force must be directed to meet its every assertion; if it comes in the temporal sphere, it must be recognized and met there. The basic issues are still theological, and, in fact, they provide the motivation for countering Catholicism's temporal advances. If the concern over the church's temporal ambitions has received more attention, it is perhaps because they have changed from time to time, while the theological differences have remained essentially the same.

We turn our attention at this point to four principal theological issues between Lutherans and Roman Catholics. No attempt is made to present a full statement of each denomination's doctrine on each point; the concern is rather to outline in general terms the basic differences and to characterize the way in which Lutherans looked at these differences. Catholic readers will at times be disturbed by what they regard as misinterpretations of Roman Catholic teaching.

A study of the theological conflict between Lutherans and Catholics properly begins with a look at differences over the sources of authority and truth, for this marks the point at which the theological positions of the two denominations go their separate ways. Lutherans believed that the separation occurring at this point makes dialogue with Catholicism futile.

In their view it prevents the possibility of reaching agreement on an initial basis for further agreement. This attitude was reflected in a *Lutheran Witness* comment of 1957 on a proposal by the Lutheran World Federation that there should be a thorough theological encounter with the Roman Catholic Church. *The Witness* commented:

> That the Roman Catholic Church will ever recede from two sources of authority, Sacred Scripture and Sacred Tradition . . . is hardly to be expected. It is from the second source that she draws some of her unscriptural dogmas.
>
> That the Lutheran Church will ever give up the position that in matters of Christian faith only the Bible is the final sacred authority is unthinkable. . . .[1]

The *sola scriptura* principle of Lutheranism emphasizes that the Holy Bible is the only final and authoritative source of saving truth. The contrasting Roman Catholic position, as it was laid down at the Council of Trent, recognized that divine "truths and rules are contained in the written books and in the unwritten traditions, which, received by the Apostles themselves, the Holy Ghost dictating, have come down to us, transmitted as it were from hand to hand."

Lutheran writers tended to emphasize with pride the *sola scriptura* principle in Lutheran theology. It therefore seems strange, as Frederick Mayer pointed out, that with its alleged emphasis on the sole authority of Scripture the Lutheran Church has in its Confessions no specific article setting forth its attitude toward Holy Scripture. Mayer cited three reasons for this unusual condition: (1) because the Roman Catholic Church had never questioned the inspiration and authority of Scripture, the Lutheran reformers could take for granted in their conflict with Rome that their opponents accepted the

---

[1] "Theological Encounter with Rome," *Lutheran Witness,* LXXVI (October 8, 1957), 491.

Bible as God's Word; (2) the Lutheran Confessions are sym-
bolical rather than dogmatical in character, and thus take
certain things for granted without attempting to present
every point of Christian faith in a systematic and comprehensive manner; (3) the interest of the Lutheran Confessions is
centered so prominently on the Christocentric approach
to the Word of God:

> They have no interest in an atomistic, prooftext, concord-
> ance approach to the Scriptures. The Confessions state
> that Scripture must always be presented according to its
> two main parts, Law and Gospel. . . . The main thought
> of all the Gospels and Epistles of the entire Scriptures is
> that we should believe that in Christ Jesus through faith
> we have a gracious God. . . .
>
> Wherever this Word is preached, it becomes the power
> of God, an active and creative Word, and engenders the
> faith which accepts the Bible as Christ's inerrant and final
> Word. . . . The Lutheran Confessions take for granted that
> a Christian accepts the Scriptures as God's Word, both as
> God speaking in this Word here and now and as God's
> Word spoken in times past through the holy writers. In
> Lutheran theology the believer does not accept the abso-
> lute authority of the Scriptures as an a priori truth, but
> because he has learned to know Christ as his divine Savior;
> has experienced the power of His Word in the Scriptures
> upon his heart; and relies implicitly on Christ's own state-
> ment concerning the divine character of the Scriptures. It
> is therefore proper to say that the formal principle of
> Lutheran theology is entirely Christological.[2]

[2] *The Religious Bodies of America* (St. Louis: Concordia, 1954),
pp. 140–142. It could be argued, as Dr. Piepkorn has pointed out
to me, that the attitude of the Lutheran Confessions toward the
Sacred Scriptures, while representing an unarticulated assumption,
is nevertheless very explicitly brought out in the unnumbered
summary concept article at the beginning of the Formula of
Concord.

It should also be pointed out, as we turn our attention to doctrinal matters, that the ideas and interpretations cited here did

Although it must be admitted that the "atomistic, prooftext, concordance approach to Scriptures" has found more than its share of followers in the Missouri Synod, especially among those engaged in polemics with Catholicism, Mayer's statement stands as a succinct expression of confessional Lutheran teaching.

Roman Catholic teaching on Scripture, tradition, and authority has been given a variety of interpretations among Lutheran observers. We shall take note later of some of the inferences that have been drawn, but it is proper to begin with the explanation provided by Mayer, the Lutheran scholar who studied this aspect of Roman Catholicism most seriously.

According to Mayer the *principium cognoscendi* of Roman Catholic theology is that the Roman Catholic Church is the only divinely recognized denomination and that reunion of Christendom can be brought about solely and alone through a return of Protestants to the Roman Catholic Church. Essential to this position is the dogma demanding obedience to the pope. The real issue from the Lutheran point of view is *sola scriptura* vs. *solus papa,* for the church, the hierarchy, and the papacy claim the power to determine doctrine. "Rome's formal principle therefore determines the place and significance

not originate with the men who are quoted. Reflected throughout their writings is the pervasive influence of the Missouri Synod's most important dogmatician, Franz Pieper. Joining the faculty of Concordia Seminary in 1878, Pieper became its president in 1887 and served until his death in 1931. He was also president of the Missouri Synod from 1899 to 1911. His monumental work, *Christliche Dogmatik* (3 vols; St. Louis: Concordia, 1917–1924; English translation, 1951–1957), is regarded as a classic late-nineteenth century (although published in the twentieth century) expression of seventeenth century Lutheran orthodoxy. The theological position developed by Pieper was formulated out of the three-cornered confrontation between Roman Catholicism, Lutheranism, and the Reformed denominations.

which it ascribes (1) to Scripture, (2) to the traditions, and (3) to reason."[3]

Accordingly, although the Roman Catholic Church affirms a high regard for the Bible, it also insists that the church has authority over the Bible and that the Bible has none over the church. Only the church can provide the supplementation necessary to offset the inadequacies and insufficiencies of the Bible. The church further claims the authority to determine the scriptural canon, to provide interpretation of the dark or difficult passages, and to regulate the use of the Bible by the laity.

In addition to the Scriptures the Roman Catholic Church also relies on the unwritten traditions, the writings of the church fathers, and the pronouncements of the church through the centuries. These traditions, given to the Apostles and their rightful successors, have been deposited in the shrine of the church and may be proclaimed as doctrine by the infallible church as the occasion demands.

> To the Protestant this appears to be a clear case of development of doctrine. But Rome answers that it is impossible for her to proclaim new doctrines. "It can, however, develop more and more the truth entrusted to it, can define it more exactly and develop the entire wealth of revelation with increasing clarity. By this process not one of the dogmas previously held is rejected, nor are any added which have not been previously taught implicitly." . . . Rome says there can be no development of doctrine, for according to John 16:12 all doctrines have always been believed implicitly even though not taught explicitly. A view held by only some in the Church, as a *pia sententia,*

[3] "The Principium Cognoscendi of Roman Catholic Theology," *Concordia Theological Monthly,* XXII (May, 1951), 321–333. After the introduction this article offers arguments similar to those in *Religious Bodies of America,* to which further reference is made here.

will not be elevated to an official doctrine until sufficient tradition has been found to support it.[4]

In his interpretation of Roman Catholic doctrine Mayer asserted further that Catholic theologians make reason a third source of knowledge.[5] Because this is not a specific claim of the church, it is more proper to refer to it here as the first of several closely related inferences drawn by Lutheran theologians as they studied Roman Catholic theology and its development. Mayer pointed out that the early apologists and the later scholastics maintained that since both reason and revelation are divine gifts, they can never be at variance with each other.

> The later Scholastics, especially Thomas Aquinas, introduced the empirical method and inductive logic of Aristotle into the realm of theology and repudiated Platonic idealism with its emphasis on intuitive knowledge, which had been held by earlier Scholastics. . . . Thomas gave a high rank to reason and the intellect, and he is today the recognized teacher of Roman theology. It is therefore not surprising that the entire theology of Rome is supported by rationalistic arguments, specious though they often are.[6]

Mayer acknowledged the Catholic contention that logic is used primarily for apologetic purposes, but he maintained that standard dogmatic works of Rome prove conclusively that throughout her theological system reason is considered a legitimate source of divine truths. This is evident especially, he added, in those teachings which have been elevated from pious opinions to dogmas of the church. Reliance on reason as a source of doctrine, he concluded, serves to enhance the authority of the church. Although it would appear that a religion of reason should lead to certainty, in reality it is a the-

[4] *Religious Bodies of America*, pp. 38–43.
[5] *Ibid.*, p. 43.
[6] *Ibid.*, pp. 43–44.

ology of doubt, for Roman Catholics expressly deny that a Christian can attain absolute assurance in matters of faith: "Since no man can be certain that his reason and intellect has correctly interpreted the empirical theological data, he is compelled to transfer to the Church the responsibility of rightly interpreting all religious facts."[7]

A second inference drawn by Lutherans was that no matter how much Catholics might affirm their belief in and loyalty to the Bible, by their unwillingness to allow it to stand alone they detract from its authority.[8] James Manz called attention to ways in which Catholics show high regard for the Bible: priests kiss it during Mass, theologians refer to it as the Word of God inspired by the Holy Spirit, the church defends scriptural inerrancy, biblical specialists have made valuable contributions to understanding and defending it against modernistic trends, twentieth-century papal encyclicals and statements of the Pontifical Biblical Commission have supported traditional Christian viewpoints concerning Scripture. Nevertheless, commented Manz, Rome's use of tradition alongside the Bible actually subverts the Word of God and puts man-made teachings into the superior position.[9]

Along the same lines Carl S. Meyer declared that Catholic criticism of the Bible raises doubts about its sufficiency. He contrasted the Lutheran and Catholic beliefs:

The Roman Catholic Church uses various arguments against the clearness of Scripture. The difficulties of the original languages, shades of meaning, symbolic language

[7] *Ibid.*, pp. 44–45.
[8] Jaroslav Pelikan, *The Riddle of Roman Catholicism* (New York: Abingdon Press, 1959), pp. 81–83. Pelikan added that the establishment of the papacy as the "living magisterium" has virtually suspended also the authority of tradition, for the pope has acquired the right to edit it or to set it aside.
[9] "Rome and the Bible," *Lutheran Witness,* LXXXI (May 29, 1962), 254–255.

in the Bible, are cited to show that the Bible needs an interpreter. When we speak of the clearness of Scripture we are not denying that portions of Scripture need explanation; we are saying that the Scriptures in their essential teachings are clear.[10]

No citations are necessary to prove that a third and most important inference was shared widely by Lutherans. The idea that tradition has been used by the Roman Catholic Church to add to clear scriptural teaching permeated all Lutheran writing on Catholicism. Doctrines on justification, the Mass, purgatory, Mary, and the papacy, particularly papal infallibility, and many others were seen as such additions to Scripture. Mayer's comment characterized the Lutheran attitude on this point:

> Paradoxically Rome forbids the teaching of any new doctrine, whereas Rome itself certainly has promulgated many new doctrines. This constitutes no contradiction for Roman theologians, who insist that the *ecclesia docens* is infallible and that all doctrines were deposited in one shrine of the Church and were implicitly held since the death of the last Apostle. . . . This is "sheer enthusiasm" and grants the Church unlimited reign in promulgating "new doctrines."[11]

This judgment by Mayer was indeed *Lutheran*, for he was referring to Luther's statement in the Smalcald Articles, one of the Lutheran Confessions:

> The Papacy also is nothing but sheer enthusiasm by which the Pope boasts that all rights exist in the shrine of his heart, and whatever he decides and commands within his church is spirit and right, even though it is above and contrary to Scripture and the spoken Word.[12]

[10] "Is the Bible Enough?" *Witness,* LXXVI (August 27, 1957), 428.
[11] *Religious Bodies of America,* p. 43.
[12] *Ibid.,* p. 37.

The Lutheran understanding of how some of these unscriptural doctrines have developed will be considered in later chapters.

One might suppose that, operating with these inferences in mind, Lutheran writers would attempt to discredit the very idea of tradition as a source of authority. They did, in fact, attempt to disparage those particular traditions which provide the foundation for specific doctrines, and in so doing they created the impression that tradition is little more than papal whim or fancy and that tradition can be invented on short order to serve the convenience of the pope or the church. In the specific instances in which doctrines were charged with being unscriptural this idea was stated in rather explicit terms. But beyond this it provided a steady undercurrent for all Lutheran writing. The characteristic Lutheran attitude was shown in a *Witness* comment following the report that on two consecutive days prior to the pronouncement of the dogma of the assumption of Mary, Pope Pius XII had been favored by appearances of the Blessed Virgin:

> The issues between the Church of the Reformation and the Roman Catholic Church are still the same today as they were in Luther's time. Rome still presumes on her own authority to lay down what is saving doctrine and conjures up the spirits of the saints to fortify her conscience-binding schemes.[13]

On the other hand, Lutherans seemed to give little consideration to the fact that the Lutheran Church itself owed something to tradition or that its doctrines and practices had in any way been influenced by some of the same traditions that had shaped Roman Catholic doctrine. This had the effect of detracting from the strong historical sense shown by the

[13] "Alleged Visions of Mary," *Witness*, LXX (October 30, 1951), 361.

Lutheran Church's acceptance of the catholic creeds and its appeal to the primitive Christian church. This perhaps explains why one is struck by the uniqueness of the comments of Berthold von Schenk, in *Christians in Conversation:*

> Unfortunately, most Protestantism tends to consider tradition and custom in a negative manner. While not actually condemning it, many Protestant theologians consider tradition, at best, to be irrelevant, holding that Church tradition and Church Scripture oppose each other, sometimes in mutually exclusive fashion. The fallacy here is that such thinking fails to realize that tradition has come down through the ages as a definite experience of the Church, and that it has in many instances aided in the comprehension of the Gospel itself.[14]

The Holy Scripture is itself a *primary* tradition, he maintained, for although inspired, it was the product of human effort. This fact should not hinder the practice of the secondary traditions which are the natural outgrowth of any human organization or group. "The proofstone for all tradition is its relevance to the Gospel and to the work of the *Logos en sarkos.*"

> It was not the intention of the early Reformation fathers to obliterate tradition, but rather to re-evaluate it in the light of the Gospel. These individuals opposed all attempts to absolutize ecclesiastical customs and rightly so. In their efforts to remove one false absolute, however, they mistakenly created a new (and perhaps far more serious) one, the woefully insufficient formula *Sola Scriptura*. This, of course, was not their intention, but it developed into a serious problem which has been divisive in Protestantism.[15]

---

[14] "Factors That Unite Us: Protestant," in *Christians in Conversation,* ed. Peter W. Bartholome (Westminster, Maryland: The Newman Press, 1962), p. 62.
[15] *Ibid.,* pp. 62–63.

Von Schenk asserted that the Bible is important, not in itself, but only insofar as it contains the message of redemption. The Bible is studied and Christians believe it to be the Word of God because it testifies to the Word made flesh; this is the scarlet thread that runs from Genesis to Revelation. It was just because of this approach to Scripture, described by Mayer as "Christocentric," that early Lutheran reformers opposed a "legalistic-biblicistic ecclesiasticism." But unfortunately, observed von Schenk, "in their zealous attempt to save the Church from rampant ecclesiasticism, the later reformers brought about a reimprisonment within the text of Holy Scripture." He pointed out that Luther's sometimes violent opposition to tradition was directed primarily against its misuse. Christocentric tradition did not meet with Luther's disapproval.[16]

The very uniqueness of von Schenk's comments amidst all the Lutheran writing on Scripture and tradition suggests that in their earnest defense of Scripture and their criticism of tradition, many Lutheran theologians have made the Bible an end in itself and have taken away some of the richness and beauty of Christian practice by also rejecting Christocentric traditions.

The Lutheran emphasis on *sola scriptura,* in contrast to Roman Catholic reliance on Scripture and traditions, had the further effect of encouraging Lutheran writers to disparage practices of Catholics in the use of the Bible. Martin Sommer even went so far as to charge that the Catholic hierarchy "hates God's Holy Book," and therefore they sow doubts about its accuracy and authenticity in the minds of their parishioners.[17] This was the underlying theme in much of

[16] *Ibid.,* pp. 64–65.
[17] "Catholic Attacks Upon the Bible," *Witness,* XXXVIII (April 15, 1919), 125–126.

what he wrote, but most writers were not quite so extreme in their judgments.

The one particular, consistent accusation of Lutherans was that the Roman Catholic Church actually did not need the Bible and had in fact prohibited its use by the laity for centuries. In quoting an article from *America* which stated that the Roman Catholic Church with her traditions and pronouncements, and with the infallible papacy, might conceivably get along if the sacred Scriptures were suddenly wiped off the face of the earth, one writer suggested that this characterizes the real attitude of Roman Catholics toward Scripture: they can do without it.[18]

The charge that the laity had been forbidden to use the Bible for centuries, and that this prohibition was still in effect in such places as Latin America and the Philippine Islands, was rather commonly accepted among Lutherans. Frederick Mayer acknowledged that the Roman Catholic Church had denied this charge, and in fact had claimed that it officially encourages Bible reading, but he pointed out that such claims must be carefully evaluated. He cited various papal pronouncements, particularly one laid down by Pope Pius IV in establishing the *Index librorum prohibitorum et expurgandorum* in 1564, which limited the use that individual Catholics could make of the Bible. He contended that this prohibition, for one, was still in effect.[19]

The objectionable limitations the Roman Catholic Church placed on Bible reading were, from the Lutheran point of view, (1) that the laity must read the Roman Catholic version which contains footnotes "designed to prevent the readers from recognizing the departures of Roman doctrine from the

[18] John H. C. Fritz, "A Church That Can Get Along Without the Bible," *Witness*, XLIII (May 20, 1924), 199.
[19] *Religious Bodies of America*, pp. 40–41.

teachings of Scripture" and in which the text is sometimes even perverted for the same reason and (2) that they must accept the Bible, not as the only rule of faith and life, but as a rule which carries authority only because it is approved by the church. Even these concessions were seen by Lutherans to be detested by the hierarchy and merely a reaction to the atmosphere of Protestantism in which Catholics must work today.[20] Another Lutheran objection was that the Catholic version of the Bible included the apocrypha, although it was asserted that this was essential, for nowhere else could the church find endorsement for some of its false teachings.[21]

With these attitudes firmly established, it is not surprising that Lutherans did not take seriously attempts of the Roman Catholic Church to encourage Bible reading. J. T. Mueller said that such encouragements Protestants may read with tongue in cheek by remembering the official Roman Catholic position.[22] Mueller urged his readers to keep in mind that Rome had not experienced a change of heart in the matter of general Bible reading by the laity, for there were still limitations placed on it, particularly in Catholic countries.[23] He was nevertheless encouraged by what Catholics had done to promote Bible reading and study in the United States. He acknowledged that this new interest of Catholics would not change dogma but that through it there might be a change of the hearts of at least some of the Catholics "who find the

[20] Theodore Graebner, "Rome and Bible Reading," *Witness*, XL (June 7, 1921), 184–185.
[21] George A. W. Vogel, "A Comparison of the King James and the Douay Version," *Concordia Theological Monthly*, VI (February, 1935), 102–103.
[22] "Catholics Urge Bible Reading," *Concordia Theological Monthly*, XIX (April, 1948), 306.
[23] "Rome Rediscovers the Bible," *Concordia Theological Monthly*, XXIII (June, 1952), 464–466.

saving Gospel in the Bible and the illuminating power of the Holy Spirit in the Gospel."[24]

As Catholic interest in biblical studies by theologians and in Bible reading by the laity increased through the years, Lutheran observers regularly took note, but always with the regret that the Scriptures were never really allowed to speak for themselves, that the interpretation of the church was always preponderant. We might properly ask whether, before the end of 1963, the church of *sola scriptura* saw in the biblical movement in the Roman Catholic Church any real, dynamic force toward healing the breach of the Reformation. The answer offered by Lutherans was perhaps best summarized by Eugene F. Klug, a professor at Concordia Seminary, Springfield, Illinois:

> While the Church of Rome has shown itself to be extremely flexible in entertaining divergent views among its theologians, allowing them to seek for new modes and expressions in keeping the church's dogma relevant to each new day, it will never allow any new thought to disturb its position of authority nor the solidarity and unity of its membership.
>
> The constant and abiding principle on which Rome lives and has its being is the final supremacy of the Church, which is the living voice of God for this day. In view of this, the significance of the Bible as God's inspired revelation to the world pales into secondary and subordinate position. Rome cannot be expected to leave the moorings which it set deeply at Trent.[25]

[24] "U.S. Catholics Honor the Bible," *Concordia Theological Monthly*, XXIV (May, 1953), 382–384.
[25] "Revelation and Inspiration in Contemporary Roman Catholic Theology," *Springfielder*, XXVI (Fall, 1962), 21.

9

THE POPE: PETER'S HEIR
OR ANTICHRIST?

IF DISAGREEMENT OVER Scripture and tradition as sources of authority marks the starting point for theological differences between Lutherans and Catholics, surely the measure of the distance between them is represented by the papacy. Martin Luther laid down a hard line in dealing with the popes of his time, and Missouri Synod Lutherans have continued to apply his judgments to the papacy in the twentieth century. One church historian reportedly has called the Missouri Synod's insistent reaffirmation that the pope is the very Antichrist *"eine missourische Schrulle,"* a crotchet of Missouri; to which a Missouri Synod theologian replied, "Well, it must then be called a Lutheran *Schrulle*. It would be queer if they who learned to know the Papacy so well should have been mistaken."[1]

Antipathy to the papacy was apparent in almost all the comments and criticisms directed toward Catholicism during the period under consideration in this study. The papacy was

---

[1] Theodore Hoyer, "The Papacy," in *The Abiding Word,* ed. Theodore Laetsch (St. Louis: Concordia, 1947), II, 750. The volumes of *The Abiding Word* were prepared in observance of the 1947 centennial of the Missouri Synod. The essays they contain were intended, not to explore new theological ideas or avenues, but to consolidate the insights the synod had developed during its one-hundred-year history, to preserve the "gist of doctrinal treasures laid down in early synodical conventions." Because the essayists were conscious of their historical, conservative function, the essays carry a tone that might be described as "rhetorical orthodoxy."

not regarded as the principal issue between the two churches, but Lutherans were convinced that it was the chief barrier to the settlement of any of the theological differences. They could never be reconciled to it, and they held no hope that it would ever become any more acceptable.

So severe was their judgment that they attempted to maintain a distinction between the papacy and the Roman Catholic Church. They recognized that the identification of the two is so close today that they cannot be separated and that the Roman Catholic Church and the papacy must stand or fall together, but they chose to regard it as a foreign body, "a deadly fungus growing on the Roman branch of the Church catholic."[2] Through this theoretical distinction they could condemn the papacy as an antichristian institution without laying the same judgment on the church. In the same way, by distinguishing between the popes and the papacy they could continue to denounce the institution and still be charitable to the individual men who represented it.

The heart of the refusal of Lutherans to accept or even to tolerate the papacy rested in their complete rejection of the claims that were made by and for it, and of the doctrinal positions to which these claims have led. We have already seen their reaction to the temporal claims of the pope. More vehemently denied were the assertions that the pope is the final authority on matters of faith and morals. As believers in the priesthood of all believers, Lutherans not only refused to allow the church and the papacy to interpret and control the Bible but they also looked upon the authoritarian structure of the Roman Catholic Church with suspicion. The power of the Roman Catholic clergy and the hierarchy is in complete contrast to the substantial autonomy of each congregation in

[2] F. W. Herzberger, "Luther's Conduct Toward Roman Catholics," *Theological Quarterly*, XXI (July, 1917), 174.

the Missouri Synod in the ordering of its internal affairs. At
the apex of the hierarchy is the pope, the ultimate authority.
As Lutherans understood it, the responsibility for all that the
Roman Catholic Church says and does on any level rests with
the papacy. Whenever they disapproved of the conduct of the
church, the blame was fixed on the pope.

Furthermore, as seen by Lutherans, not only has the
Roman Catholic Church substituted tradition for Scripture,
but tradition itself has been displaced by the claim that the
pope is infallible when he speaks *ex cathedra* in matters of
faith and morals. One Lutheran put it this way:

> The infallibility of the pope provides the church with a
> living tradition. Whether or not it is true that Pope Pius
> IX declared, "Tradition? I am the tradition!" it is certain
> that by introducing this new authority into the teaching
> of the church modern Roman Catholicism has found a way
> to substitute clear and distinct doctrines for the ambiguous
> statements of Scripture and tradition.[3]

Lutheran writers devoted little effort to debating the dogma
of infallibility. Generally it was dismissed as "a convenient
claim invented and drilled into the minds of the 'faithful' to
secure acceptance of any doctrine the Church may wish to
proclaim."[4] The reason they gave little attention to refuting
it is that their arguments had to rest on Scripture, and they
judged the Roman Catholic Church to be using a different
foundation for this teaching.[5] Theodore Hoyer saw no point
in discussing it:

---

[3] Jaroslav Pelikan, *The Riddle of Roman Catholicism* (New
York: Abingdon Press, 1959), pp. 82–83.
[4] Otto E. Sohn, *Lutheran Witness*, LXXIII (August 17, 1954),
285.
[5] That the claim could be refuted scripturally was shown by
Carl S. Meyer, *Witness*, LXXVI (November 19, 1957), 572.

We need not spend many words on this latest papal fiction. Only one Bible passage is quoted by Romans to support this teaching, Luke 22:32, where Jesus says to Peter: "I have prayed for thee that thy faith fail not." And even Roman exegesis has rarely dared so fantastic a flight as this.

He contended that this text as a basis for papal infallibility had even been refuted by a Catholic theologian in 1869, before the promulgation of the infallibility decree.[6]

Several writers referred to tradition to show the error of the infallibility claim. W. G. Polack pointed out that "nineteen centuries of the Christian era were drawing to a close before this dogma was foisted upon the Roman Catholic Church." He acknowledged that before it became official it had been taught, even by Thomas Aquinas, but that there was too much opposition to make it official. In 1870, however, "the well-oiled papal steam roller ruthlessly flattened out all opposition."[7] Hoyer declared that "the most hideous and naked exercise of Papal infallibility was necessary before that infallibility could be elevated into a dogma." In addition, he charged that the Vatican Council was not regularly constituted, that the Italians held a "monstrously predominating majority," that the participants "were dominated by the Propaganda in the most scandalous manner," and that the whole apparatus of the pope's political power was used to intimidate and repress all those who opposed the decree. He concluded that the only real foundation for the doctrine that the pope is infallible is the pope's own assertion to that effect.[8]

The Vatican Council which promulgated the decree of

---

[6] "The Papacy,"*Abiding Word,* II, 744.

[7] "When Is the Pope Infallible?" *Witness,* LXVII (January 27, 1948), 27–28.

[8] "The Papacy," *Abiding Word,* II, 746.

infallibility was discussed by Richard Sommerfeld, a Concordia Senior College professor, in a little booklet, *The Case Against the Infallibility of the Pope*.[9] Sommerfeld cited some of the arguments advanced in support of papal infallibility and then reprinted a translation of a lengthy speech by Bishop Strossmayer of Diakovar, Bosnia.[10] The speech, a fervent attack on the proposed doctrine, was interrupted with frequent cries of objection or disapproval. Sommerfeld reported that after the Bishop had made his "eloquent, historically factual, and Scripturally correct address," the delegates met in secret session and took a preliminary vote. The first tally showed 451 for, 88 opposed, and 62 in favor with reservations. Fifty-six bishops sent a written protest to the pope, but he ignored it, and the next day these bishops and six others left Rome, alleging that their respective dioceses needed their attention. Sommerfeld noted that when the final ballot was cast, there were only two dissenting votes; most of those who had opposed it, including Strossmayer, had submitted. He concluded that nothing has changed since 1870. Then, "in the face of clear and known falsehood and deceit a man stood up and spoke bravely what was in his heart and conscience," but he submitted as millions do today, either knowingly or in ignorance.[11]

Some Lutheran writers could not resist using the infallibility claim as a general basis for attacking the pope on unrelated matters. During World War I, for example, Martin Sommer asked why, if the pope is the supreme authority, he did not say who was right and who was at fault in the war.[12] But

---

[9] *The Case Against the Infallibility of the Pope* (St. Louis: Concordia, n.d. [1962]).

[10] *Ibid.*, pp. 10–27.

[11] *Ibid.*, pp. 27–28.

[12] "The Papacy a Failure," *Witness*, XXXVI (October 30, 1917), 337–338.

when they chose to, most of them recognized, as Polack explained, that the pope does not claim to be infallible in his personal life, nor in his opinions as a private instructor, nor in his official decisions, sermons, addresses, letters, and the like. They acknowledged that the claim of infallibility does not extend to matters of church discipline, church law, church government, church administration, and not even to all dogmatic teachings of the pope, but only to those matters covered when the pope speaks *ex cathedra.* Polack noted that according to some opinion within the Roman Catholic Church, infallibility applies only to those cases in which the pope chooses to make use of it and declares positively that he is imposing on all the faithful the obligation of belief under pain of heresy and exclusion from the church.[13] These exceptions provided small satisfaction to Lutherans who were convinced that the pope had no right to speak from a position of infallibility on anything.

Because they denied the authority and the infallibility of the papacy, Lutherans naturally objected to the teaching that there is no salvation outside the church over which the pope presides. Such claims by the Roman Catholic Church were given frequent attention and were always denounced. In commenting on a Catholic pamphlet which explained that only a person who *knowingly* and *willfully* separates himself from the Roman Catholic Church cannot be saved, Carl S. Meyer pointed out that "whatever hedging is made in an attempt to soften the absoluteness of the papal pronouncements, the fact remains that according to the teachings of the Roman Church salvation is to be found only in that church." He called attention to the biblical teaching that there is salvation

[13] "When Is the Pope Infallible?" *Witness,* LXVII (January 27, 1948), 27–28.

only in Christ, and in his church, that is, his body, made up of all believers and only believers.[14]

The suspension of Father Leonard Feeney, S.J., a chaplain to Catholic students at Harvard University, by Cardinal Richard Cushing in 1949 for teaching that outside the Roman Catholic Church there is no salvation did nothing to soften Lutheran resentment. Even though the Cardinal declared that because of great offense against the cause of the Roman Catholic Church, Father Feeney had lost the right to perform any priestly function, Lutherans were convinced that Catholic teaching had not changed. William Arndt contended that where Rome is in power, the same teaching is maintained in all its terrifying aspects, but where Rome is not in power and the people are intelligent and use independent judgment, "the door is pointed to which Roman Catholic theology can open when the charge of fanaticism is raised and pressed."[15]

The papal claims rejected by Lutherans that have been cited thus far were all claims made by the papacy as it existed. For most writers these were not the most important claims however; they preferred to challenge the very foundation on which the papacy justifies its existence. They were unable to find either scriptural or historical evidence that Jesus had founded his church on the Apostle Peter or that the papacy represented the extension of Peter's primacy in the church. They could not accept the assertion that the popes through history were the successors of Peter as the bishop of Rome.

The words of Jesus "And I say to thee that thou art Peter, and upon this rock will I build My Church, and the gates of hell shall not prevail against it" (Matthew 16:18) are cited

---

[14] "Let's Investigate," *Witness,* LXXVI (July 30, 1957), 380.
[15] "Outside the Roman Catholic Church There Is No Salvation," *Concordia Theological Monthly,* XX (June, 1949), 468–469.

by Catholics as the principal scriptural basis for their claims. If Lutherans were to refute the Catholic teaching, they had to deal directly with this text and the application given to it by Catholics. Although several theologians did this, Theodore Hoyer made the most complete analysis, and it serves here as a summary view of the way in which at least some Lutherans regarded the Roman Catholic interpretation.

Hoyer began by acknowledging that Jesus did indeed address these words to Peter and to no other person and that in so doing he was distinguishing Peter above the other disciples. The question is, Why did he make this distinction? The reason, according to Hoyer, is that Peter was the first disciple to be ready to confess his faith in Jesus.

> Even the Catholic will have to admit that Christ's words to Peter require as their logical *prius* the confession of Peter; that if Peter had not spoken as he did, the Lord would not have spoken to Peter as He did. We have no right to assume that the Lord had any other reason to speak as He did; there is nothing in the text to warrant that. If anything like the primacy of Peter as conceived by the Roman Church is laid down here, other Scripture must be adduced, and history will have to be called upon for its witness to substantiate the claim.[16]

But, observed Hoyer, other Scripture does not produce any substantiation for Peter's primacy; in fact it indicates just the contrary. If Jesus had really meant Peter, why did he not say, "Thou art Peter, and on thee will I build My Church?" The distinction in the Greek text between *Petros* and *petra* must be taken to mean that Jesus intended a difference between the two. Furthermore, the confession of Peter as recorded in the accounts of Mark and Luke do not say a word about the church being built upon Peter. On the contrary, in his letter

16 "The Papacy," *Abiding Word*, II, 730.

to the Ephesians, Paul writes of the church being built on the "foundation of the Apostles and Prophets, Jesus Christ Himself being the chief Cornerstone." And St. John's account of the new Jerusalem (Revelation 21:10–14) describes the wall of the city as having "twelve foundations, and in them the names of the twelve Apostles of the Lamb."[17]

Moreover, according to Hoyer's explanation, there is no evidence in Scripture that the other Apostles recognized Peter as their primate; the evidence is all to the contrary. Jesus himself put all the disciples on the same plane. Neither was Peter given any indication that such a primacy had been given to him. In fact, "in the whole New Testament none of the Apostles or of the disciples anywhere, at any time, or in any way, give even the least hint of a primacy of Peter."[18]

Asserting that surely total silence is tantamount to proof, Hoyer nevertheless returned for further consideration of the *Petros-petra* distinction. He found it illuminating that Jesus had given Peter his new name, but that whenever he found the old sinful nature of Peter cropping up again he referred to him as Simon.

> Why does Jesus here . . . call him Peter? Because of his confession; . . . by this confession, by his faith in the Son of God, he had become a Peter, a rock man, who stood on the Rock Jesus Christ. It is not to the natural Peter that Jesus speaks, but to the regenerated Peter; not to the fisherman, but to the confessor; not to Simon Bar-jona, but to Peter the rock man. And on the same Rock on which Peter stood, and thus became a rock man, on Jesus Christ Himself, the Lord will build His Church.

This interpretation, Hoyer maintained, agrees with other Scripture, for Christ himself is referred to as the Rock on

---

[17] *Ibid.*, II, 730–731.
[18] *Ibid.*, II, 731–733.

which the church is built. In his first epistle Peter himself described Jesus by this term.[19]

Therefore the conclusion reached by Hoyer was that Christ is the Rock on whom the church rests and that by confessing Christ, Peter and the Apostles become a part of the larger foundation of the church, all resting on Christ. By their confession they bear up others who were won by them for Christ, and so "all Christians can become Peters and part of the foundation, bearing up others by their confession of Christ." The sole distinction of Peter is that which priority in confessing Christ before others gives him. The Roman Catholic interpretation of this passage, then, "is fraud and can be adduced from this text only by jugglery."[20]

Hoyer found evidence that some Roman Catholics themselves had admitted that "rock" in the Matthew text should be understood to mean the faith Peter had confessed. He quoted Archbishop Kenrick of St. Louis to this effect. The speech to which he referred was prepared for the Vatican Council in 1870 but was not actually delivered. In it Archbishop Kenrick asserted that in both honor and jurisdiction he accepted the primacy (but not the lordship) of the pope, but he denied that primacy could be proved from Scripture. Hoyer also referred to the contention of Bishop Strossmayer at the 1870 Vatican Council that neither Scripture nor tradition would support the idea that "rock" referred to Peter. Cardinal Newman, Hoyer added, had admitted in his *An Essay on the Development of Christian Doctrine* that neither

---

[19] *Ibid.,* II, 734.

[20] *Ibid.,* II, 736–737. Hoyer's interpretation is essentially the same as the one attributed to Luther and other reformers, although it is not in strict agreement with the argument in the Lutheran Confessions. In his *Treatise on the Power and Primacy of the Pope* Melanchthon asserted that the church is built, not on the man Peter, but on the ministry of his confession.

the Bible nor tradition would furnish adequate proof for Roman Catholic doctrine of the pope's supremacy.[21]

Other Lutheran theologians interpreted the text and commented on the Roman Catholic application of it in much the same way. Edward W. A. Koehler, a theology professor at one of the synod's teacher-training institutions, stated in addition that Peter was an emotional man, not firm or stable enough that Christ would have ventured to build his church on him and make him the infallible teacher of all Christendom.[22] William Arndt commented that even if "rock" means Peter, we still have nothing but the statement of Our Lord that he is going to use Peter "in an eminent degree" in the erection of his holy church here on earth.[23] Walter A. Maier contended that neither Christ, nor the Apostles, nor Peter himself claimed that Peter was pope. He contrasted the life of Peter with the papacy and concluded that when "popery" is mentioned in the Bible, it is spelled "A-n-t-i-c-h-r-i-s-t."[24]

If scriptural evidence to support the belief that Peter was the first pope was lacking, neither could Lutheran observers find such evidence in history. Hoyer, Arndt, and Koehler all stated that it could not be proved that Peter had ever even been in Rome. Hoyer agreed that it is fair to assume that Peter may have died there, but among the church fathers it was not so stated until about 170 A.D. Nor was there

---

[21] *Ibid.,* II, 737–738. Hoyer's otherwise excellent essay is weakened by the fact that it is not documented; its historical accuracy is open to some question, for the bibliography indicates that he used articles by William Dallmann for historical data. Dallmann's articles are poorly documented.

[22] "Upon Whom Did Christ Promise to Build His Church?" *Witness,* XLV (July 13, 1926), 225–227. Reprinted as a tract.

[23] "Was St. Peter the First Pope?" *Witness,* XLI (February 14, 1922), 49–51.

[24] "Peter Never Pope," *Walther League Messenger,* XXX (February, 1922), 249.

evidence that there was a Roman bishop in Peter's days, for the terms "bishop" and "presbyter" had been used interchangeably.[25]

Polack argued that the claims of the church concerning the primacy of Peter were not accepted in the first six centuries by many of the church fathers. He cited a book, *Quaestio,* which appeared in 1870, written by Roman Catholics who had examined carefully the opinions of the church fathers on the subject. Of the eighty-five church fathers who were quoted, eight said "rock" meant all the Apostles, sixteen said it meant the Lord himself, forty-four considered it to be the faith Peter had confessed, and seventeen applied it to Peter. Thus, sixty-eight of the eighty-five rejected the Roman Catholic claim. Among those who rejected it were Tertullian, Origen, Cyprian, Hilary of Poitiers, Ambrose, Athanasius, John Chrysostom, Augustine, Pope Leo I, and Pope Gelasius. Polack concluded that the Lutheran position is therefore the one that is in agreement with most of the church fathers.[26]

Hoyer discussed the early history of the papacy in more detail, and, incidentally, contradicted the allegation passed along by Polack that Leo I and Gelasius were in disagreement with the basic Roman Catholic teaching. In fact, he indicated that the letters of Gelasius (492–496) claim almost everything that the Vatican Council of 1870 decreed.[27] The interpretation of the early history of the papacy advanced by Hoyer is that it was primarily a product of Rome's force of persistence.

No matter how much a claim was opposed at first, it kept on asserting it. If the objection was too strong, it kept

[25] "The Papacy," *Abiding Word,* II, 740–741.
[26] "Was the Papacy Founded in Matthew 16:16–18?" *Witness,* LXVII (February 24, 1948), 55–56.
[27] "The Papacy," *Abiding Word,* II, 723.

silence for a while, but at the first opportune moment re-
iterated the old claim. This everlasting hammering away
at the same idea through the centuries has made Rome
what it is.

Methods used by popes, he said, included distortion of Scripture, forgery of existing church orders, and invention of new
canons and decretals. Through their unwavering, obstinate
persistence and the ability to wait, the papacy was eventually
brought to the point where, until the late Middle Ages, there
was little or no opposition to it.[28]

The question of the primacy of Peter and the legitimacy of
the claims of the popes to be his successors was not, however,
the principal issue as far as Lutherans were concerned. Even
if there had been a clear scriptural statement designating
Peter as the first bishop of Rome, and if the succession of
such bishops in the early centuries had been clearly recorded,
there would still have been pronounced differences between
Lutheran and Catholics over the papacy (assuming of course
that the Reformation had occurred). Similarly, the historic
corruption of the popes in the Middle Ages, which Lutheran
writers were so quick to identify as being characteristic of the
papacy in its true form, was not the decisive factor in the
Lutheran judgment. Certainly such revelations as were
brought out by Graebner in *The Dark Ages* and by Dallmann
in *How Peter Became Pope* contributed to Lutheran antipathy to the papacy. But a millenium of personally impeccable
popes would not have substantially affected the acceptability
of the papacy to Lutherans, although it might have compelled
them to express their objections in more temperate terms.

From the Lutheran point of view the pope is to be judged
by just one thing: his doctrine. The test is simply, How do the
teachings of the pope square with Scripture? When Luther

[28] *Ibid.,* II, 712–725.

concluded that scriptural and papal teachings were in conflict, he recognized that a turning point had been reached in his career, for he wrote to Spalatin on March 13, 1519: "I am studying the decretals of the Popes, preparing for my disputation, and (I whisper it in your ear) I do not know whether the Pope is Antichrist or his apostle."[29] Before long his reservations were removed; his judgment was expressed in the Smalcald Articles of 1537:

> This teaching shows forcefully that the pope is the very Antichrist, who has exalted himself above and opposed himself against Christ, because he will not permit Christians to be saved without his power, which, nevertheless, is nothing and is neither ordained nor commanded by God.[30]

The Lutheran Church-Missouri Synod has historically identified itself with this judgment. Lutheran theologians not only have reaffirmed Luther's assertions but they also have approached the question from various angles and with different emphases and have consistently come up with the same judgment. Moreover, the judgment has not been made only by individual theologians. It was formally incorporated into the Brief Statement of the Doctrinal Position of the Missouri Synod adopted in 1932. The Brief Statement asserts:

> As to the Antichrist we teach that the prophecies of the Holy Scriptures concerning the Antichrist, 2 Thess. 2:3–12; 1 John 2:18, have been fulfilled in the Pope of Rome and his dominion. All the features of the Antichrist as drawn in these prophecies, including the most abominable and horrible ones, . . . are the outstanding characteristics of the Papacy. . . . Hence we subscribe to the

---

[29] *Ibid.*, II, 710.
[30] Smalcald Articles, Part II, Article IV, 10–14. This judgment may well have been justified by circumstances in Luther's own experience and time; whether he would have wanted it to stand as a dogmatic statement is of course uncertain.

statement of our Confessions that the Pope is "the very Antichrist."[31]

We turn here again to the argumentation developed by Hoyer as representative of the method used by Lutheran theologians in reaching this harsh judgment. Hoyer maintained that although the papacy has no foundation in Scripture, it does appear in Scripture. In 1 John 2:18 the term "antichrist" is used in a general sense as referring to anyone who is a false teacher. But it is also used in the special sense, for it says, "Ye have heard that Antichrist will come," which indicates that the Antichrist has been referred to in a prophecy. It could be the prophecy in Daniel 11:36–39, which speaks of a king who will do his own will, exalting himself above every god and speaking marvelous things against the God of gods. Or it might be the "man of sin" referred to by Paul in 2 Thess. 2:3–10, who also opposes and exalts himself above God. Both of these texts, in addition to several others, contain descriptions of the Antichrist.

These descriptions, or "marks" of the Antichrist, were tested against political tyrants, against infidels and scoffers, against Mohammed, and in modern times against atheism, but they do not fit in any of these cases because they are all outside of the church. For reasons apparent in the texts, Antichrist must be someone within the church who can be guilty of a falling away, a special apostasy. The way to determine who is the Antichrist, according to Hoyer, is to test the possible candidates against the doctrine which is the essence of Christian teaching. That doctrine is justification by faith in Christ without works. Whoever threatens and attacks this doctrine harms the church most.

The Council of Trent of course has anathematized this doctrine, so the conclusion is easily drawn:

[31] Brief Statement of the Doctrinal Position of the Lutheran Church-Missouri Synod, Article 43.

That is the very heart of the Papacy: denial of justification by faith. The whole machinery of the Papacy is organized against this doctrine. There are a host of teachings promulgated by the Papacy which by no stretch of the imagination can ever be brought into harmony with this cardinal doctrine. . . . Nor do they ever pretend that they can be harmonized; they want to have nothing to do with justification by faith. The whole edifice of the Papacy falls if justification by faith is admitted.[32]

This judgment having been reached, it was then confirmed by specifically applying to the papacy each of the marks of the Antichrist given in any of the appropriate texts. Most frequently Lutherans relied upon 2 Thess. 2:3-12 and found that the marks there do indeed apply to the pope: he sits in the temple of God where he claims to be the head of the church and excommunicates all who do not acknowledge his supremacy; he claims divine attributes, divine prerogatives, and divine authority. The pope is the very Antichrist.[33]

This is admittedly a harsh and severe judgment to render against the head of the largest church within Christendom. It prompts certain questions: Was it taught within the synod? What status did it have as doctrine? Has there been any desire in recent years to back away from it or to mitigate its severity?

That the pope was the very Antichrist was an integral part of Missouri Synod teaching for the better part of the period covered in this study. It was taught in an informal way through the numerous comments in editorials in which certain statements or incidents were taken to prove that "the Antichrist is at work" or that "we have no reason to change our doctrine that the pope is the very Antichrist." No regular reader of the *Lutheran Witness* could have been unaware that this was official and current teaching of the synod.

[32] "The Papacy," *Abiding Word,* II, 747–751.
[33] *Ibid.,* II, 751–761.

Furthermore, it was taught through the Bible class materials produced by the synod. Lessons included in courses prepared for use in 1932, 1933, 1941, 1945, and 1953 all contained the standard interpretations of the appropriate texts.[34] Lengthy articles in the *Concordia Theological Monthly,* written by professors at the St. Louis seminary, show that any pastors who continued their theological education through this medium received repeated instruction on the subject. Articles such as Paul E. Kretzmann's "The Progressive Revelation of the Antichrist"[35] gave no indication that the official teaching was being softened. Presumably the faculty members who wrote the articles taught the same things in their classrooms. It would seem proper to infer that the pastors who were the products of Concordia Seminary could be expected to teach in turn what they had been taught.

The inclusion of the article on the Antichrist in the Brief Statement referred to above indicates that the teaching enjoyed official status in the Missouri Synod. More important was the fact that it was already a part of the Lutheran Confessions, to the doctrinal content of which every clergyman and congregation is bound. Furthermore, the Common Confession adopted by the synod in 1950 as a basis for doctrinal fellowship with the American Lutheran Church contained this assertion:

> Among the signs of His approaching return for judgment the distinguishing features of the Antichrist, as portrayed

---

[34]William H. Luke, *Junior Bible Student,* XXI (January, 1932). Theodore Graebner, *Bible Student,* XI (April, 1933). Theodore Graebner, *Bible Student,* XII (October, 1933). Arthur E. Neitzel, *Bible Student,* XX (January, 1941). Theodore Graebner, *Bible Student,* XXIV (July, 1945). John M. Weidenschilling, *Bible Student,* XXXI (January, 1953).

[35] *Concordia Theological Monthly,* XIII (February, 1942), 120–136.

in the Holy Scriptures, are still clearly discernible in the Roman papacy, the climax of all human usurpations of Christ's authority in the Church.[36]

A Statement on the Antichrist adopted by Joint Committees of the Synodical Conference in 1958 essentially reaffirmed the confessional position. This statement was never acted upon because the Wisconsin Synod, the other large body in the Synodical Conference, withdrew before it came up for final action in a Missouri Synod convention,[37] but it does represent the conclusions reached by a special committee that studied the question.

These examples indicate that it was maintained as official teaching through the years. It was not, however, regarded as a fundamental doctrine, for, according to Hoyer:

> Knowledge of this article is not needed to plant and keep saving faith in the heart. A Christian may know Christ as his Savior and be saved by Him even though he does not recognize the Antichrist in the Papacy. It is not an article on which saving faith rests, with which Christianity stands or falls.[38]

President John W. Behnken quoted this statement in replying to a sarcastic request by *Our Sunday Visitor* for clarification of the Antichrist doctrine; he concluded his reply with this comment:

> Please do not consider this attitude a concession. It is a direct expression of classic Lutheran principle regarding the relationship of exegesis and dogma to saving faith. Is it too much to hope that Roman Catholics . . . may one day assume the same position in regard to assertions of papal authority? If there were such a possibility, the greatest

[36] *Proceedings of the Forty-First Regular Convention of the Lutheran Church-Missouri Synod,* 1950, p. 572.
[37] *Witness,* LXXVIII (March 10, 1959), 104–105, 117.
[38] "The Papacy," *Abiding Word,* II, 764.

stumbling block could be removed from inauguration of discussion between Roman Catholics and Lutherans regarding Christian doctrine.[39]

Terming the teaching nonfundamental was not considered a concession by Hoyer either. He asserted that the Christian who does not recognize the truth of the Antichrist teaching is in greater danger than others of being led astray by the errors of the papacy.

> And a religious teacher, a pastor, who knows the Pope's teaching and practice and yet does not recognize him as the Antichrist is a poor theologian. . . . And it is very difficult to see how pastors can rightly perform their duty of warning the soul committed to their care against the abominations and seduction of the Papacy if they themselves have not recognized the Papacy as the Antichrist.[40]

It would appear that by endorsing the teaching on the Antichrist in articles and editorials, by teaching it, and by reaffirming it at synodical conventions, the Lutheran Church-Missouri Synod was showing little desire to back away from the harsh judgment that had been rendered through the years. In this case the appearance may well be deceiving. In looking for a softening of approach one should not expect a repudiation of the official position. The confessional principle of the Lutheran Church-Missouri Synod prevented it from renouncing the Smalcald Articles. Nevertheless, in a quiet way the Antichrist teaching was given less emphasis, and a more conciliatory tone was adopted. Increasingly this statement of Luther came to be regarded as an historical judgment rather than a doctrinal statement.

The last major exposition of the Antichrist teaching

---

[39] "President Behnken Refutes 'Sinister Charge,' " *Witness,* LXXVIII (December 29, 1959), 610, 620–621.
[40] "The Papacy," *Abiding Word,* II, 764.

appeared in 1953. Although the writer concluded that there is strong foundation in prophecy and history for the view that the pope is the very Antichrist, and that the marks of the Antichrist are seen more clearly in the papacy today than they were at the time of the Reformation, he acknowledged two difficulties: Does the pope deny that the Son of God has come into the flesh? Do the claims of the popes actually amount to an exalting of themselves over everything that is called God and is worshipped? Identifying the pope as the Antichrist, he added, involves a frightfully earnest responsibility.[41] These acknowledgments are in marked contrast to the glib or even vindictive manner in which the judgment had usually been pronounced previously.

After this, aside from official consideration by the synod, the teaching on the Antichrist scarcely received attention. In 1958 Carl S. Meyer presented an objective, historical survey of the modern papacy from Pius IX to Pius XII without mentioning it.[42] The accession of John XXIII prompted a reminder of the Antichrist teaching in the *Witness,* but the old denunciatory tone was lacking. Again the distinction between the pope and the papacy was noted.[43] The *Cresset,* in expressing genuine sorrow at the death of Pius XII and extending best wishes to his successor, commented that "few non-Roman Christians find it as easy as did their fathers to identify the papacy with the anti-Christ." But it added that if sitting in the temple of God and showing himself forth as

[41] Henry Hamann, "A Brief Exegesis of 2 Thess. 2:1–12 with Guideline for the Application of the Prophecy Contained Therein," *Concordia Theological Monthly,* XXIV (June, 1953), 418–433.
[42] "The Modern Papacy," *Concordia Theological Monthly,* XXIX (April, 1958), 241–260.
[43] Lewis W. Spitz, "Pope John XXIII," *Witness,* LXXVII (November 18, 1958), 538.

being God is a mark of the Antichrist, Rome cannot escape responsibility for making that identification seem plausible.[44]

A more significant example in the trend toward backing away from the hard judgment is the Bible class guide on Paul's epistles to the Thessalonians. The familiar Antichrist text was simply used to discuss the identifying marks of the "man of sin." This was added: "NOTE: Luther stated that the prophecy was fulfilled in the papacy, and called the pope (not the man, but the office) the Antichrist."[45] The accompanying guide included these suggestions to teachers:

> State that Luther and the Lutheran confessions see in this passage a prophecy of the papacy. You may even briefly point out a few of the identifying marks. Then state that this identification is not your purpose in this lesson. You want to learn rather what Paul intended to teach by including this prophecy.[46]

Moreover, the pastoral approach of John XXIII to the papacy evoked favorable comment in the *Cresset,* the *American Lutheran,* and the *Witness.* In a column in the *American Lutheran* an anonymous pastor described in an interesting way why he had invited his congregation to pray for the dying Pope John. He had been prompted to do so, he said, by the words at the close of the Order of Holy Communion, "Lord, now lettest Thou Thy servant depart in peace according to Thy Word."[47]

[44] "Rome Elects a New Bishop," *Cresset,* XXII (December, 1958), 3–4.

[45] Robert Hoyer, *Adult Bible Discussion Guide,* V, Part 9 (May 29, 1960), p. 41.

[46] Robert Hoyer, *Teachers Guide* to *Adult Bible Discussion Guide,* p. 40. The guide also referred the teacher to the various parts of the Lutheran Confessions which deal with the Antichrist in case he wished "to state more strongly the Confessional Lutheran position" (*ibid.,* p. 42).

[47] "We Prayed for the Pope," *American Lutheran,* XLVI (July, 1963), 10.

In contrasting these comments with those of an earlier era one might deduce that the teaching on the Antichrist has indeed softened in recent years. Such a conclusion must rest on the assumption that the hard line of the earlier years was taught earnestly and with conviction. Without calling into question the honesty or sincerity of the earlier writers, we can discern three conditions about the manner in which it was taught and the reasons for teaching it which cast doubt upon this assumption.

First, the mental framework of the men who pronounced the judgment in their editorial comments was such that by using the standard interpretation of the proper texts they could easily conclude that the pope was indeed the Antichrist. Furthermore, the religious and political climate in which they matured provided them with evidence which did little to contradict this conclusion. It therefore became a standard part of their journalistic rhetoric, used in some articles in almost the same manner in which one uses simple punctuation in a sentence and paragraph. This is an impression gained, not from reading an article or two that they wrote, but by surveying in a comparatively short time what they produced through three or four decades.

Second, as it was being taught, regular reference was made to the fact that this teaching was a part of the Lutheran Confessions. Typical was the argument used by Paul E. Kretzmann in answering objections to it: "As for Lutheran theologians, doubt or hesitation is hardly excusable, since our Confessions make such clear statements concerning the Antichrist that the issue is clear-cut."[48] Similarly, in discussing the teaching on the Antichrist in the *Seminarian,* Herbert Bouman, a Concordia Seminary professor, dealt essentially with two questions: How do the Confessions treat the Scripture

---

[48] "Papam Esse Verum Antichristum," *Concordia Theological Monthly,* IV (June, 1933), 434.

doctrine of the Antichrist? What does this mean for those who pledge their allegiance to the Confessions? He commented that "when the adherents of the Lutheran Reformation framed the expressions of their Scriptural convictions in the Lutheran Confessions, they did not hesitate to apply what they learned from Scripture about the Antichrist to the historical situation that confronted them." Noting that four of the Confessions label the pope the Antichrist, he asserted that if we stand where the reformers stood, and the papacy stands now as it did then, we must make the same identification.[49] One wonders what the explanation of the basic texts would have been if the reformers had not made this application.

Third, in surveying the polemics on the Antichrist one discovers that much of what was written was apparently prompted, not by anything in particular that the pope had done, but rather by doctrinal differences within the Missouri Synod. In the early 1940's, when the Missouri Synod was engaged in doctrinal discussions with the American Lutheran Church for the purpose of eventually establishing church fellowship, a dissident group within the synod opposed such talks on the grounds that they would lead to unionism. Before fellowship could be established, they insisted that there must be complete agreement, even in regard to nonfundamental doctrines. They questioned, in fact, the idea that a doctrine could be termed nonfundamental.

The teaching on the Antichrist was among those seized upon by the dissident group to show that doctrinal differences existed between the Missouri Synod and the American Lutheran Church. The controversy continued for more than a dozen years and is too complicated to summarize here, but

[49] "The Doctrine of Anti-Christ with Special Reference to Subscription to the Lutheran Confessions," *Seminarian,* XLVI (December, 1954), 27–31.

essentially the dissidents raised two complaints: (1) the American Lutheran Church considers the teaching that the pope is the Antichrist to be an *historical judgment,* not a *doctrine,* and (2) the American Lutheran Church allows that in the future a still more comprehensive fulfillment of the Antichrist prophecies *may occur,* but the Missouri Synod teaches that they *have been fulfilled* in the pope of Rome.

The arguments of the dissidents were presented in a memorial brought to the 1950 convention of the synod. One of the signers of the memorial was Paul E. Kretzmann.[50] Although he had left the faculty of St. Louis seminary by 1950, Kretzmann had been a professor there and had contributed several of the articles on the Antichrist carried in the *Concordia Theological Monthly* in 1942 and 1943, when the Antichrist issue was emerging.

In 1942 and 1943 the *Confessional Lutheran,* the magazine published by the dissidents, also devoted extensive attention to the Antichrist question.[51] Kretzmann was a contributor to the discussion here and was obviously in sympathy with the *Confessional Lutheran*'s position. It is clear that the *Confessional Lutheran* Antichrist articles were inspired by the negotiations with the American Lutheran Church, not by anything done by the Roman Catholic Church or the pope. The heat and the duration of this intrasynodical dispute kept the Antichrist question in the foreground and compelled the Missouri Synod to restate its position in much more severe terms than would have been likely otherwise.

For these three reasons we may conclude that the papacy

[50] *Proceedings of the Forty-First Regular Convention of the Lutheran Church-Missouri Synod,* 1950, pp. 590–597. This was by no means the only place where their views were presented.
[51] Articles on the subject appeared in the following issues of the *Confessional Lutheran:* III (April, May, June, October, November, and December, 1942); IV (March and May-June, 1943).

as the Antichrist had been little more than a popular abstraction long before it was recognized that the literal application of it in the practical situation had ceased to make sense. This conclusion does little to diminish the obstacle that the papacy presents to meaningful encounter between Lutherans and Roman Catholics. The teachings, the claims, and the history of the papacy still make it unacceptable to Lutherans.

10

FAITH AND WORKS:
THE CENTRAL ISSUE

How can unrighteous man find favor with a God who demands righteousness? For both Lutherans and Catholics this is a central theological concern. Both churches teach that man is sinful, that God is righteous, and that reconciliation between God and man can come only after man's sins are no longer a barrier between them. Only the "justified" man can stand in God's favor.

But how does man become just? Their differing responses account for the essential disagreement that prevails between the two churches. The theological systems of both Lutheranism and Catholicism are outgrowths and developments of the answers they give to this central question. It is of course beyond the scope of this study to describe in detail the way the whole matter of sin and grace is treated by either group. The concern here is primarily to examine the way in which Lutherans have regarded the theology of Roman Catholicism on this subject. As the various points of conflict are touched upon, it must be remembered that no attempt is being made to present the complete doctrine of the atonement for either side.

In seeking to understand the reaction of Lutheran theologians to Roman Catholic teaching it is helpful to know the perspective from which they observed and studied it. Their perception and evaluation of it was shaped by their earnest conviction that the Lutheran Church is "the true visible church" and that its doctrine on justification is its most significant and distinctive mark. They did not hesitate to express in blunt terms their certainty of the purity and fullness of the teachings of the Lutheran Church.

> The Lutheran Church, the true visible Church on earth, faces the contemporary world to bring it to Christ with the means of grace as its only equipment. The Lutheran Church has the one philosophy of effective action of the Church in relation to the world. It knows that it must use the means of grace to bring men to God. It has them purely and fully.[1]

This idea had been proposed already in 1866 by the Missouri Synod's venerable founder, C. F. W. Walther. He advanced the thesis that if the Evangelical Lutheran Church possesses pure gospel preaching and unadulterated administration of the holy sacraments, it is the true visible church of God on earth. In reviewing this thesis and Walther's affirmative conclusion Paul F. Koehneke acknowledged that objection had been raised to calling the Lutheran Church *the true visible church*. To the critics who would substitute the indefinite article he addressed the question, "Where is there another church body on earth which is orthodox to the same extent as the Lutheran Church is? We do not deny the possibility, but at present we know of none."[2] The natural result of this attitude among Lutherans was a readiness to equate difference with error.

The second characteristic affecting the perception of Lutherans was the emphasis they placed on the doctrine of justification by faith alone. The Lutheran teaching that man is justified by faith alone was not regarded simply as *an* article of faith; it was *the* article of faith. William Arndt, a Con-

---

[1] Edwin E. Pieplow, "The Means of Grace," in *The Abiding Word,* ed. Theodore Laetsch (St. Louis: Concordia, 1947), II, 322.

[2] "The Evangelical Lutheran Church, the True Visible Church of God," in *The Abiding Word,* ed. Theodore Laetsch (St. Louis: Concordia, 1946), I, 307.

cordia Seminary professor, was not exaggerating when he wrote that "in speaking of this doctrine, the Church and her eloquent theologians, like enthusiastic organists, pull all the stops and play fortissimo."[3] Among Lutherans justification by faith was referred to as *articulus stantis et cadentis ecclesiae,* the article by which the church stands and falls.[4]

The two beliefs, that the Lutheran Church possesses the pure and full truth and that man is justified by grace through faith alone, provided the dominant motif in Lutheran writing throughout the greater part of the period under consideration here. The theme was implicit in the editorials and articles in the Lutheran periodicals to which reference has been made in the previous chapters. In the more formal doctrinal essays and expositions of Lutheran teaching the errors of other faiths were cited explicitly to emphasize in contrast the truth of the Lutheran doctrine. Because of the basic differences on the question of justification, Lutheran theologians made frequent reference to Roman Catholic teaching on this point. These doctrinal essays and Mayer's more extended discussion of the subject are the principal references in this chapter. It should be noted that these essays generally reflected the theological position set forth by Franz Pieper in his comprehensive *Christian Dogmatics* cited earlier. (See footnote 2, Chapter Eight.)

The starting point in discussing the matter of justification is the teaching on sin, and it is here that Lutheran differences with Roman Catholicism were seen to begin. Mayer believed that there was an irreconcilable clash between Catholicism and Lutheranism on the entire doctrine of sin. In the Lutheran view original sin means that the totality of man's nature has been corrupted. It refers to man's total depravity and

[3] "The Doctrine of Justification," *Abiding Word,* II, 236.
[4] Frederick E. Mayer, *The Religious Bodies of America* (St. Louis: Concordia, 1954), p. 142.

alienation from God, his lust, his inborn egotistic drive, "the sin which embraces everything that man thinks and does without faith in God, the sin that subjects man to God's wrath." On the other hand, Roman Catholicism thinks of original sin essentially as deprivation rather than depravity; it defines sin "chiefly in terms of isolated acts, some more, others less grievous; some venial, others mortal."[5]

As a rule Lutherans do not even distinguish between mortal and venial sins, for all sins are viewed as potentially mortal. When one accepts Christ, however, they can no longer destroy him; they become venial sins. This means, not that they are of a less sinful nature, but that they are fully pardoned. The Roman Catholic doctrine which terms a venial sin a slight offense against the law of God was regarded as vicious because "it deceives man about the enormity of his smallest sin and deadens his conscience."[6]

Mayer pointed out that Luther's divergent view of sin was at the bottom of practically all his theological controversies with Rome, especially in the areas of Christ's work, of justification, and of faith. Luther was convinced of the twofold character of sin, guilt and bondage, and he believed that Christ's work had both paid man's debt and freed him from the powers that had held him captive. Mayer saw this to be an important distinction: "This aspect of Christ's work was a complete departure from the Roman view, oriented entirely in the doctrine of righteousness by man's work as a complement to Christ's sacrifice. Roman theology rejects the forensic character of justification and views it as progressive sanctification."[7]

In the Lutheran point of view, being freed from the bond-

---

[5] *Ibid.*, pp. 49, 129.
[6] Theodore F. A. Nickel, "Sin," *Abiding Word,* II, 164.
[7] *Religious Bodies of America,* pp. 129–130.

age of sin means that man is truly liberated also from the burden of the law and is free to serve his fellowman. Good works are the natural outgrowths of the new freedom and are not oriented toward or motivated by anything legalistic. The consequences of the Catholic concept of sin were seen to be quite in contrast. Because Catholics regard sin as simply voluntary transgressions against God, they are more concerned with individual sins, and from the Lutheran point of view they "thoroughly atomize the concept of sin." Depending on the attendant circumstances, the intention, and other considerations, they have determined various categories and catalogs of sin. Thus the effect of this atomizing of sin actually amounts to a denial of the need for an absolute Redeemer. The legalistic emphasis, coupled with man's freedom of will, ascribes to him the ability to cooperate in his own salvation.[8] Accordingly, Lutherans consistently maintain that although Catholics are taught to believe in Christ, they are also taught that they can save themselves by their good works. The simplistic assertion that Lutherans believe in salvation by faith and Catholics in salvation by works rested on this interpretation of the differing teachings on sin.

The Roman Catholic concept of the grace of God was also seen to be in sharp disagreement with Lutheran, and therefore with scriptural, teaching. Lutheran theology emphasized the Reformation watchword, *sola gratia,* by maintaining that the sinner is justified solely by God's unmerited grace through faith in Christ's all-sufficient work. No matter how it was expressed, this was always the central teaching in Lutheran doctrine. But, as interpreted by Mayer, Catholicism does not accept this simple definition of grace. Either they define it as "some infused quality, virtue, or power in man," or they ascribe man's justification in part to God and in part to man.

[8] *Ibid.,* pp. 49–50.

Citing St. Augustine, Mayer argued that grace is not grace unless it is entirely grace. "Grace cannot be quartered, or halved, or treated in any piecemeal fashion. We obtain everything by grace, or we get nothing at all."[9]

In discussing the Roman Catholic teaching on the work of Christ, Mayer conceded that it might be possible for a Catholic to understand it in the truly evangelical sense and that many undoubtedly do so and rely solely on grace as God's favor in Christ's all-sufficient work.

> But the leading dogmaticians understand it to mean that Christ has gained sufficient graces (or virtues) for man, whereby men are enabled to acquire holiness and salvation by their own works. . . . While Rome today teaches that Christ is the Propitiation for both original and actual sins, it nevertheless states that Christ purposed *primarily* to remove original sin not because it is the greater sin, but because it is universal. Accordingly Roman theologians can still maintain that although Christ has removed the guilt of original sin, the expiation of actual sins is primarily man's own obligation.[10]

In his essay on "The Grace of God" Theodore Hoyer accused Catholics of confusing the cause and the effect of saving grace. It is scriptural teaching that God does impart to man the quality by which he can and does love God, and this quality is called grace. But it is an effect of saving grace, not saving grace itself. The fundamental error of Catholics, according to Hoyer, is that they make the *effects* of divine grace in man the basis of his justification and salvation. In so doing they undermine the very foundation on which our justification and salvation rest.[11]

Mayer acknowledged that the various points of view repre-

[9] *Ibid.*, p. 127.
[10] *Ibid.*, p. 51.
[11] *Abiding Word*, II, 202–203.

sented among Roman Catholic theologians show some inconsistency and disagreement on the matters of justification and grace, but he suggested that the scriptural teaching can never be reached because of the definite limitations prescribed by the necessity of adhering to the Tridentine decrees. He pointed out that the distinction between *actual* and *sanctifying* grace seems to be receiving greater emphasis. Modern Roman Catholic theologians, he said, seem to be leaning toward ascribing as much as possible to God and as little as possible to man, and generally they hold that for all "salutary acts" actual grace is absolutely necessary. Actual grace in this sense refers to grace that is intrinsically efficacious, bestowed gratuitously as a gift of God. Even though modern Roman Catholic theology ascribes the granting of such grace, the beginning of faith, exclusively to God, Mayer contended that "the standard doctrine that man's justification is dependent on his good works is not in the least modified," principally because it does not exclude human merit and allows for the possibility of human cooperation.[12]

In contrast to the Lutheran doctrine of justification, in which it is taught that "God imputes Christ's all-sufficient sacrifice to the sinner and thereby forgives all his sin or declares him just," Roman Catholic doctrine, according to Mayer, distinguishes between forgiveness, which is the eradication of sin, and justification, a moral change. It teaches that because of the merits of Christ God bestows a supernatural quality upon the soul which makes man just and an heir of heaven. The infusion of this grace completely changes the sinner from an unjust to a just person.[13]

Lutheran criticism of Roman Catholic teaching on grace was three-pronged. Naturally they judged it to be unscriptural

---

[12] *Religious Bodies of America,* pp. 52–53.
[13] *Ibid.,* pp. 54–55.

and therefore in error. Furthermore, they repeatedly denounced the official condemnation of the Lutheran doctrine at the Council of Trent. One writer remarked that the Roman Catholic Church is not alone in its "officially avowed opposition to the Scriptural doctrine that justifying or saving faith is essentially confidence, trust, in the atoning work of Christ as set forth in the Gospel." But, he added, no other church "has gone to the extreme of cursing and damning this teaching."[14]

The third criticism of Roman Catholic doctrine was that because it teaches that a man must be saved by his own works, it is of necessity a theology of doubt. So many conditions and restrictions determine the meritoriousness of a work that a Catholic can never be sure of his salvation.[15] Theodore Hoyer commented that although they teach that God will be gracious, they require that a person must do penances and good works to show that he is worthy of divine grace.

> God will be gracious to you if you repent and lead a respectable life. That means—doesn't it?—Heaven's gates are open; God invites you to come; but when you get there, you are told: Entrance costs you so and so much; you must pay remorse, repentance, good works, before you can enter.

This teaching, he said, denies the universality of divine grace and makes it conditional. In so doing the papacy deliberately keeps people in doubt and terror of conscience.

> The careless, the indifferent are not greatly disturbed, it is true; but the best among them, those who are seriously concerned about their salvation, suffer under the thought: Before you can rely on God's promises and comfort in the assurance of His grace, you must do your part and prove that you are worthy of receiving His grace. . . . No doubt

---

[14] Edwin L. Wilson, "Faith," *Abiding Word,* I, 202–203.
[15] Mayer, *Religious Bodies of America,* pp. 55–56.

many souls who are nominally members of the Roman Church, and others who teach that error, by a fortunate inconsistence actually do rely on the grace of God in Christ. . . . But for the soul that follows such teaching only two ways are open: Either despair, because he cannot do what is required of him, or self-righteous reliance on his own works, which again will cost him his salvation.[16]

Another writer asserted that in Roman Catholic theology *sola gratia* had been replaced by *monstrum incertitudinis* and that therefore "precious souls are driven back to slave under the lash of the Law, where there is no certainty of salvation, nay, where there is no salvation at all!"[17]

William Arndt, in commenting on the uncertainty that results from failure to distinguish between justification and sanctification, insisted that this is not merely an unfortunate departure from correct terminology. Although it is of the gravest consequence, he saw it to be in keeping with the general tendency of Catholic theology "which avoids leading the Christian to joyous certainty concerning his state of grace."[18] In contrasting this characteristic of Roman Catholic teaching with Lutheran teaching James Manz noted that although there are warnings in Scripture against falling away, and although we must guard against a false sense of security, "rightly understood the Christian's assurance of salvation is a most precious and strengthening truth in times of pain, trial, and heartache."[19]

In their respective theologies both Lutherans and Catholics recognize that if sinners are to profit by the merits of Christ's work and resurrection, they must in some way receive them

---

[16] "The Grace of God," *Abiding Word,* II, 225–226.
[17] A. E. Wagner, "The Certainty of Salvation," *Abiding Word,* I, 225–226.
[18] "The Doctrine of Justification," *Abiding Word,* II, 254.
[19] "Can I Be Sure of Salvation?" *Lutheran Witness,* LXXXI (March 6, 1962), 101.

directly. The means by which God imparts Christ's merits have come to be known among Lutherans as the means of grace. In Lutheran theology the means of grace are the gospel and the sacraments.

The phrase "means of grace" is used less precisely in Roman Catholic theology. Theodore Graebner declared that a "farrago of unprofitable, self-contradictory, man-made dogmas" had been substituted for the simple means of grace. Included in the list he quoted from a Catholic textbook were prayer, sacraments, sacramentals, religious ceremonies, genuflections, vestments, liturgy, processions, pilgrimages, the ecclesiastical year with its holy days, rogation days, the Corpus Christi, the devotion of the Sacred Heart, and the entire system of seasons and days.[20]

The differences over the means of grace are far more significant than mere problems of definition or terminology. Not only do Lutherans insist that the means of grace must be limited to the Word and sacraments but they disagree with Catholics over the use of the Word and the celebration of the sacraments. In listing the means of grace in Catholic theology Graebner noted that one was conspicuously absent— the Word.[21] This was generally regarded by Lutherans as being consistent with the theology of the church on the question of grace; if forgiveness is not dependent on what God does, there is no need for the sinner to hear what God says. It is the satisfaction that he can render that earns him merit, and for this he does not need the Word of God.

> The Roman Church does not believe in the efficacy of the Word of God. It is not a means of grace to the poor deluded followers of Rome. Rome denies that God offers

[20] "The Means of Grace in Roman Theology," *Concordia Theological Monthly,* X (April, 1939), 241, 250.
[21] *Ibid.,* p. 242.

in the Word the grace which Christ merited. . . . Therefore the preaching of the Word of God has rarely found a place in the service of the Catholic Church. We hear the priest mumbling Latin prayers, chanting Latin liturgies, we see him swinging incense before the altar, we hear him reading Mass, but we strain our ears in vain to hear him preach the Gospel.

. . . If the Bible contained only the Law of God, the Pope and his henchmen would not be so eager to suppress it. But the Bible contains also the Gospel, and that is what makes it so dangerous to Rome.[22]

Concerning the sacraments as means of grace Lutherans were in general disagreement with Roman Catholic doctrine, and their teaching was at specific variance on the two rites designated as sacraments by both churches. In Lutheran teaching, the necessity of faith in making beneficial use of the Word and the sacraments is stressed. It is taught that the Word both requires and engenders faith, and the sacraments are regarded as the "visible" Word. Because the Spirit is always present in the Word and the sacraments, they are always efficacious regardless of man's attitude, but their salutary use requires that the recipients believe.[23] Lutherans therefore rejected the Roman Catholic teaching that the sacraments contain the grace which they represent and that they bestow it *ex opere operato,* "in virtue of the act performed." The salutary effect, according to Catholicism, does not depend on the faith of the recipient. Yet, depending on the specific sacrament, worthy reception depends on receiving it in the right disposition. The requirements vary according to the specific sacrament.[24]

The second criticism of Roman Catholic teaching on the

---

[22] Pieplow, "The Means of Grace," *Abiding Word*, II, 336.
[23] Mayer, *Religious Bodies of America,* p. 159.
[24] *Ibid.*, pp. 57–60.

sacraments concerned what Mayer called the "integral relation between Rome's sacramentalism and sacerdotalism."
With the exception of baptism and matrimony the sacraments
may be administered only by those who have qualified by taking holy orders; they are nevertheless necessary for salvation.
This places the salvation of each individual in the hands of
the hierarchy. By wielding the power of the interdict the
church can in theory at least force all of its members to conform to its demands.[25]

The doctrine of intention was a third point at which Lutheran observers directed their attacks. Mayer accused
Roman Catholic theologians of inconsistency. On the one
hand, in his interpretation, they claim that the objective efficacy of a sacrament is assured by the *opus operatum* theory,
but on the other they make the efficacy dependent on the disposition of both the administrant and the recipient. Although
attempts have been made to give reassurances to those in
doubt about the intention of the priest from whom the sacrament was received, such reassurances, according to Mayer,
run counter to papal and conciliar decisions. If this is so, a
person can never be really sure that the sacrament was validly
administered. True objectivity and real certainty, in the
Lutheran view, can be obtained only when the heart relies
firmly on the promises of God.[26]

Roman Catholic teaching on the Lord's Supper, or the
Eucharist, provoked three objections from Lutherans, all
three of which were responses to teachings derived from
the doctrine of transubstantiation. According to this doctrine
the act of consecration by the priest permanently changes the
bread and wine into the body and blood of Christ. Two of
the teachings that have developed out of this doctrine require
little more than mention: withholding of the cup from the

[25] *Ibid.*, p. 58.
[26] *Ibid.*, pp. 59–61.

laity and adoration of the Eucharist under its aspect as Real Presence. Although they were frequently attacked, they did not prompt much serious consideration among Lutherans. They were flatly rejected as unscriptural.[27] Mayer attributed their inclusion in Roman Catholic teaching to "a definite trend of Romanticism in Roman theology, which attempts to objectify and materialize the spiritual without sacrificing the mysterious and miraculous." The Eucharist therefore provides a way of bringing the supernatural Christ physically into the world.

Most seriously criticized was the third teaching, that the Eucharist is offered by man to God for the sins of the living and of the dead, and thus, as Lutherans saw it, in some way adding to the once-and-for-all sacrifice of Jesus on Golgotha. According to Mayer this teaching, the "heart and core of the Roman cultus," rests on the belief that man stands in a three-fold relationship of obligation to God. He is God's creature, he is a sinner, and he is the recipient of God's blessings. In each of these relations he owes God something. Prayers and good works are figurative sacrifices, but they are insufficient. An actual sacrifice is required as a sensible gift and serves as a recognition of God's supreme dominion and an appeasement to his anger. Mayer described in some detail the arguments used to support the sacrifice of the Mass, and the supposed benefits derived from it. Probably because he concluded that this teaching had no scriptural foundation, he did not bother to refute it.[28]

This teaching was nevertheless attacked frequently by Lutheran writers. Representative of the Lutheran criticism was that expressed by James Manz. He contended that it

---

[27] For examples of Lutheran criticism see Ottomar O. Krueger, "The Lord's Supper," in *The Abiding Word* (St. Louis: Concordia, 1960), III, 448–454; and Carl A. Eberhard, "The Lord's Supper," *Witness*, LXXIX (November 15, 1960), 598–599.

[28] *Religious Bodies of America*, pp. 63–72.

"overshadows and colors all the truths still held by Rome." According to Manz, in changing the Lord's Supper from a gift of God into an act of man, it represents, as Luther said, the whole work-righteousness orientation of Roman Catholicism. Furthermore, the faith that should be directed toward Jesus Christ alone is focused on the act of sacrifice.[29]

Several Lutherans took exception to the view that the sacrifice in the Mass is completely objectionable and should be condemned outright. Jaroslav Pelikan observed that when it is stated carefully that the daily offering up of the body of Christ is a "re-presentation" by which the Christian continues to plead the merits of the perfect sacrifice, the practice may not seem as dangerous as most Protestants make it. But, he added, it is usually not stated that carefully, and it has now in effect become an extension or repetition of that sacrifice. He contended that the fine distinction between these interpretations had been obscured partially through the emphasis placed on the Mass at the expense of communion.[30] Arthur Carl Piepkorn, while rejecting the idea that the celebration of the Holy Eucharist is an expiatory sacrifice that can be applied to the sins of the living and the dead, asserted that the idea of sacrifice should not be completely ruled out. The very name Holy Eucharist indicates that it is properly regarded as a sacrifice of praise and thanksgiving, a Eucharistic sacrifice.[31]

[29] "The Sacrifice of the Mass," *Witness,* LXXXI (April 3, 1962), 167.
[30] *The Riddle of Roman Catholicism,* New York: Abingdon Press, 1959), pp. 117–118. The "re-presentation" should not be understood in the Reformed sense of "representation."
[31] "Sacrament, Sacrifice, and Stewardship," *Una Sancta,* XVIII (St. Simon and St. Jude, Apostles, 1961), 16–25; originally presented as the doctrinal essay at the 1960 convention of the Michigan District of the Lutheran Church-Missouri Synod.

Another Lutheran theologian suggested that there was some room for further discussion and possible agreement on this point. Berthold von Schenk expressed his views in an address to a colloquy of Protestants and Catholics in 1960. Referring to the Order of Holy Communion as the Lutheran Mass, he alleged that although it is centered on justification, it is also sacrificial as well as sacramental. Although his argumentation on this point is not clear, he suggested later that the Catholic position has been pushed too far by "well-meaning but misdirected people" and that the position taken at Trent would allow for the idea that the sacrifice in the Mass is the visible sacrifice human nature requires as representative or commemorative of the one great sacrifice: "In this manner the Holy Mass in no wise takes away from that sacrifice of Jesus Christ. Furthermore, the sacrificial gift and the sacrificing priest are the same as on the cross, for it is one and the same sacrificial gift." The manner is different, but it is in effect the same sacrifice once offered on the cross. "This is the total offering which happened in history, and in the Mass this Offering is represented." Von Schenk believed that a reevaluation of their positions by both sides could lead to a better understanding on this point.[32]

The differences over the sacrament of baptism were not as pronounced, and therefore they were not discussed as frequently, but differences nevertheless did prevail. J. T. Mueller argued that even though Catholics baptize according to the proper forms, they have perverted the doctrine "so greatly that it is only by the grace of God and contrary to Rome's teaching if a baptized Romanist finds comfort in his Baptism." The three objections he offered were (1) the *ex opere*

---

[32] "Factors That Unite Us: Protestant," in *Christians in Conversation,* ed. Peter W. Bartholome (Westminster, Maryland: The Newman Press, 1962), pp. 67–78.

operato principle eliminates the doctrine of salvation by faith; (2) by teaching that baptism wipes out all original sin they in effect are teaching that the evil lusts and desires remaining in the baptized are no longer sin, and they are thus giving him a sense of "carnal security"; (3) by teaching that by committing a mortal sin the baptized person breaks the baptismal covenant and must turn to the sacrament of penance for his salvation.[33] These views may have been commonly held, but the fact that they were infrequently expressed suggests that Lutherans generally were not greatly disturbed about Roman Catholic teaching on Baptism.

One additional subject related to the larger question of sin, grace, and justification remains to be mentioned. Walter F. Wolbrecht aptly summarized the Lutheran attitude on the doctrine of purgatory:

> The Lutheran Church today just as determinedly as the Lutheran Church of the Reformation era opposes the purgatory of Rome as a devilish device of the Antichrist, which has nothing but garbled Bible passages, questionable proofs from the Apocrypha, fallacious proofs from reason, and no proofs from Scripture to back it.[34]

Manz reflected a traditional Lutheran inference when he noted that there is "little doubt that financial gain through masses for the dead in purgatory fostered the spread of this practice." In commenting on the daily Masses he asked, "And who can say how much money pours into the Church of Rome as a result of this false, unbiblical doctrine?" His main criticisms of the purgatory doctrine were that it tends to keep people in the church on a false principle by inducing them to pray for the dead, that it inclines to dull the sense of Christian propriety because it allows for purification after death, and

[33] "Holy Baptism," *Abiding Word,* II, 409.
[34] "The Doctrine of the Last Things," *Abiding Word,* I, 559.

that it tends to obscure and destroy faith in Jesus Christ as the real source of salvation.[35]

Other Roman Catholic teachings and practices related to the central question also received extensive treatment in Lutheran literature. There is no need here to discuss such things as indulgences, the treasury of merits, and penance. From the Lutheran point of view it was charged that they all provide the wrong answers to the central question and therefore detract from the work that Christ has done for man. They merely provide additional evidence, of which enough has already been cited, to support Mayer's conclusion:

> Lutheranism and Romanism are poles apart in the doctrine of justification, and there can never be rapprochement as long as this wide theological chasm remains concerning such vital points as the author of our justification; the nature and function of faith; the meaning of grace; the Scriptural definition of justification; the relation of justification to sanctification.[36]

---

[35] "Is There a Purgatory?" *Witness,* LXXXI (April 17, 1962), 186–187.
[36] *Religious Bodies of America,* p. 56.

11

MARY: CHRISTIAN PROTOTYPE
OR COREDEMPTRIX?

As JUDGED BY Lutherans, the culmination of the false
teachings of the Roman Catholic Church lies in its dogmas
on the Blessed Virgin Mary. They appear to Lutherans to
have no foundation in Scripture and only dubious support in
tradition. The antichristian papacy has furthermore fostered
and cultivated devotion to Mary to such dimensions that it
detracts from the redemptive work of Christ and raises the
real possibility that coredemption by Mary may be proclaimed an article of Roman Catholic faith. It therefore constitutes nothing less than a direct attack on the scriptural
teaching that man can find salvation only through the merits
of Christ.

The broader matter of veneration of saints and relics also
received a considerable measure of criticism and scorn from
Lutherans. The various practices allowed and advocated by
the Roman Catholic Church were condemned as superstitious, idolatrous, and paganistic, and were sometimes taken
as evidence that these terms applied also with full force to
the church itself.[1] But the veneration of Mary, resulting in her
elevation to an extremely lofty position, was taken much more
seriously and was frequently denounced by Lutherans as
"Mariolatry."

The unacceptability of much Roman Catholic teaching on

[1] See for example Theodore Engelder, "Papists and Other Idola-
ters," *Concordia Theological Monthly,* II (August, 1931), 622–
625; also Theodore Graebner, "Superstition," *Lutheran Witness,*
XXXIX (November 23, 1920), 378.

Mary can best be understood when it is seen as the com-
pound, consummate error in Catholic theology. The compos-
ite judgment of Catholic Mariology by Lutheran theologians
showed it to be unscriptural, a product of papal pre-
sumption, and a denial of the doctrine of justification. An
analysis of the various aspects of this judgment reveals the
intensity of the antipathy among Lutherans to this aspect of
Catholicism.

The general charge that the teachings on Mary were unscriptural rested on two criticisms. First, Lutherans asserted
that the elaborate Mariology that had been developed simply
lacks foundation in Scripture. It is nothing more than "teaching for doctrines the commandments of men."[2] But more
important, it amounts to a perversion of true scriptural
teaching. In discussing the possibility that the coredemption
of Mary might be proclaimed as dogma, Roland Seboldt
acknowledged that Catholics attempt to establish some
ground in Scripture for the development of Mariology, just
as they try to give all their teachings some scriptural base. But
he showed how this can be done only by relying on papal
elaborations concerning biblical references to Mary.[3] When
a given doctrine lacks the support of a direct scriptural statement, it may be that it is "clearly implied in the light of what
the church has clarified."[4] Seboldt analyzed the Scripture
texts used by Mariologists to support the idea of Mary's coredemption and found that without the papal explanations they
all failed to support the interpretations given them. He concluded that if these texts are interpreted to bring out their
intended meaning, one will find that there is no proof of any
special relations between Jesus and Mary during his earthly

[2] William Arndt, "The Assumption of Mother Mary," *Concordia Theological Monthly,* XII (November, 1941), 872.
[3] *Christ or Mary?* (St. Louis: Concordia, 1963), pp. 29–33.
[4] *Ibid.,* p. 7.

career and that the gospels show forth the glory of Christ, not of Mary as Catholics would have it. The Catholic Mary is therefore not the Mary of the Scriptures. "The theological traditions have overshadowed the beautiful Mary of the Scriptures, the chosen instrument for the Incarnation. The Roman Catholic view is not that of the historical Mary, but the 'theological' Mary, who plays a significant role in the salvation of mankind."[5] The Scripture texts analyzed by Seboldt had been discussed frequently by earlier Lutheran writers who had drawn similar conclusions.

Absence of biblical foundation for the teachings on Mary automatically precludes the possibility of acceptance by Lutherans, but nevertheless some Lutheran writers attempted to determine the extent of support the church's tradition provides for the continuing Mariological development. Seboldt called attention to several apocryphal references that had a direct influence on it, but he found that Mary played no special role in postapostolic times. He thought it to be significant that she is included in the Apostles' Creed, along with Pilate, as a witness to the true humanity of Jesus, but with no separate honor of her own. The early fathers Justin Martyr, Irenaeus, and Tertullian had developed the parallel between Eve and Mary similar to the one drawn by Paul between Adam and Christ, but the first real move to elevate Mary to a special position Seboldt attributed to the ascetic ideals of the fourth century, when the virginity of Mary was in the process of acquiring a value in itself.[6]

The first real turning point in the church's attitude toward Mary, according to Seboldt, came in 431 A.D. with the decision at the Council of Ephesus that Mary was indeed *Theotokos,* the Mother of God. Although the purpose of the decision was to stress that Christ is truly God, not to glorify Mary,

[5] *Ibid.,* pp. 46–51.
[6] *Ibid.,* pp. 10–11.

it opened the way for further Mariological development in the subsequent centuries. In 649 A.D., at the First Lateran Council, the perpetual virginity of Mary became a dogma. During this time both the immaculate conception and the assumption of Mary began to achieve some acceptance. The veneration of Mary had been firmly established by the end of the eighth century and was widely practiced during the Middle Ages.

The second major point in the development of the church's Marian teachings came in 1854 with pronouncement of the dogma of the immaculate conception in the papal bull *Ineffabilis Deus*. From this point on, as described by Seboldt, the discussion has turned to Mary's coredemptive role, an idea that has been gaining support in Roman Catholic circles. It was given specific impetus in 1950 by the proclamation of the dogma of the bodily assumption of Mary into heaven, the third peak in the development of Mariology.[7]

Most other writers were neither as informed nor as careful as Seboldt in discussing the part played by tradition in the growing veneration of Mary. One, in commenting on the 1950 pronouncement, *Munificentissimus Deus*, which made the assumption of Mary an official dogma, traced the idea back to a reference made in 400 A.D. to a legend that Mary had been taken mysteriously into heaven. He thought it was strange that four centuries should have elapsed between the event and the first known reference to it. The elaboration on that legend came 200 years later by Gregory of Tours, who gave no source for his information. By the mid-eighteenth century it had gained enough support to be declared a pious opinion; in 1950, by a "diabolical alchemy" and a mighty "presto," a fiction became a fact.[8] Another tract by the

[7] *Ibid.,* pp. 11–23.
[8] [Herman W. Gockel], "Proclaiming Fiction a Fact" (St. Louis: Concordia, n.d. [1951]), 8-page tract.

same author shows how Lutherans were unable to compre-
hend the concept of tradition in Roman Catholic theology:
"Some early church fathers who wrote learned essays on the
subject of theology found it hard to believe that Jesus, the
sinless Son of God, could have been born of a sinful mother.
Somehow that just couldn't be!" By ignoring the specific teaching on the immaculate conception, the writer attempted to
show the logical necessity of proclaiming Mary's parents
sinless also.[9] In similar fashion the writer of a booklet, *The
Truth About the Virgin Mary,* tried to argue that, according
to logic, if Mary was holy she could not have died. The
Roman Catholic acknowledgment that she did indeed die
should therefore be taken as proof that she was not holy.[10]

The particular situations that prompted these men to write
had so agitated them that they were not able to discuss the
problem detachedly. Furthermore, along with most other
Lutheran observers, they were not familiar enough with
Roman Catholic theology and its principles to be able to comment on the Mariological development in an informed manner. More knowledgeable writers did not concern themselves
so much with challenging the alleged support in tradition for
the new doctrines on Mary. They simply described how,
through a blending of reason and the exercise of papal
powers, reinforced by popular piety and hierarchical pressures, doctrines on Mary had developed and might develop
further in the future.

Frederick Mayer, for example, asserted flatly that there is
a total lack of scriptural and historical evidence for the dogma

[9] [Herman W. Gockel], "Was Mary Born Without Sin?" (St.
Louis: Concordia, n.d. [1953]), 6-page tract. These two tracts
were very widely distributed; more than 700,000 copies were
sold by Concordia Publishing House.
[10] Paul E. Schuessler, *The Truth About the Virgin Mary* (St.
Louis: Concordia, n.d.), pp. 9–10.

of the assumption.[11] Therefore reason must be called in:

> The dogma of Mary's Assumption is supported by the following syllogism: It is not fitting that the Mother of God be contaminated by sin. In view of His future suffering, Christ preserved her from original sin. Having no sin, she was immortal by absolute right, but sharing in all the work of Christ, she was united with Him in His death and likewise in His ascension.[12]

He then described the "theological" grounds advanced by Roman Catholic theologians to support the dogma of the assumption. Since they have already established that Mary was sinless, they can argue that she was not subject to death as punishment. In fact, as the Mother of God, she had a supernatural claim to a complete exemption from the necessity of death. Her death was necessary only as evidence that she was not greater than her Son and that as her nature was truly human, so also was the nature of her divine Son. Her assumption into heaven after her death spared her the degrading decomposition of the body that is the penalty and curse of sin. Because of her relation to Jesus she must of necessity be spared this corruption. The idea of her incorruption was supported by the belief in her perpetual virginity, and since incorruptibility and resurrection are correlative concepts, death simply could not hold her body until the resurrection of all

[11] *The Religious Bodies of America* (St. Louis: Concordia, 1954), p. 111.

[12] *Ibid.*, p. 44. Mayer had anticipated the dogma of the assumption in "The Dogma of Mary's Assumption: A Symptom of Antichristian Theology," *Concordia Theological Monthly,* XXI (March, 1950), 181–189. Here he discussed the procedure by which it would become dogma as being symptomatic of Rome's *formal* and *material* principles, that is, that the church establishes doctrine above and contrary to Scriptures and it directs its faithful to seek their salvation by means beyond Christ alone.

mankind. On such rationalistic "theological" arguments the doctrine of the assumption rests.[13]

But in additon to reason another element was needed. The second general criticism of Lutherans was that for Mariological development to proceed, it depended on the encouragement and sanction of the papacy and ultimately on the dogmatic pronouncements of the popes, for scriptural statements on Mary had to be studied in the light of papal statements.[14] As tradition evolved and new dogmas were added, more papal statements provided further light for additional interpretations. Seboldt described how this was happening currently in regard to the proposed dogma of the coredemption of Mary.

> The present status of coredemption leaves room to pursue theological studies according to the pattern of the centuries. Pious ideas and tradition form a basis of study. Detailed scholarship on the question follows. After many efforts of scholarship have been published, appeals are made to the papacy for a dogmatic definition. After the question is generally accepted, a papal proclamation follows, defining the dogma. This was precisely the pattern for the dogma of the immaculate conception in 1854, and for the assumption in 1950. The question of the coredemption is in the pattern now.

Not only is the pattern being followed, Seboldt observed, but when the current studies have run their course, the culmination will be another papal definition, another dogma, and an even greater climax in the development of the Mary cult.[15]

The papal action in each case in which a pious opinion has been elevated to the status of dogma has not been prompted solely by theological studies. Popular piety and pressures

[13] *Ibid.*, pp. 111–112.
[14] Seboldt, *Christ or Mary?*, p. 6.
[15] *Ibid.*, pp. 57–58.

from the hierarchy have given the pope added impetus to make his pronouncements. In 1945, according to the *Concordia Theological Monthly, America* pleaded with its readers to request the Holy Father to make the doctrine of Mary's assumption an official dogma, and it complained that the movement toward this end had received little support in the United States.[16] The next year Arndt reported that the pope was listening to opinions on when the assumption should be made dogma.[17] After the pronouncement Mayer wrote that the church had abandoned even its theoretical reliance on Scripture and tradition as sources for its teachings and substituted for them the current views of the hierarchy. The pope did not proclaim the dogma of the assumption until a poll of the hierarchy showed that they favored it.[18]

This development was seen to lead to the third evil in the development of Mariological doctrine. Mayer concluded that Mariology is a denial of Christology and therefore is mythology. For the first time a myth has become a dogma of the church, which makes "the chasm between Roman theology and Bible-centered theology . . . absolutely unbridgeable."[19] Four years earlier he had written: "The fact dare not be overlooked that Rome does direct the sinner to Christ. It is still a Christian Church. But it is a miracle of God's grace that Romanists still find Christ as the only and all-sufficient Redeemer under the mass of Mariological appendage."[20] He never withdrew the earlier judgment, but it must have been severely tested in his mind as devotion to Mary increased. In

[16] J. T. Mueller, "The Dogma of the Assumption," *Concordia Theological Monthly,* XVI (December, 1945), 873–875.
[17] "The Assumption of Mother Mary," *Concordia Theological Monthly,* XVII (November, 1946), 862.
[18] "The Dogmatic Foundation for Rome's Marian Cult," *Concordia Theological Monthly,* XXV (June, 1954), 468–471.
[19] *Ibid.*
[20] "The Dogma of Mary's Assumption," 187.

fact, Roman Catholic teaching on Mary was a constant source of puzzlement to all Lutherans. They simply could not reconcile the devotion to Mary with Christian teaching. For them it was a question of Christ *or* Mary, not Christ *and* Mary. Addressing prayers to her was interpreted simply as substituting her for Christ as mediator. Substitution of any human for Christ was seen as a clear attack on the doctrine of justification.

Sincere and informed Catholics must have been puzzled by the attitude of Lutherans toward their veneration of Mary. Catholics insist that the purpose of giving honor to Mary is to enhance, not to diminish, the glory of Christ. Even in speaking of her as a mediator, Catholics deny any intention of substituting her for Jesus. The veneration of Mary, in their view, is a direct way of worshiping Christ. Why should Lutherans not accord her the same position and the same honor? Why should they be so severely critical of Catholics who give the Blessed Mother her due? Part of the answer has already been given. Lutherans rejected the sources of authority upon which Mariology had been built, and they denied the prerogative of the papacy in promoting it. But there was more to it than this.

For one thing, Lutherans did not see any need for raising Mary to a position above that clearly ascribed to her in the Bible. If it were a fact that Mary was sinless, surely the Scriptures would say so. She was given her role to perform, and she did so with dignity and humility. That Jesus was born of a sinful mother adds, in fact, to the assurance that he was born for all mankind. "It belongs to the humiliation of the Son of Man that Mary was born a sinful being. We need not misinterpret the Scripture by claiming for her a sinlessness and holiness."[21]

[21] Carl S. Meyer, "Born of Mary for All," *Witness*, LXXVII (December 2, 1958), 572.

Lutherans believe that Mary should be called blessed, not because of her own grace or achievement, but because God did a great work through her:

> She is not venerated as the virgin mother of God who dispenses her grace together with that of Christ to men, but she is held in honor as the servant who was granted the grace of bearing our Savior into human flesh and life. . . . In calling her blessed we ascribe all glory to God for his grace working in her life as the mother of the God-man, Jesus Christ.[22]

In addition, as Lutherans looked at Roman Catholic teaching and practice it was difficult for them to find the distinction between veneration, superveneration, and worship that is technically made in Roman Catholic theology. It appeared to them that Mary had been placed on the same level as Christ. They were repulsed by the popular sentimental piety of Catholics in their devotion to Mary. Incidents, remarks, and publications intended to promote this kind of piety rankled them. An example of such promotion was seen in Bishop Fulton Sheen's comment that Mary is the mother of all of us, for if we must be born again, how can we be born again without a mother? This assertion was labeled "Mariolatry."[23] Jaroslav Pelikan contended that the theologians and the hierarchy, the very ones who ought to watch and to warn against excesses in sentimental piety, were themselves guilty of encouraging it. He referred to the alleged visions of Pius XII in the week that he proclaimed the dogma of the assumption.[24] The prayer composed by the pope in honor of Mary's assumption was disturbing to Lutherans. One writer remarked that

[22] Seboldt, *Christ or Mary?*, p. 56.
[23] Paul M. Bretscher, "Mariology and Mariolatry," *Concordia Theological Monthly*, XXV (February, 1954), 150–153.
[24] *The Riddle of Roman Catholicism* (New York: Abingdon Press, 1959), p. 140.

Hollywood could not have done better in its adulation of a cinema starlet.[25] The entire text of the prayer was included in a footnote in Mayer's *Religious Bodies of America*.[26]

By describing the forms that veneration of Mary takes in Roman Catholic piety, Seboldt emphasized the extent to which the stated theology of the highly trained professional, who may make the proper distinctions in the understanding of Mary, is at variance with Marian devotional life:

> Though even her role in redemption is proclaimed to be "subordinate," in practice she receives the worship of the richest liturgical content, along with special festivals. The veneration of Mary is addressed to the person of Mary, the Heart of Mary, the image of Mary, to the name of the most holy Mary. Daily devotions to her are practiced: the Ave Maria, Salve Regina, Angelus Domini or Regina Coeli, the Litany, the little Office of the Madonna, the Rosary, the Crown of Seven Sorrows. Saturday is dedicated to Mary as Sunday is to Christ. May, September, and October are consecrated to her. The annual feasts of the Annunciation, Immaculate Conception, and Assumption are high festivals. Perpetual worship of Mary is the project to which special orders are consecrated. Marian congresses are devoted to the glorification of Mary. Such devotion to the Virgin gives strong evidence that in practice she is elevated above the subordinate role almost to the level of equality with God.[27]

Pelikan pointed out that just as the dogma of the Roman Catholic Church has always run the danger of glorifying Christ so much that it separates him from the humanity he was to save, so it is running a similar danger in glorifying Mary. Increasingly the attributes ascribed to her seem closer to those of Christ than to those of common mortals.[28]

[25] Schuessler, *The Truth About the Virgin Mary*, p. 25.
[26] Pp. 112–113.
[27] *Christ or Mary?*, p. 44.
[28] *Riddle of Roman Catholicism*, p. 137.

James Manz warned of a further danger in addressing prayers to Mary. True prayers should be offered to God in Christ's name, but prayers to her tend to center man's thoughts on himself, for a person can request Mary's favor, help, and intercession without a sense of repentance and without faith in Jesus Christ. Such prayers tend to replace Christ as the Judge, Savior, and Hearer of prayer.[29]

A further reason for the criticism of the Marian teachings lay in the sincere concern over the consequences to which they might lead and, in fact, appeared to be leading already. Lutheran writers pondered the serious effect that they might have on the future of Roman Catholic theology and on Lutheran teaching and practice. The concern for Roman Catholic theology was that the trend would continue in the direction that it had been going for centuries: moving further and further away from scriptural teaching, depending increasingly on reason, popular piety, and papal pronouncements, and detracting more and more from the person and work of Christ. That Mary was already regarded as having shared in Christ's redemptive work, especially in the so-called mystical experiences—birth, presentation, death, resurrection, and ascension—was readily acknowledged. Mayer called attention to the names by which Roman Catholics address her: *salvatrix, reparatrix, restauratrix, liberatrix, reconciliatrix, redemptrix.* In these capacities she is regarded, not as the cause of man's salvation, but as the mediatrix in man's redemption by Christ.[30]

After the assumption of Mary became dogma, speculation increased on the possibility that an additional pronouncement would make her officially the coredemptrix. In 1952 Julius A. Friedrich wrote in a letter to the *Concordia Theological*

[29] "The Virgin Mary," *Witness,* LXXXI (May 1, 1962), 208–209.
[30] *Religious Bodies of America,* p. 110.

Monthly that it is hardly correct to assume that "papistic Mariolatry" has culminated in the proclamation of the assumption of Mary: "Roman logic demands that two more papal bulls must follow before the . . . structure is complete, namely, one regarding Mary as Co-Redeemer . . . and another . . . as Consummator of the Trinity."[31] In 1954 it was seen as a distinct possibility that the pope might use that Marian year to proclaim in official dogma that Mary is coredemptrix.[32] Pelikan observed in 1959 that the titles comediatress and coredemptress were already being used with official approval. He intimated that the official proclamation might not be very far off.[33]

In 1963 the possibility of such action prompted publication of the little book *Christ or Mary?* Reference has already been made to some of the observations and conclusions reached by the author. Although only sixty pages in length, it is a perceptive study of Marian history and of the developments in Mariological research within Roman Catholicism that lead to the conclusion that "in the pattern of papal history, the definition of coredemption will be made." Whether it takes a decade or a century, "Mary will be declared co-redemptrix!"[34]

Such an official declaration would present an additional obstacle to faith in Christ alone and would be a direct blow at the doctrine of justification through the merits of Christ. It would necessitate what W. H. T. Dau had called "a diplomatic egg-dance of Catholic dogmaticians." This description had been used in the speculation in 1924 over the possible proclamation of the assumption of Mary. Dau said that they

[31]*Concordia Theological Monthly*, XXIII (March, 1952), 217–219.
[32] Paul M. Bretscher, "Will Mary Be Proclaimed Co-Redemptrix in 1954?" *Concordia Theological Monthly*, XXV (June, 1954), 471–473.
[33] *Riddle of Roman Catholicism*, p. 137.
[34] Seboldt, *Christ or Mary?*, p. 58.

would have to prove "that Mary is actually elevated to equal-
ity with her Son and yet is not equal to her Son, that the
Trinity has received an accession of a new element and yet
is not changed into a Holy Quartet."[35] Paul Bretscher concluded that if, by official dogma, Mary is made coredemptrix,
"the split between Roman Catholicism and Protestantism will
become absolute and the anti-Christ character of Roman
Catholic speculative theology will be past redemption."[36]

This conclusion was a bit more pessimistic than that
reached by Seboldt. He saw it as paradoxical that the development of Mariology and the expression of a new evangelical
theology bearing the theme of justification by faith should be
contemporaneous movements within Roman Catholicism.
The warm response to both the new evangelical strain and to
the Mariological developments forced him to the conclusion
that many movements, even those approaching the point of
contradiction, can grow within the church as long as they do
not challenge the absolute authority of the papacy.[37] The hope
of Lutherans has been that the evangelical ideas will attract
the greater following.

The Catholic emphasis on Mary was not without its effect
on Lutheran teaching and practice, but the nature and the
extent of that effect is difficult to assess. There is always the
danger that strong opposition to certain teachings and practice will lead to extremes in the other direction. From the
writings in Missouri Synod literature it appears that there
was no concerted effort to downgrade or destroy the honor
which Scripture accorded to Mary, but neither was there willingness to allow her any kind of special position as the mother
of Christ. One senses in surveying the bulk of literature on

[35] *Theological Monthly,* IV (February, 1924), 54.
[36] "Will Mary Be Proclaimed Co-Redemptrix in 1954?" 473.
[37] *Christ or Mary?,* pp. 5–6.

the subject that the honor that was granted her was granted with reticence.[38]

Some comments by Arthur Carl Piepkorn intimate that he believed Missouri Synod teaching was more narrow than was desirable. He criticized both excessive veneration and excessive downgrading, calling them sources of concern and scandal to Christians "who stand committed to the Book of Concord and to the Book of God." In a chapel address given at Concordia Seminary on the Feast of the Visitation and reprinted in *Una Sancta,* he asserted that the purpose of Mary in Scripture is to point to her Son and that what she reflects from his radiance is all appropriate. Then he reacted to excessive downgrading of the role of Mary:

> Nor ought we to feel any particular compulsion to execrate pious opinions long held by Christians. We need not feel obligated to blacken her reputation and to invent transgressions for her to have committed, as if somehow we were saved by the sinfulness of the Blessed Virgin rather than by the sinlessness of her Son.

In referring to Martin Luther's position on Mary, Piepkorn pointed out that although he objected to exaggerations of devotion, three years before his death Luther was still affirming in print the opinion that he had worked out in detail and with theological ingenuity twenty-five years earlier. In Luther's opinion, according to Piepkorn, "through the merits of her Son-to-be the Blessed Virgin was marvelously preserved from the taint of sin from the first moment of her existence as a human being." Piepkorn contended that pious opinions in themselves are not evil. It is only when they are elevated to the status of dogma that they must be declared antichris-

---

[38] Dr. Piepkorn has pointed out to me that the Lutheran liturgy and Lutheran hymnology pay extensive tribute to Mary. For reference see Arthur Carl Piepkorn, "Mary's Place Within the People of God," *Marian Studies,* XVIII (1967), p. 78.

tian and diabolical.[39] For these remarks Piepkorn was accused by the *Confessional Lutheran* of fostering a "Mary cult" at the St. Louis seminary.[40]

Because Piepkorn's views concerning Mary were more generous than those usually expressed in synodical literature and because he was in a position of influence as a seminary professor, it is desirable to take another look at them. An opportunity to do this was provided in a *Seminarian* article in which he discussed the attitude of the Lutheran Confessions toward Mary. He reported that the Confessions credit Mary with being worthy of highest honors; they assert that she prays for the church and that she is indeed *Theotokos*. They affirm the virgin birth, but not the immaculate conception, although Piepkorn added that Luther's private writings might allow the immaculate conception as a pious opinion. The reformers were concerned with being strictly biblical in their approach to Mary. Piepkorn believed that following the Confessions and the Bible would lead to an "evangelical Mariology," the best defense against both "the extravagance of vulgar Roman Catholic piety and the Christological corruptions of Protestantism." We would do well, he asserted, to recover the generosity characteristic of our spiritual forebears in the sixteenth and seventeenth centuries. That generosity "left room for wide differences of exegesis, pious practice, and theological opinion, as long as binding dogmas or heretical conclusions were not inferred from them."[41]

Because of their deep-seated conviction that Mariology represents the consummate error in Roman Catholic theology, it is not likely that such generosity will become widespread among Missouri Synod Lutherans. Rather to be hoped

[39] "Blessed Art Thou Among Women," *Una Sancta,* XV (Feast of the Visitation, 1958), 4–7.
[40] *Confessional Lutheran,* XIX (December, 1958), 121–130.
[41] "Eve Reversed," *Seminarian,* LI (February, 1960), 6–19.

for is that Lutherans should emphasize the real significance of Mary for Christ. Pelikan asserted that her significance is twofold. As she was truly human, she "is warrant for the Christian declaration that our Lord was a true man, flesh of our flesh and bone of our bone." As the prototype of the Christian believer she offers a splendid example to follow; her own true humanity must be recaptured by Christians today.

> Protestant thought can speak frankly about her faith and its struggles, about her apparent misunderstanding of her Son's true mission, about the refusal of Jesus to make any physical relationship to him (even hers) a mark of true blessedness, about her doubts and her victory over those doubts. These are all themes in the biblical portrait of Mary, themes which appear in the lives of Christian believers everywhere. When the New Testament urges that Christians consider the cloud of witnesses who surround them as they run the race of faith, it certainly includes the first witness of the life and work of Jesus Christ—his mother. Not as a semi-divine being, but as an outstanding member of the communion of saints, she is blessed among women.

When Protestants begin to say this out loud in their teaching and worship, Pelikan declared, they will be better prepared to deal with their Roman Catholic brethren. They will be able to say that because their regard for Mary is so deep, they must protest against the cult of the Blessed Virgin.[42] This, in a defensive sort of way, is what Lutherans have been doing. When it is done affirmatively, it stands a chance of appealing to the evangelical-minded in the Roman Catholic Church. It must also be done patiently, for the trend established in a decade of centuries will not be easily reversed.

[42] *Riddle of Roman Catholicism,* pp. 141–142.

12

TO THE EDGE OF REAPPRAISAL

THE FORTY-SEVEN-YEAR PERIOD treated in this study marks the four-hundredth anniversary of that dramatic and critical span between the hammer blows at Wittenberg and the closing of the doors at Trent. The conflict between Lutherans and Catholics that developed then has continued to the present. No one would claim now that the later period compares in importance with the former, but the story told here would not be complete without some assessment of the significance it holds for future relations between the two groups.

Circumstances in the late 1950's and early 1960's brought Lutherans to the point where they were compelled to reappraise their traditional approaches and attitudes toward Roman Catholicism. Some of the events and developments that made reappraisal necessary have already been discussed. Our chapter "Moving Toward Evangelical Concern" indicated some of the ideas of those who were particularly sensitive to the need for such reappraisal. We turn our attention now to Vatican Council II as the experience that moved Missouri Synod Lutherans, willingly or reluctantly, to the edge of reappraisal, the point at which they stood at the end of 1963.

The underlying assumption on which the traditional atttitudes and approaches of Lutherans toward Catholicism were based was that *Rome never changes*. Proclamations and pronouncements of the Roman Catholic Church of any era, for any circumstances, were assumed to remain in full effect unless they had been specifically rescinded. Any deviation from the officially stated position was regarded as a ploy by which the church hoped to gain an advantage. Those who opposed the church must ever be on the alert lest they be duped; a Roman tentacle was waiting to seize or destroy them at the first opportunity.

Any talk of reform in the Roman Catholic Church or of reunion with it was therefore easily dismissed: reform was impossible and reunion unthinkable. The very concept of reunion of Lutherans and Catholics was an abstraction, a proposition that could be dealt with only in hypothetical terms. Invitations to return to the fold of the church were treated by Lutherans with abhorrence. Sommer referred to one such invitation as "the deceitful imitation of the call of the Good Shepherd by which the sheep are to be lured into the thicket where the wolf lurks."

> Remember that a return to the Pope means a return to bondage under him who burned innocent and faithful Hus at the stake, rejoiced over the massacre of thousands of godly men and women on that bloody night of St. Bartholomew, waged cruel persecution against millions of faithful Christians in Spain, France, Germany, England, and the Netherlands till this savagery rivaled, if it did not surpass, that of the Roman emperors who hunted down the early Christians.[1]

The terms under which any reunion with Rome would have to take place were simply unacceptable, even when considered only as an abstraction. W. G. Polack made this clear in his comments on a series of prayers used in the Roman Catholic Church during the Church Unity Octave. He rejected such phrases as "communion with the Apostolic See," "submission to the authority of the Vicar of Christ," and "find their way back to the Holy Church."[2]

[1] "The Pope's Invitation," *Lutheran Witness*, XLIII (July 29, 1924), 280.
[2] "Rome and Church Unity," *Witness*, LXIV (January 30, 1945), 36.

On occasions when an invitation from the pope to all non-Catholics to reunite with the Roman Catholic Church was given a rhetorical response, that response itself was phrased in hypothetical terms. Paul M. Bretscher, a St. Louis professor, stated the Missouri Synod's position most pointedly in such a response to a papal invitation:

> We, too, deplore the schisms and divisions in Christendom, and we say with the confessors who in 1530 signed the *Augsburg Confession* . . . that "we are prepared to confer amicably concerning all possible ways and means, in order that we may come together, as far as this may be honorably done, and, the matter between us on both sides being peacefully discussed without offensive strife, the dissension, by God's help, may be done away and brought back to one true accordant religion; for as we are all under one Christ and do battle under Him, we ought to confess the one Christ . . . and everything ought to be conducted according to the truth of God."

Bretscher specified what Lutherans meant by the "truth of God" when he stated the terms under which they would take the pope's plea seriously: (1) the pope must be ready to renounce the titles and honors which he claims to hold by divine right, (2) he must be ready to declare that his position in the church is of human origin, (3) his church must disavow the dogma of infallibility of the pope, (4) he must give assurance that the bodily assumption of Mary will not be made a dogma, and (5) he must be prepared to confer with non-Catholic Christians as a brother in Christ.[3] Obviously the pope could no more readily accept these terms as a basis for discussion than Lutherans could submit completely to the papacy. Neither Lutherans nor Catholics were able to propose terms acceptable for negotiation. Even rapprochement, much less reunion, seemed out of the question.

[3] "To the Pope's Christmas Message," *Concordia Theological Monthly,* XXI (February, 1950), 134–136.

The event to which Lutherans repeatedly referred as symbolic of the unbridgeable hiatus between themselves and the Roman Catholic Church was the Council of Trent, 1545–1563. It was this council that had definitely fixed the doctrines of the church, and it was therefore taken as "an accurate portrait of the policy and purpose of Popery."

> Those doctrines and that policy show that it is unscriptural, self-righteous, superstitious and idolatrous, intolerant, and antichristian, a system that means, in its natural outworking, destruction to Christianity, Church, and State.[4]

Who would want reunion with such a church? Before such a possibility could be given even a second thought, the Roman Catholic Church would have to give definite indication of change, and *Rome never changes.*

It is therefore not surprising that Lutherans were unmoved by the flash of inspiration that prompted Pope John XXIII to announce his intention of calling an ecumenical council for the purpose of discussing reform and reunion. The aged "caretaker" pope had been in office only ninety days when he announced his decision. No one, not even Catholics, knew what to expect. The first reaction among Lutherans was skepticism mixed with caution. A month after the Pope's announcement on January 25, 1959, the Missouri Synod's President, John W. Behnken, raised some questions in the *Lutheran Witness:*

> Will it in any measure or to any degree be that "general, free, Christian Council" which the Augsburg Confession hoped for and every Lutheran must desire? Will it offer an opportunity for a full and free witness to that truth which made the Reformation necessary, the truth which alone can recreate unity according to God's good pleasure?

Indications were that the Roman Catholic Church would dominate the council, and it appeared that there would be

[4] Louis Buchheimer, "The Council of Trent," *Witness,* XXXVI (December 11, 1917), 387–388.

no intention to determine "who is right and who is wrong." Behnken therefore urged Lutherans not to set their hopes too high, to keep a sober check on their enthusiastic dreams, and to follow where the Lord leads.[5]

Lewis W. Spitz judged the decision of the Pope to be a shrewd move in line with the current popularity of ecumenicity. The Pope's council, he said, would claim its share of conversation, and Rome never misses a chance for favorable publicity. He observed that even if others would be invited, it still would not be a free council, "for at best the erring children of non-Roman churches can be invited to return to the bosom of the mother church."[6] J. T. Mueller passed along an article which recalled that Lutherans had gone to the Council of Trent because they did not want to miss the opportunity publicly to witness to the gospel. They returned home when they were not permitted to take part in the business of the council. Perhaps, suggested the writer, this should be considered in connection with the council called by Pope John.[7]

The council received little attention during the preparatory stages, but as the opening of the first session approached, Lutherans began to watch for some indication of the direction it might go. By this time they had apparently become well enough acquainted with John XXIII to look forward to it with some hope. The *Cresset,* while acknowledging that the barriers seemed insuperable, expressed some unthinkable thoughts:

> The Roman Catholic Church is our mother, from whose house we are, for the time being, absent in obedience to our Lord's demand, "He that loveth father or mother more

[5] "Pope John's Ecumenical Council," *Witness,* LXXVIII (February 24, 1959), 74.
[6] "The Pope's Council," *Concordia Theological Monthly,* XXX (May, 1959), 321–322.
[7] "The Roman Catholic Church, the Ecumenical Movement, and the World Council of Churches," *Concordia Theological Monthly,* XXXI (January, 1960), 55–56.

than me is not worthy of me." We hope for the day when the invisible fellowship which we share with all Christians will once more be a visible reality in the fellowship of one Holy, Catholic, and Apostolic Church.[8]

But the *Cresset* also revealed its Lutheran orientation by advancing an unrealistic proposal. It suggested as the starting point for discussion the doctrine of authority in the church and the whole problem of the role of Mary in the redemption drama. If the authority of Scripture and the uniqueness of Jesus Christ are not asserted, "if it concerns itself with lesser issues, we will be able to see it as nothing more than the international convention of another Christian sect."[9]

The *American Lutheran* attempted to provide its readers with information that would be helpful in understanding the council. It reported that it would be a denominational, rather than an ecumenical, council, that it would be big and would attract much attention, and that there would be something on the agenda for everyone. In listing some of the topics for consideration it observed that the principal aim was to promote the development of the Roman Catholic faith. Reunion was not the main issue, but it did not lie wholly outside the scope of the council's concerns. It urged that appeals to pray for the council be heeded.

> Our Roman Catholic-fellow-Christians are not merely neighbors; they are brothers in Christ, even though they may be separated brothers and on some doctrines heretical brothers. To the extent that the Gospel of God's grace in Christ is proclaimed as the Gospel in the Roman Catholic denomination and the sacraments are administered there as sacraments, . . . the Roman Catholic community is part of the one, holy, catholic and apostolic Church.[10]

[8] "The Vatican Council," *Cresset,* XXV (October, 1962), 4–5.
[9] *Ibid.*
[10] "The Coming Roman Catholic Council," *American Lutheran,* XLV (October, 1962), 3–5.

Writing in the *Lutheran Witness,* Curtis Huber emphasized the challenge that the council presented to Lutherans. The vigorous biblical research going on in the Roman Catholic Church was taken to mean that Lutherans would have to renew their scholarly efforts if they were to evaluate the scholarly claims of Catholics. The housecleaning in Rome, even though it was not likely to remove many offenses to the faith, served as a reminder to Lutherans of their responsibility to perfect their theology.[11]

Alfred P. Klausler, the editor of the *Walther League Messenger,* remarked that although it was too early to tell what the significance of the council would be, Lutherans should make no mistake about its importance. He indicated that there would be little chance for a radical change in doctrine but that some efforts might be made to ease tensions between Catholics and Protestants and also to heal the breach with the Eastern Orthodox Church. He warned that if any new doctrines hostile to scriptural teaching should be created, then the church "stands in danger of becoming a sect and will perhaps even read herself out of Christendom."[12]

The first session of the council apparently created enough interest among Lutherans to prompt the *Witness* to bring its readers up-to-date and to fill in details they might have missed. This task was performed by Gilbert A. Thiele of Concordia Seminary. Thiele was most impressed with the stress the council was placing on the study of Scripture for guidance, for "all doctrine and practice can only be blessed when renewed attention to God's Word becomes the order of the day." He added that no one in or out of the Roman Catholic Church should expect doctrines on Mary, the papacy, the Roman Catholic sacraments, grace, or justification, to be

[11] "The Challenge of Rome's Council," *Witness,* LXXXI (November 27, 1962), 583.
[12] *Walther League Messenger,* LXXI (December, 1962), 4.

reversed, dropped, or significantly reinterpreted. "The pope will not use his infallibility to declare himself fallible." At the same time no new doctrines on Mary or new condemnations of Protestants were expected. He commented that it was too early to speak of progress but that the course the council was taking indicated that Catholics would attempt to appear less exclusive.[13]

In the second article in the series Thiele explained the structure and operation of the council. He pointed out that showing an interest in it was not the same as glossing over the deep and abiding separation prevailing in matters of faith and practice. He proposed that Lutherans develop an attitude toward the council that would keep them from unnecessary criticism, encourage justified constructive criticism, and keep them from disappointment if the council would not bring the results for which Christians pray and work.[14]

In commenting on the work of the council the *American Lutheran* referred to the surprise of millions of non-Catholics in learning that the Roman Catholic Church is not the huge monolithic structure they had always thought, even though not much had really happened at the council. It also took favorable note of the good spirit of the increasing dialogue between Lutherans and Catholics.[15] In the same issue Richard Koenig expressed encouragement over the apparent rebuffs to Cardinal Ottaviani, the bulwark of conservatism at the council. Koenig reflected what must have been characteristic Lutheran astonishment that the central theme of "reform" was being stressed over and over again. "Who would have envisioned something like this happening ten years ago while

[13] "The Vatican Council: 1. Background," *Witness,* LXXXII (January 8, 1963), 8–9.
[14] "The Vatican Council: 2. Structure, Operation, and Results," *Witness,* LXXXII (January 22, 1963), 32–33, 46.
[15] "The State of the Church," *American Lutheran,* XLVI (January, 1963), 3–4.

Pius XII reigned?"[16] In its progress report on the council the following month the *American Lutheran* editorialized that "Rome will never be the same again" and that the freedom of speech and the differences of opinion at the council had shattered the naive myth of the monolithic uniformity of the church.[17]

Comments in the same vein continued throughout 1963. The *Concordia Theological Monthly* reprinted a perceptive article by George A. Lindbeck of the Yale Divinity School, in which he observed that the mere fact that the council had been convoked was encouraging. He suggested that there was good reason to believe that the council represented the end of the Counter-Reformation and urged Lutherans not to underestimate the council's immense transforming power.[18]

In speaking to a convention of the English District of the Missouri Synod, John H. Tietjen, editor of the *American Lutheran,* called attention to the significance of Vatican II as a renewal effort by the Roman Catholic Church. He quoted from an address by Professor Lindbeck:

> If the process which has now started continues, we may be confronted surprisingly soon with a transformed Catholicism which we shall have to recognize as much more clearly Christian than that to which we have been accustomed. In some ways and places, it may become more effective than we are in bringing the good news of love, peace and salvation to the world. Having overcome much of its authoritarian rigidity and intellectual arteriosclerosis, it may prove a much more uncomfortable and disturbing factor in our pastoral and theological work than it has been in most of the Protestant past.

[16] "One Church," *American Lutheran,* XLVI (January, 1963), 16.

[17] "Vatican II: Progress Report," *American Lutheran,* XLVI (February, 1963), 3–7.

[18] "The Second Vatican Council," *Concordia Theological Monthly,* XXXIV (January, 1963), 19–24.

Tietjen warned against both overestimating and underestimating the results of the council, and urged Lutherans to pray for it, to hope for it, and to seek to understand it.[19]

Lutherans never lost sight of the relation between John XXIII and the council. The *Witness* credited him with setting up the machinery for building bridges of understanding so that the divisive issues might be discussed without prejudice and blinding emotion.[20] At his death the *American Lutheran* commented:

> Pope John embodied the love so characteristic of his name-sake Apostle. It will be a good day for the Church of Christ everywhere if the new pope can embody the universal mission and the doctrinal depth of the apostle whose name he has chosen to bear.[21]

Much emphasis, deservingly so, has been placed on Vatican Council II as the force that compelled Lutherans to reappraise their position and attitudes toward Catholicism. But an important qualification and reminder must be interjected to keep the picture in balance. The fresh air that John XXIII had wanted to let into the Roman Catholic Church was also in the atmosphere outside Lutheran windows. Traditional attitudes and established practices had already come in for reevaluation before the first session of the council was convoked. The new approach was apparent during the 1960 presidential campaign. How much change would have developed among Lutherans if the Vatican Council had not been convened no one can say.

But the Vatican Council was convened, and it became the symbol of a new spirit. The cautious hope of Lutherans per-

---

[19] "Helsinki, Rome, Montreal," *American Lutheran*, XLVI (July, 1963), 6–10, 19–20.
[20] *Witness*, LXXXII (June 25, 1963), 291.
[21] "The New Pope and the Council," *American Lutheran*, XLVI (August, 1963), 7.

sisted as the second session opened in late 1963. Miracles were not happening, but none were expected. Slight progress was regarded as an improvement on none at all. Rhetorical criticism and negative comments were absent from the pages of Lutheran periodicals. The November 26, 1963, *Lutheran Witness,* in taking note of the "new Rome" that was beginning to emerge from Vatican Council II, asserted that Protestants, Lutherans specifically, "will have to work toward updating long-cherished opinions and fixed ideas of Roman Catholicism."[22] This was official acknowledgment that Lutherans had moved, by late 1963, to the edge of reappraisal. Reform and reunion were no longer abstractions; they had become concrete possibilities and had to be dealt with as such.

[22] "Protestants and the 'New Rome,'" *Witness,* LXXXII (November 26, 1963), 549–550.

13

REAPPRAISAL

Reappraisal of their traditional attitudes and practices was not a matter of choice for Lutherans. It was dictated by historical circumstances. Whatever the situation had been in the earlier years, during the period 1917 to 1963 the initiative in the relations between Catholics and Lutherans lay with the Catholics. The essentially negative outlook of Lutherans, whose principal aim seems to have been to avoid deterioration of the status quo, had been shaped largely in opposition to policies and practices of the Roman Catholic Church. As long as Catholicism appeared to remain the same, there was no compelling need for Lutherans to change their position. But when the Roman Catholic Church launched an effort at renewal and reform, that which Lutherans had been opposing began to change. Abstract opposition to concepts that were no longer abstract had to be abandoned. Reappraisal for the purpose of determining a new course of action and new goals pertinent to the real situation became necessary.

Reform and reunion were not the only ideas that Lutherans had come to treat as abstractions. The Reformation itself had become an abstract concept, something to be gloried in for its own sake. The biblical and historical research that accompanied the new spirit in the early 1960's compelled both Lutherans and Catholics to look at the Reformation as a real event. From a reappraisal of the purposes of the Reformation naturally followed a reappraisal of the historic separation between the Lutheran and Roman Catholic churches.[1]

[1] See for example Jaroslav Pelikan, *Obedient Rebels* (New York: Harper, 1964).

New understandings of the past contributed in turn to new attitudes toward present differences. Extraneous factors also appear to have influenced significantly the demand for reappraisal. Perhaps the most important was an increasing awareness among Christians that as a minority in the world they could ill afford the luxury of hostile separation. This awareness served as a catalyst in bringing about a willingness to take a new look at the divisions within Christianity.

It must be acknowledged that no matter how much its credibility was challenged by the events and the spirit of Vatican Council II, the old conviction that *Rome never changes* naturally did not disappear immediately or completely. An idea that has been unchallenged and unquestioned for decades and generations will put up a good fight for its life. Nevertheless, only a person who was committed to the theory that history is a mass of dark conspiracies, and who therefore refused to heed evidence contrary to his fancies, could continue to assert, without reappraisal, that Rome was not changing.

Reappraisal by Lutherans in the years following 1963, no matter how urgent, could only come by challenging the old attitudes and practices so deeply ingrained by this time. The mental set of most Lutherans had been nourished on the diet of anti-Catholicism provided by the journalistic critics and the party-line polemicists in former years. Before they could believe that any good thing could come out of Rome, their way of thinking required a complete remodeling. Until such remodeling could be achieved, ideas about Catholicism or Catholics that differed from the traditional viewpoint were certain to be viewed with suspicion.

Furthermore, Catholicism was so distasteful to many Lutherans that, historically, many of them had felt constrained to prove their true Lutheranism by avoiding "Romanizing tendencies," that is, any practice generally associated with the Roman Catholic Church. A conscious effort was made to prove that the Lutheran Church was less like the Roman Catholic Church than any other denomination, that "both as to doctrine and practise in general the Lutheran Church is in a class by itself."[2] This assuredly had an inhibiting effect on Lutheran liturgical practice and probably contributed to an imbalance in teachings related to the role of good works in the life of the Christian, to the motherhood of the Virgin Mary, and to the Real Presence in the Lord's Supper.

Concern over "Romanizing tendencies" was not restricted to the congregational level. In 1956 the synodical convention, in response to a memorial presented by a congregation, resolved:

> That the pastors, teachers, and theological students who have a special interest in liturgics continue to be warned to exercise an appropriate measure of caution in these matters, so that the consciences of our people and clergy be not disturbed, and that our Synod be on guard lest "Romanizing tendencies" develop in our midst.[3]

The next convention passed a resolution urging continued examination of the problem of "Romanizing tendencies." Synodical and district officials were instructed to be on the alert to the dangers involved and to deal "properly and promptly whenever evidence of them is apparent."[4] Possibly it was the sentiment reflected in these resolutions that induced Arthur Carl Piepkorn to point out that one characteristic of the Lutheran liturgical movement was "a cordial lack of enthusiasm for Roman Catholicism." Rather, he said, a pref-

[2] Oscar E. Feucht, "Is the Lutheran Church Like the Catholic Church?" *Lutheran Witness,* XLVIII (October 29, 1929), 353–354; LI (March 29, 1932), 127.

[3] *Proceedings of the Forty-Third Regular Convention of the Lutheran Church-Missouri Synod,* 1956, pp. 550–551.

[4] *Proceedings of the Forty-Fourth Regular Convention of the Lutheran Church-Missouri Synod,* 1959, pp. 194–195.

erence for primitive or historical practices prevails, and when
an option exists, the tendency is to choose the practice which
differs from Roman Catholic practice.[5]

Antagonism toward Roman Catholic teaching and practice
had contributed through the years to the creation of a caricature of Catholicism which did little justice to the real character of the church. This caricature had in turn deepened the
initial antagonism. Of course no one outside a particular
church can really understand and appreciate the teachings
and practices of the church in the same way as its own members. But despite affirmations to the contrary, it could easily
have been inferred from much of the Lutheran writing in this
period that the Roman Catholic Church does not even fit
within the realm of Christianity. Such declarations of faith as
this one by Father Gustave Weigel simply did not come
through in Lutheran literature:

> The starting point in Catholic dogma is Christology. In
> this field Catholic doctrine is unambiguous and crystal
> clear. For us Jesus of Nazareth, born of the Virgin Mary,
> is true God and true man: the ontological Savior of a lost
> human race in an action which began at His conception
> and continues through time and eternity. The saving action
> of Christ after His sojourn on this earth is continued in
> His mystical prolongation, the visible, organized Church,
> acting through divine energy in efficacious symbolism.[6]

Although Weigel continued by immediately asserting that
when all this is stated in detail, papacy, Mariology, and sacramental rite and theory inevitably follow, his statement
placed an emphasis on the work of Christ that Lutherans

[5] "The Lutheran Liturgical Movement," XVII, *Una Sancta* (St.
Luke the Evangelist, 1960), 5–12.
[6] Review of Pelikan, *The Riddle of Roman Catholicism* (New
York: Abingdon Press, 1959), in *America,* CI (September 12,
1959), 693.

would not expect to find in Catholicism, based on the descriptions of Catholic theology provided by their interpreters.

A reappraisal by Lutherans would necessarily involve a closer look at what is taught in Roman Catholicism. By beginning their studies with its teachings on the person and work of Christ they might succeed in replacing the traditional caricature with a more accurate understanding, and thus the traditional attitudes might be displaced. Nevertheless, even among those most anxious for a reappraisal, one seemingly insuperable barrier stood in the way: the Council of Trent. Lutherans, no matter how open they were to the idea of change in Catholicism, could not forget that the doctrine of justification had been anathematized at Trent.[7] In a little booklet on this council Herbert Mayer asserted that "had things gone differently at Trent, it is conceivable that the modern history of the Christian Church would be marked by a much greater degree of unity." One of the purposes of this booklet was to help Protestants gain a better understanding of the Roman Catholic Church through a look at this critical event in its history. After explaining the principal decisions and accomplishments of the council, Mayer declared that the modern history of the Roman Catholic Church began with the Council of Trent and that it is still shaped and colored essentially by its canons and decrees.[8]

The overriding significance of the Council of Trent forced Lutheran observers to check their enthusiasm over the good things they saw happening in Roman Catholicism. In recognizing the salutary effects of the liturgical movement, of bibli-

[7] See for example Oswald C. J. Hoffmann, "Vatican II and the Reformation: 1963," *Arena,* LXXII (October, 1963), 18–19.

[8] *The Story of the Council of Trent* (St. Louis: Concordia, 1962), 20 pages. For a more detailed, scholarly look at one aspect of this council see Richard Baepler, "Scripture and Tradition in the Council of Trent," *Concordia Theological Monthly,* XXXI (June, 1960), 341–362.

cal studies, and of the desire for dialogue with other Christians, James Manz felt compelled to point to the continuing significance of Trent.

> Yet Rome's official curse upon the Biblical doctrine of justification still stands. Unless we grasp this fact, we shall never understand the Reformer's identification of the papacy with the Antichrist. And the teaching of righteousness by works is evident in thought and life on the grass roots level.[9]

Efforts to minimize the importance of the Council of Trent also ran into obstacles. Richard Koenig reported in the *American Lutheran* on his attendance at a colloquium at Harvard University at which the speaker had been Cardinal Augustin Bea, assumed to be among the more liberal in the hierarchy. The feeling of strangeness at attending this mixed gathering was heightened by what the Cardinal said and how he said it.

> As he spoke of these things with genuine sincerity and love, mixed with delightful flashes of humor, one could sense that a real miracle has taken place. There is now, in our time, in our age, a Spirit of unity making itself felt even across the great gulf that separates Protestant and Roman Catholic. . . .
>
> But the Cardinal's comments regarding the future emphasized the distance the two confessions are from one another. In one of the most puzzling portions of his three addresses . . . the Cardinal went out of his way to emphasize that nothing could be changed in those doctrines which the church regards as essential parts of her divinely revealed Faith. He mentioned in particular *the doctrines formulated by the Council of Trent*. For a long time it has been fashionable to speak of Tridentine and post-Tridentine Catholicism, using the first term pejoratively.

[9] "Rome Has Not Changed," *Witness,* LXXXI (February 20, 1962), 81.

The distinction was useful in softening some Roman Catholic positions vis-a-vis Protestants. The Cardinal seems now to have blocked this approach with his extremely conservative statement.

Koenig inferred that the Cardinal may have opened the door again to a solution of some knotty doctrinal questions when he emphasized later that the hands of the church were not tied and that "the Church can and must restate its dogma for the present age and remove misunderstandings." Nevertheless, Koenig's optimism had obviously been shaken.[10]

Pelikan, too, saw the Council of Trent as an insurmountable barrier, "even if the current reinterpreters of Trent are right—and they do seem to stretch the decrees beyond the breaking point." Additional obstacles cited by Pelikan were the Vatican Council of 1870 and the dogmas of the immaculate conception and the assumption of Mary.[11] These four milestones in Roman Catholic history were consistently regarded by Lutherans as the principal stumbling blocks in the path to agreement.

By 1963, then, Lutherans had reached a critical juncture. They were faced with the distinct necessity of reappraising their traditional position, but reappraisal was complicated by their deep and abiding differences. The historical relations between Lutherans and Catholicism as they have been described in this study offer some guidance and instruction for determining the character and direction that a reappraisal might take. We are today not so far removed from 1963 that this guidance and instruction lacks current significance, nor need it apply only to Lutherans. As new relations are beginning to develop, both Lutherans and Catholics can profit from some simple guidelines shaped out of the historical experi-

---

[10] *American Lutheran,* XLVI (May, 1963), 5, 25.
[11] *The Riddle of Roman Catholicism,* p. 238.

ence. To the reader who is familiar with the story that has been told here they may seem obvious or even anticlimactic; there may nevertheless be merit in drawing them together in summary form.

The first step in developing improved relations between Lutherans and Catholics requires meetings between representatives of the two sides, and these are already occurring. Whether these meetings are called discussions or dialogues or encounters, real reappraisal can come only through regular and forthright confrontation. Theologians, pastoral clergy, and laity can all profit from the exchange of beliefs and ideas. Vigorous study of the Scriptures should always be the starting point for each confrontation. The emphasis must be on determining anew what Scriptures say, not on simply reiterating what has always been said. Lutherans should not allow the renewed biblical interest and the biblical resources of Catholics to go unexploited; Catholics can profit from the Lutheran tradition of biblical scholarship.

As confrontations between Lutherans and Catholics take shape, it makes sense to identify as the starting points for discussion those beliefs that are held in common by the two denominations. From this common ground it will be natural for the discussion to move quickly to points of disagreement, but more can be achieved in reaching theological understanding if it is recognized that Lutherans and Catholics are brothers in Christ, even though at present they are separated brothers.[12] Lutherans should pay close attention to what is being said and written by Catholic theologians. There is much latitude for movement within the structure of Roman Catholic theology, and perceptive Lutheran theologians should observe

---

[12] The fine spirit that can prevail in Lutheran-Roman Catholic confrontations is described by Robert W. Bertram, "Chronology of the Notre Dame-Valparaiso Dialogue, 1957–1964," mimeographed report (April 8, 1964).

how their counterparts are maneuvering within this structure. Respect for the integrity of Catholic theologians requires that their statements be accepted at face value. Catholic theologians may also be surprised at the differences in viewpoint they might find among Lutherans.

It is not to be expected of course that all differences and disagreements can be overcome or even smoothed over through confrontation. No matter how abiding they might be, they should be faced in an evangelical spirit. As this point was defined earlier, this means that what is said and written should be done so in the spirit of the gospel by showing a readiness both to seek and to grant forgiveness and to work toward unity in Christ. Vindictiveness, ridicule, suspicion, and scorn have accomplished nothing constructive in the past and will not do so in the future. The elimination from the Lutheran vocabulary of the pejorative term "Romanizing tendency" would be one step in the right direction. The correctness of practices and teachings should be determined independent of their relation to the Roman Catholic Church.

Moving away from theological matters, another guideline calls for Lutherans who have not already done so to reevaluate their almost irrational fear of Roman Catholic political principles and machinations in the light of the demonstrated loyalty of the church and its members in the United States. Too much time and energy in the past has been spent charging windmills. For their part, Catholics might be encouraged to work toward bringing their church's stated position into line with its practical subscription to American political principles. The Declaration on Religious Freedom and its application to the American scene by prominent Catholic spokesmen represent a noteworthy effort in this direction.

The time has come for both sides to cease dealing in abstractions and to turn to the real situation. The Reformation was a concrete event in history; it was both the cause and effect of other concrete events, and should be understood as such. *Reform* is real. *Renewal* is real. The overtones of the term *reunion* are at present unacceptable to Lutherans; perhaps the emphasis should be on *unity*. But unity is not an abstract concept; it is a distinct, concrete goal. A Lutheran reappraisal incorporating these guidelines would constitute an affirmation rather than an abandonment of the Reformation or of Lutheran principles. A Catholic reappraisal along these lines could mean that the church is coming to grips with the issues raised by the Reformation.

Four hundred years after the Reformation the Council of Trent was regarded as a closed story, an event that had accomplished its purpose. Four hundred years after the Council of Trent the Reformation was continuing, showing promise of achieving in some form and in some undetermined time the purposes for which it had been begun.

BIBLIOGRAPHY

BOOKS

The Abiding Word. Vol. III. St. Louis: Concordia Publishing House, 1960.

Buchheimer, Louis (ed.). *Great Leaders and Great Events.* St. Louis: Concordia Publishing House, 1922.

————. *Sermons on Romanism.* St. Louis: Rudolph Volkening, n.d. [1917].

Dallmann, William. *How Peter Became Pope.* St. Louis: Concordia Publishing House, 1931.

Engelder, Theodore; Arndt, William; Graebner, Theodore; and Mayer, Frederick E. *Popular Symbolics.* St. Louis: Concordia Publishing House, 1934.

Graebner, Theodore. *The Dark Ages.* St. Louis: Concordia Publishing House, 1917.

————. *The Pope and Temporal Power.* Milwaukee: Northwestern Publishing House, 1929.

Jahsmann, Allan Hart. *What's Lutheran in Education?* St. Louis: Concordia Publishing House, 1960.

Koenker, Ernest B. *The Liturgical Renaissance in the Roman Catholic Church.* Chicago: University of Chicago Press, 1954.

Laetsch, Theodore (ed.). *The Abiding Word.* Vols. I–II. St. Louis: Concordia Publishing House, 1946–1947.

Marty, Martin E. "A Dialogue of Histories," in *American Catholicism: A Protestant-Jewish View.* Philip Scharper (ed.). New York: Sheed and Ward, 1959.

Mayer, Frederick E. *The Religious Bodies of America.* St. Louis: Concordia Publishing House, 1954.

Pelikan, Jaroslav. *Obedient Rebels.* New York: Harper, 1964.

Pelikan, Jaroslav. *The Riddle of Roman Catholicism*. New York: Abingdon Press, 1959.

Pieper, Franz. *Christian Dogmatics*. Vols. I–III. St. Louis: Concordia Publishing House, 1950–1957. (English translation of *Christliche Dogmatik*. St. Louis: Concordia Publishing House, 1917–1924.)

Rehwinkel, Alfred M. *The Voice of Conscience*. St. Louis: Concordia Publishing House, 1963.

Seboldt, Roland H. A. *Christ or Mary?* St. Louis: Concordia Publishing House, 1963.

Von Schenk, Berthold. "Factors That Unite Us: Protestant," in *Christians in Conversation*. Peter W. Bartholome (ed.). Westminster, Maryland: The Newman Press, 1962.

BOOKLETS AND TRACTS

Bohlmann, Ralph. *Treasury of Merits*. St. Louis: Concordia Publishing House, 1963.

Dau, W. H. T. *Weighed and Found Wanting: An Inquiry into the Aim and Methods of the Ku Klux Klan*. Fort Wayne: American Luther League, 1923.

[Gockel, Herman W.] *Proclaiming Fiction a Fact*. St. Louis: Concordia Publishing House, n.d. [1951].

————. *Was Mary Born Without Sin?* St. Louis: Concordia Publishing House, n.d. [1953].

Gotsch, M. L. *The Reformation and Its Blessed Fruits*. St. Louis: Concordia Publishing House, 1925.

Graebner, Theodore. *The White House and the Vatican*. St. Louis: Concordia Publishing House, n.d. [1940].

Hallerberg, William. *Protestantism vs. Romanism*. St Louis: Concordia Publishing House, n.d. [ca. 1925].

Heintze, R. W. *Was the Reformation Needed?* New York: American Lutheran Publicity Bureau, n.d.

[Hoffmann, Oswald C. J.] *The Split Between Roman Catholicism and Christ*. New York: The Lutheran Press, n.d. [1945].

Hoyer, Theodore. *Why I Am Not a Roman Catholic.* St. Louis: Concordia Publishing House, 1953; 4th printing, 1960.

Mayer, Frederick E. *To Sign or Not to Sign?* St. Louis: Concordia Publishing House, 1946.

Mayer, Herbert T. *The Story of the Council of Trent.* St. Louis: Concordia Publishing House, 1962.

Meyer, Carl S. *A Catholic President?* St. Louis: Concordia Publishing House, n.d. [1960].

Petersen, Lorman M. *A Critical Analysis of "A Manifesto" by "Protestants and Other Americans United for Separation of Church and State" and Its Relation to the Lutheran Church-Missouri Synod.* Peoria, Illinois: Committee on Parish Education and Youth Work, Central Illinois District, The Lutheran Church-Missouri Synod, 1949.

Quadricentennial Reformation Series, 1517–1917. New York: American Lutheran Publicity Bureau, 1917. Officially adopted by the Central Committee on the Missouri Synod. Titles:

Brunn, Arthur. *The Bible Church.*

Dallmann, William. *Luther and America.*

Dau, W. H. T. *The Character of Luther.*

————. *Luther on the Bible.*

Eckhardt, H. P. *The Reformation and the Open Bible.*

Graebner, M. *The Separation of Church and State.*

Lindemann, Paul. *The Formation, Deformation, and Reformation of the Church.*

Schumm, F. C. G. *The Augsburg Confession: The First Protestant Confession of Faith.*

Volk, Jno. H. *Some Present-Day Fruits of the Reformation.*

Walker, H. H. *Luther in His Home.*

Scharlemann, Martin H. *The Last Word.* St. Louis: Concordia Publishing House, n.d.

Schuessler, Paul E. *The Truth About the Virgin Mary.* St. Louis: Concordia Publishing House, n.d.

Seboldt, Roland H. A. *Your Roman Catholic Neighbor.* St. Louis: Concordia Tract Mission, n.d.

Sommerfeld, Richard. *The Case Against the Infallibility of the Pope.* St. Louis: Concordia Publishing House, n.d. [1962].

Spitz, Lewis W. *Saint Paul versus Pope John.* St. Louis: Concordia Publishing House, n.d. [1959].

PERIODICALS

American Lutheran. Vols. I–XLVI. 1917–1963.

Arena. See *Walther League Messenger.*

Concordia Theological Monthly. Vols. I–XXXIV. 1930–1963. (Edited by the faculty of Concordia Seminary, St. Louis; this is essentially a continuation of *Theological Quarterly* and *Theological Monthly.*)

Confessional Lutheran. Vols. I–XXIV. 1940–1963.

Cresset. Vols. I–XXVII. 1937–1963.

Lutheran Education. Vols. LXXXIII–XCIX. 1947–1963. (Continuation of *Lutheran School Journal.*)

Lutheran School Journal. Vols. LVI–LXXXII. 1921–1947.

Lutheran Witness. Vols. XXXVI–LXXXII. 1917–1963.

Seminarian. Vols. XXXIV–LV. 1943–1963.

Springfielder. Vols. XXIII–XXVII. 1959–1963.

Theological Monthly. Vols. I–IX. 1921–1929.

Theological Quarterly. Vols. XXI–XXIV. 1917–1920.

Una Sancta. Vols. IV–XX. 1943–1963.

Walther League Messenger. Vols. XXVI–LXXII. 1917–1963. (Published as *Arena* after September, 1963.)

References to specific articles in the above periodicals are given in the notes to the text.

REPORTS, YEARBOOKS, PROCEEDINGS, AND OFFICIAL STATEMENTS

Bertram, Robert W. "Chronology of the Notre Dame-Valparaiso Dialogue, 1957–1964." April 8, 1964. (Mimeographed.)

Brief Statement of the Doctrinal Position of the Lutheran Church-Missouri Synod. 1932.

Hochwalt, Frederick G. "Some Educational Problems with Reference to Church and State: As a Catholic Sees It." *Papers and Proceedings of the Forty-Eighth Annual Convention, National Lutheran Educational Conference.* Cleveland, 1962.

Huegli, Albert G. "Church and State in Education: As a Protestant Sees It." *Papers and Proceedings of the Forty-Eighth Annual Convention, National Lutheran Educational Conference.* Cleveland, 1962.

Miller, Arthur L. "Current Issues in Church-State Relations." *Legal Aspects of Lutheran Parish Education.* Peter W. Zadeik, Jr. (ed.). River Forest, Illinois: Twenty-First Yearbook of the Lutheran Education Association, 1964.

Mueller, John Theodore. "Lutheranism in Its Fundamental Opposition to Romanism, Calvinism, and Modernism." *Proceedings of the Twenty-Third Convention of the Central Illinois District,* 1942.

Proceedings of the Triennial Synodical Conventions of the Lutheran Church-Missouri Synod. 1917–1963.

Report of the 1948 Educational Conference. River Forest, Illinois: Board for Parish Education, The Lutheran Church-Missouri Synod, 1948.

BIBLE CLASS MATERIALS

Graebner, Theodore. *Bible Student.* Vol. XI. April, 1933.

————. *Bible Student.* Vol. XII. October, 1933.

————. *Bible Student.* Vol. XXIV. April, 1945.

Hoyer, Robert. *Adult Bible Discussion Guide.* Vol. V, Part 9. May 29, 1960.

Luke, William H. *Junior Bible Student.* Vol. XXI. January, 1932.

Neitzel, Arthur E. *Bible Student.* Vol. XX. January, 1941.

Weidenschilling, John M. *Bible Student.* Vol. XXXI. January, 1953.

RADIO AND TELEVISION TRANSCRIPTS

Hoffmann, Oswald C. J., and Hochwalt, Frederick G. "CBS Reports: Should Private and Parochial Schools Receive Federal Aid?" April 6, 1961.

Maier, Walter A. The Lutheran Hour. January 1, 1940.

Marty, Martin E. "The Church and the Council: A Non-Catholic View." The Catholic Hour. May 12, 1966.

OTHERS

The Theodore Graebner Papers, Manuscripts, and Correspondence, on file at Concordia Historical Institute, St. Louis, Missouri. Access to this collection was granted under the rules of the depository.

BIOGRAPHICAL NOTES

Brief biographical sketches of the Lutheran spokesmen who played the most significant roles in the story related in this book are given below. Cited first in each sketch is the synodical institution from which the individual graduated. The degrees listed are the highest earned degrees and honorary doctorates awarded by synodical or affiliated colleges and seminaries. Pastoral, teaching, leadership, and chief editorial positions are noted next. Because most of the men were prominent in the various aspects of the total work of the synod, it is not possible to list all their editorial associations, offices, and memberships on boards and committees, nor is an attempt made to include their books and other writings.

ARNDT, William F. (1880–1957). Concordia Seminary, St. Louis, 1903. D.D., Concordia College, Adelaide, Australia, 1930; Ph.D., Washington University, St. Louis, 1935. Served parishes in Tennessee, Missouri, and New York, 1903–1912. Professor at St. Paul's College, Concordia, Missouri, 1912–1921, and Concordia Seminary, St. Louis, 1921–1951. Editor of *Theological Monthly,* 1926–1929, and *Concordia Theological Monthly,* 1938–1950.

BEHNKEN, John W. (1884–1968). Concordia Seminary, St. Louis, 1906. D.D., Concordia Seminary, St. Louis, 1934; LL.D., Valparaiso University, 1953. Pastor in Houston, Texas, 1906–1935. President, Texas District, 1926–1929; vice-president, Lutheran Church-Missouri Synod, 1929–1935; president, 1935–1962; and honorary president, 1962–1968.

BRETSCHER, Paul M. (1893–   ). Concordia Seminary, St. Louis, 1915. Ph.D., University of Chicago, 1936; S.T.D., Concordia College, Adelaide, Australia, 1964; Litt.D., Valparaiso University, 1965. Parish pastor in Milwaukee, Wisconsin, 1918–1923. Professor at Concordia Teachers College, River Forest,

Illinois, 1915–1918 and 1923–1941, and Concordia Seminary, St. Louis, 1941–1966.*

DALLMANN, William (1862–1952). Concordia Seminary, St. Louis, 1886. D.D., Concordia Seminary, St. Louis, 1926. Served congregations in Missouri, Maryland, New York, and Wisconsin until his retirement in 1940. President, English Synod, 1899–1901; vice-president, Lutheran Church-Missouri Synod, 1926–1932. Instrumental in assisting the church in its transition from German to English. Popular speaker and writer.

GRAEBNER, Theodore C. (1876–1950). Concordia Seminary, St. Louis, 1897. D.D., Concordia College, Adelaide, Australia, 1930. Teacher at Walther College, St. Louis, 1897–1900, and at Lutheran Ladies' Seminary, Red Wing, Minnesota, 1900–1906. Pastor in the Chicago area, 1906–1913. Professor at Concordia Seminary, St. Louis, 1913–1950. Coeditor, *Lutheran Witness,* 1914–1949.

HOFFMANN, Oswald C. J. (1913–   ). Concordia Seminary, St. Louis, 1936. M.A., University of Minnesota, 1935; D.D., Concordia Seminary, St. Louis, 1952; LL.D., Valparaiso University, 1952. Professor at Bethany Lutheran College, Mankato, Minnesota, 1936–1940; University of Minnesota, 1940–1941; and Concordia Collegiate Institute, Bronxville, New York, 1941–1948. Director of public relations, Lutheran Church-Missouri Synod, 1948–1963. Lutheran Hour speaker, since 1955, full-time since 1963.

HOYER, Theodore (1883–1963). Concordia Seminary, St. Louis, 1905. D.D., Concordia College, Adelaide, Australia, 1943. Pastor in Kansas and Colorado, 1905–1927. Professor at St. John's College, Winfield, Kansas, 1927–1930, and Concordia Seminary, St. Louis, 1930–1957.

HUEGLI, Albert G. (1913–   ). Concordia Seminary, St. Louis, 1936. Ph.D., Northwestern University, 1944; LL.D., Concordia Teachers College, River Forest, Illinois, 1964. Professor at St. John's College, Winfield, Kansas, 1938–1940, and Concordia Teachers College, 1940–1961. Vice-president for academic affairs, Valparaiso University, since 1961.

KLAUSLER, Alfred P. (1910–   ). Concordia Seminary, St. Louis, 1932. M.A., Loyola University; Litt.D., Valparaiso University, 1967. Pastor in Montana, 1934–1942. Chaplain, U.S. Army, 1942–1946 and 1961–1966. Walther League executive, 1946–1966, and editor of the *Walther League Messenger*, 1946–1966. Executive secretary, Associated Church Press, since 1966.

MAIER, Walter A. (1893–1950). Concordia Seminary, St. Louis, 1916. Ph.D., Harvard University, 1929; D.D., Concordia College, Adelaide, Australia, 1943. Executive secretary of the Walther League, 1920–1922, and editor of the *Walther League Messenger*, 1920–1945. Professor, Concordia Seminary, St. Louis, 1922–1950. Lutheran Hour speaker, 1935–1950.

MANZ, James G. (1914–   ). Concordia Seminary, St. Louis, 1943. S.T.D., Chicago Lutheran Theological Seminary, Maywood, Illinois, 1953. Pastor in the Chicago area since 1943.

MARTY, Martin E. (1928–   ). Concordia Seminary, St. Louis, 1952. Ph.D., University of Chicago, 1956. Served parishes in the Chicago area, 1952–1963. Associate editor of the *Christian Century* since 1956. Professor at the University of Chicago, since 1963.

MAYER, Frederick E. (1894–1954). Concordia Seminary, St. Louis, 1915. D.D., Concordia Seminary, Springfield, Illinois, 1945. Pastor in Illinois, 1915–1925. Professor at Concordia Seminary, Springfield, 1925–1937, and Concordia Seminary, St. Louis, 1937–1954. Managing editor of *Concordia Theological Monthly*, 1949–1954.

MEYER, Carl S. (1907–   ). Concordia Seminary, St. Louis, 1930. Ph.D., University of Chicago, 1954; D.D., Concordia Seminary, Springfield, Illinois, 1964. Principal of Luther Institute, Chicago, 1943–1954. Professor at Bethany Lutheran College, Mankato, Minnesota, 1934–1943, and Concordia Seminary, St. Louis, since 1954. Editor of *Concordia Historical Institute Quarterly*, since 1956.

MILLER, Arthur L. (1907–   ). Concordia Teachers College, River Forest, Illinois, 1927. Ph.D., University of Chicago, 1951. Teacher and principal of a Lutheran school in Chicago, 1927–

1946. Executive secretary of the Board of Parish Education of the Lutheran Church-Missouri Synod, since 1946.

MUELLER, Arnold C. (1891–   ). Concordia Seminary, St. Louis, 1914. M.A. Ed., Saint Louis University, 1953; D.D., Concordia Seminary, St. Louis, 1953. Served congregations in Canada, Pennsylvania, and Indiana, 1914–1933. Synodical Sunday School editor, 1933–1966.

MUELLER, John Theodore (1885–1967). Concordia Seminary, St. Louis, 1907. Ph.D., Webster University, Atlanta, Georgia, 1923; Th.D., Xenia Theological Seminary, Pittsburgh, Pennsylvania, 1927. Pastor in Michigan and Illinois, 1913–1920. Professor at Wittenberg Academy, Wittenberg, Wisconsin, 1911–1913, and Concordia Seminary, St. Louis, 1920–1955.

PELIKAN, Jaroslav J., Jr. (1923–   ). Concordia Seminary, St. Louis, 1946. Ph.D., University of Chicago, 1946; LL.D. Valparaiso University, 1966; D.D., Concordia Seminary, St. Louis, 1967. Professor at Valparaiso University, 1946–1949; Concordia Seminary, St. Louis, 1950–1953; University of Chicago, 1953–1962; and Yale Divinity School, since 1962.

PIEPKORN, Arthur Carl (1907–   ). Concordia Seminary, St. Louis, 1928. Ph.D., Oriental Institute, University of Chicago, 1932. Pastor in Missouri, Minnesota, and Ohio, 1930–1940. Chaplain, U.S. Army, 1940–1951. Professor at Concordia Seminary, St. Louis, since 1951.

POLACK, W. Gustave (1890–1950). Concordia Seminary, St. Louis, 1914. Litt. D., Valparaiso University, 1942. Pastor in Evansville, Indiana, 1914–1925. Professor at Concordia Seminary, St. Louis, 1925–1950. Associate editor, *Lutheran Witness,* 1925–1950; editor, *Concordia Historical Institute Quarterly,* 1927–1949.

REHWINKEL, Alfred M. (1887–   ). Concordia Seminary, St. Louis, 1910. M.A., University of Alberta, 1919; LL.D., Valparaiso University, 1947. Pastor in Canada, 1910–1922. Professor, Concordia College, Edmonton, Alberta, 1922–1928; president, St. John's College, Winfield, Kansas, 1928–1936; professor, Concordia Seminary, St. Louis, 1936–1965.

SCHENK, Berthold von (1895–   ). Concordia Seminary, St. Louis, 1918. Th.D., University of Marburg, 1955. Served congregations in Missouri and New Jersey, 1918–1940; pastor of the Lutheran Church of Our Savior, New York, N.Y., 1940–1961.

SEBOLDT, Roland H. A. (1924–   ). Concordia Seminary, St. Louis, 1946. S.T.M., Concordia Seminary, St. Louis, 1958. Pastor in Texas and Illinois, 1946–1963. Book editor, Concordia Publishing House, since 1963.

SOMMER, Martin S. (1869–1949). Concordia Seminary, St. Louis, 1891. Litt.D., Valparaiso University, 1937. Pastor in St. Louis, 1891–1920. President of the English District, 1914–1919. Professor at Concordia Seminary, 1920–1949. Coeditor of the *Lutheran Witness,* 1914–1949.

SPITZ, Lewis W. (1895–   ). Concordia Seminary, St. Louis, 1918. Ph.D. University of Chicago, 1943; D.D., Concordia Seminary, Springfield, Illinois, 1964. Pastor in Wyoming and Nebraska, 1918–1925. Professor at St. Paul's College, Concordia, Missouri, 1925–1946, and Concordia Seminary, St. Louis, since 1946.

STREITELMEYER, John H. (1920–   ). Valparaiso University, 1942. M.A., Northwestern University, 1947; Litt.D., Concordia Seminary, St. Louis, 1963. Professor at Valparaiso University and editor of the *Cresset* since 1947.

INDEX